D0635806

IRELAND IN THE MIDDLE AGES

British History in Perspective
General Editor: Jeremy Black

PUBLISHED TITLES

Rodney Barker *Politics, Peoples and Government*
C. J. Bartlett *British Foreign Policy in the Twentieth Century*
Jeremy Black *Robert Walpole and the Nature of Politics
in Early Eighteenth-Century Britain*
Anne Curry *The Hundred Years War*
John W. Derry *British Politics in the Age of Fox, Pitt and Liverpool*
William Gibson *Church, State and Society, 1760–1850*
Brian Golding *Conquest and Colonisation: the Normans
in Britain, 1066–1100*
S. J. Gunn *Early Tudor Government, 1485–1558*
Richard Harding *The Evolution of the Sailing Navy, 1509–1815*
Ann Hughes *The Causes of the English Civil War*
Ronald Hutton *The British Republic, 1649–1660*
Kevin Jefferys *The Labour Party since 1945*
T. A. Jenkins *Disraeli and Victorian Conservatism*
D. M. Loades *The Mid-Tudor Crisis, 1545–1565*
Diarmaid MacCulloch *The Later Reformation in England, 1547–1603*
A. P. Martinich *Thomas Hobbes*
W. M. Ormrod *Political Life in Medieval England, 1300–1450*
Keith Perry *British Politics and the American Revolution*
A. J. Pollard *The Wars of the Roses*
David Powell *British Politics and the Labour Question, 1868–1990*
David Powell *The Edwardian Crisis*
Richard Rex *Henry VIII and the English Reformation*
G. R. Searle *The Liberal Party: Triumph and Disintegration, 1886–1929*
Paul Seaward *The Restoration, 1660–1688*
Robert Stewart *Party and Politics, 1830–1852*
John W. Young *Britain and European Unity, 1945–92*

History of Ireland
D. G. Boyce *The Irish Question and British Politics, 1868–1996 (2nd edn)*
Seán Duffy *Ireland in the Middle Ages*
David Harkness *Ireland in the Twentieth Century: Divided Island*

History of Scotland
Keith M. Brown *Kingdom or Province? Scotland and the Regal Union,
1603–1715*

History of Wales
A. D. Carr *Medieval Wales*
J. Gwynfor Jones *Early Modern Wales, c.1525–1640*

941.5
D874

IRELAND IN THE
MIDDLE AGES

SEÁN DUFFY

WITHDRAWN

LIBRARY ST. MARY'S COLLEGE

IRELAND IN THE MIDDLE AGES

Copyright © 1997 by Seán Duffy

All rights reserved. No part of this book may be used or reproduced in any manner whatsoever without written permission except in the case of brief quotations embodied in critical articles or reviews. For information, address:

St. Martin's Press, Scholarly and Reference Division, 175 Fifth Avenue, New York, N.Y. 10010

First published in the United States of America in 1997

Printed in Hong Kong

ISBN 0–312–16389–4 (cloth)
ISBN 0–312–16390–8 (paperback)

Library of Congress Cataloging-in-Publication Data
Duffy, Seán.
Ireland in the Middle Ages / Seán Duffy.
p.   cm. — (British history in perspective)
Includes bibliographical references (p.   ) and index.
ISBN 0–312–16389–4 (cloth). — ISBN 0–312–16390–8 (pbk.)
1. Ireland—History—1172–1603.   2. Ireland—History—English
Conquest, 1166–1186.   3. Ireland—History—To 1172.
4. Civilization, Medieval.   I. Title.   II. Series.
DA934.D94   1997
911.5—dc20   96–25753
                                                              CIP

For my mother and father

CONTENTS

Preface   ix

Maps   xi

Introduction   1

1   **Dwellers at the Earth's Edge**   7

2   **A Kingdom Unique to Itself?**   28

3   **Adventus Anglorum**   57

4   **From Kingdom to Lordship**   81

5   **Colonial Domination and Native Survival**   111

6   **A Colony in Retreat**   134

7   **Equilibrium**   156

Notes and References   182

Select Bibliography   201

Index   206

PREFACE

This book is not intended to supersede any of the many histories of medieval Ireland already available, several of which are works of such importance that they are likely to remain indispensable to students of the subject for generations to come. However, some of the best work on the subject is out of print, other volumes are by now somewhat dated, and much that remains is work of such formidable scholarship that it is not readily accessible to the beginner. It is for this reason that I have had the temerity to undertake the present volume. Its aims are modest. They are, first, to provide a brief survey of Irish history in the first half of this millennium, written in a style and format that will make this quite difficult subject intelligible to those previously unacquainted with it; second, to incorporate the findings of recent research in the field; and third, to offer – such as it is – my own reinterpretation of the evidence. I hope that this will mean that it contains something of use for both raw recruit and weary veteran alike. There are, however, large gaps in the narrative. I have had limited space to devote to the church, and even less room for society and economy. I can but apologize for this, which is the consequence of trying to cover such a broad time-span in a volume of this size (though in the Bibliography I refer readers to some of the more important works in the field).

Many debts are incurred in compiling a volume even of these dimensions. My primary debt is to all those scholars, living and dead, whose work I have borrowed to build the narrative. I have tried to acknowledge the extent of my indebtedness in the Notes, but I fear that this is not enough. So many of the ideas that one thinks are one's own are the product of reading other people's work over the years, or of attending their public lectures, or of conversations with them. Where my theft has gone unacknowledged below I apologize here. Several scholars have had a more direct involvement. Professor James Lydon, Dr Ailbhe Mac Shamhráin, Dr Máire Ní Mhaonaigh, Ms Linzi Simpson and Dr Brendan Smith have read drafts of the book in whole or in part and made many helpful comments. As I have in many instances stubbornly refused to take their advice, the exoneration normally pronounced at this point needs to have even greater force than usual.

The dedication expresses a debt of another kind.

SEÁN DUFFY
Dublin, January 1996

MAPS

Ireland *c.* 1000 AD

(includes the main place-names and population names mentioned in the text)

TÍR
CONAILL
(Ua
Domnaill)
Derry

Earldom
of ULSTER

Carrickfergus

TÍR EÓGAIN
(Ua Néill)

Armagh
Downpatrick

Sligo

Ua Conchobair

BRÉIFNE

LOUTH

ROSCOMMON

Drogheda

CONNACHT
(De Burgh)

MEATH

Tuam

Trim

Athlone

Galway

Loughrea

OFFALY

Dublin

Ua Briain

KILDARE

DUBLIN

THOMOND

CARLOW

Limerick

KILKENNY

TIPPERARY

WEXFORD

LIMERICK

Cashel

Wexford

KERRY

CORK

Waterford

DESMOND

WATERFORD

Cork

Mac Carthaig

Ireland *c.* 1250 AD

(includes the main place-names and lordships mentioned in the text)

Ireland *c.* 1500 AD

(includes the main place-names and lordships mentioned in the text)

INTRODUCTION

> This then I note as a great defect in the Civill policy of this
> kingdom, in that for the space of 350 yeares at least after the
> Conquest first attempted, the English lawes were not communi-
> cated to the Irish, nor the benefit and protection therof allowed
> unto them, though they earnestly desired and sought the same.
> For, as long as they were out of the protecion of the Lawe, so as
> every English-man might oppresse, spoyle, and kill them without
> controulment, howe was it possible they shoulde bee other then
> Out-lawes & Enemies to the Crown of England? If the King
> woulde not admit them to the condition of Subiects, how could
> they learn to acknoledge and obey him as their Soveraigne?
> When they might not converse or Commerce with any Civill
> men, nor enter into any Towne or Citty without perrill of their
> Lives; whither should they flye but into the Woods and
> Mountaines, and there live in a wilde and barbarous maner? ...
> In a word, if the English woulde neither in peace Governe them
> by the Law, nor could in War root them out by the sword; must
> they not needes bee prickes in their eyes, and thornes in their
> sides, till the worlds end? and so the Conquest never bee
> brought to perfection.[1]

The above are the words of Sir John Davies, James I's attor-
ney-general for Ireland, taken from his history of that country
which he published in 1612. Davies's book is a remarkable
piece of work, still valuable now nearly four centuries later,
and his analysis of England's Irish problem has in many
respects stood the test of time, to the extent that its self-
explanatory (if rather cumbersome) title, *A Discoverie of the
True Causes why Ireland was never entirely Subdued and Brought
under the Obedience of the Crowne of England*, could serve as a

publisher's blurb for almost every subsequent work on the subject. Like Davies's work, most histories of medieval Ireland, after providing an account of the English invasion in the late twelfth century, have as their overriding theme an explanation of why that initial conquest failed. This book is no exception, and that, perhaps, is as it should be, since the English invasion and long drawn-out conquest was, most scholars would argue, the most important development in Irish secular affairs during the Middle Ages (having an impact far greater than that of the earlier Viking invasion).[2]

What I attempt to do below, though, is to broaden the chronological scope of the work, so that the English invasion is not, as it is sometimes made to appear, the starting point of Irish history, but rather one – the major – turning point in that story. The metamorphosis wrought by the event radically altered the relationship between Ireland and the other kingdoms and principalities in this archipelago, and it irrevocably changed the ground rules of Irish politics. At the same time Ireland enjoyed a long and complex relationship with its sister island before that invasion took place, and Irish politics did not begin in 1169. Therefore, one must guard against the assumption that everything which occurred after that date is a product of the new age; such an awareness can only come from an examination of the pre-invasion precedent, and this I attempt to do below, in so far as space allows.

If I have followed Sir John Davies in devoting considerable space to a discussion of the 'causes why Ireland was never entirely subdued', I have followed him in another respect also. As is clear from the above quotation, Sir John was by no means unsympathetic to the situation of those Irish who opposed the English attempt to conquer the country. He, of course, favoured that conquest, yet felt that the Irish had been rather hard done by over the years and that, had other policies towards them been pursued, their subjection to English rule would have occurred many generations earlier. Some other writers on medieval Ireland, both before and after Davies, have been less than sympathetic to the native Irish and their work has suffered as a result, to the extent that the picture of Irish society which they sometimes present is one of unremitting chaos and bloodshed, and their discussion of Irish political affairs after the late twelfth century is occasionally conducted with only limited reference to the Irish themselves. These are not histories of Ireland; they are histories of the English colony in Ireland. It is Dublin-centred history, and the Irish are on the outside looking in. In a volume of this size I do not have the luxury of dealing with native Irish affairs as generously as I would have wished, but, in so far as it proved practicable, I have attempted to bring them in from the wings: if they are not yet centre-stage, they are, I hope, a little bit closer to it.

There is more than one reason why the Irish have been relegated to second place in the history of their own country. It is partly to do with the fact that many of the experts on Gaelic Ireland have preferred to concentrate their efforts on an earlier period of Irish history. It is partly to do too with the sources for the subject. Historians are only as good as their sources and cannot write history if the evidence for it is lacking. As regards medieval Ireland, the documentary, archaeological, architectural, and artifactual sources for the history of the English colonial community there are far more wide-ranging and accessible than they are for Gaelic Ireland. The documentary sources for the Anglo-Irish colony are in part the legacy of its administrators in both Dublin and Westminster. These administrative records are relatively easy to use (once the language barrier has been overcome) and they have enabled historians to build up a much more comprehensive picture of colonial affairs than of the affairs of the native Irish. The latter, by contrast, have left little in the way of conventional administrative records, but a great mass of annalistic material and literature, and it is difficult to know how best this intractable material can be exploited.[3]

Here, the language barrier has played an important part. The comments of Francis John Byrne, one of the leading authorities on early medieval Ireland, that the subject 'is interesting and important enough to demand the serious attention of a sympathetic historian ... whoever he may be, he must at least pay the subjects of his study the elementary courtesy of learning their language',[4] apply equally to later medieval Ireland, and yet it is fair to say that many of the leading scholars in the field have failed this test. This has meant that, with a handful of exceptions, historians who have dealt with the native Irish in the later Middle Ages have had to do so without the use of the literary remnants of their civilization, and this has undoubtedly hindered an understanding of the subject. They have had to construct a history based on external observations on the Irish and on translated annalistic material. The result is that the frequently unsympathetic and uncomprehending view of the contemporary external commentator on native Ireland has sometimes found its way into modern secondary literature on the subject, and the impression, which annals of their nature tend to give since they are often no more than a catalogue of battles, of a turbulent and anarchic society, has been clearly visible on the pages of modern historiography.

Another reason for the disproportionate attention devoted to colonial as opposed to native Ireland has, frankly, to do with the predisposition of those scholars who work in the field. Throughout the twentieth century some of the greatest historians of later medieval Ireland have felt more comfortable in an Anglo-Irish environment (and it must be said in their defence that they readily acknowledged as much). This is as much a feature of the work of such stalwarts as Eric St John Brooks, H. G. Richardson, G. O. Sayles, and G. J. Hand,[5] as it is of their great predecessor Goddard Henry Orpen in his monumental four-volume study, *Ireland under the Normans, 1169–1333*, published 1911–20, a work whose importance for the development of Irish historical scholarship could not be overestimated. Orpen has not been given due credit for the efforts to which he went, both in this monograph and in numerous articles, to understand native Ireland, yet, whatever the depth of his knowledge on the subject, one always senses that he never quite warmed to it: his heart lay with the colonists, and his work remains the story of the extirpation of what he calls Irish tribalism and the imposition of the 'Pax Normannica'.

Orpen's approach produced a reaction in the work of Eoin Mac Neill, in his *Phases of Irish History*, which appeared in 1919, and Edmund Curtis, whose *History of Medieval Ireland* was published in 1923 (and of which a thoroughly revised edition appeared in 1938). While differing from Orpen in some significant matters of interpretation, and in particular in the attitude to and emphasis they chose to place on Gaelic Ireland, both men were happy to acknowledge their indebtedness to Orpen, and their criticisms were mercifully free of that rancour which has bedevilled other branches of Irish historiography. This is exemplified by the fact that Orpen's spiritual successor, Jocelyn Otway-Ruthven, dedicated to Curtis (a predecessor as Lecky Professor of History at Trinity College, Dublin) her magisterial *History of Medieval Ireland*, a work which, though it remains as essential a narrative of post-invasion Ireland as when it first appeared in 1968, is unashamedly anglocentric in tone, to the extent that the one introductory chapter devoted to Gaelic Ireland is the work of another scholar (the late Kathleen Hughes).

If Otway-Ruthven inherited Orpen's mantle, the successor to Curtis is another Lecky Professor, James Lydon, whose work, while frequently focusing on Anglo-Irish affairs, including his *Lordship of Ireland in the Middle Ages* (1972), and his *Ireland in the Later Middle Ages* (1973), exudes Curtis's empathetic attitude to the inhabitants and civilization of Gaelic Ireland. The best features of Otway-Ruthven's and Lydon's work have been inherited by their students Robin Frame and Katharine Simms, the former in his *Colonial Ireland, 1169–1369* (1981) and his *English Lordship in Ireland, 1318–1361* (1982), which, as their names suggest, concentrate on Anglo-Irish affairs, and the latter in her *From Kings to Warlords* (1987), the only thorough examination of later medieval Gaelic society to appear since Kenneth Nicholls's pioneering *Gaelic and Gaelicised Ireland in the Middle Ages*, published in 1972. One may add here the work, especially on ecclesiastical history, of Aubrey Gwynn and John Watt,[6] the recent and important study, by Marie Therese Flanagan, of the English invasion, entitled *Irish Society, Anglo-Norman Settlers, Angevin Kingship. Interactions in Ireland in the Late Twelfth Century* (1989), and considerable insights on late medieval Ireland provided by Art Cosgrove and, in many challenging and important publications, Steven Ellis.[7]

With this generation of scholars the earlier barrier between Anglo-Ireland and Gaelic Ireland may with confidence be said to be breaking down. It is no longer acceptable to treat the affairs of one in a vacuum. Both natives and newcomers in medieval Ireland mingled in their daily lives; they must mingle too on the pages of history.

1

Dwellers at the Earth's Edge[1]

Surely the most incisive commentary on Ireland and on Irish life ever produced is *Topographia Hiberniae,* an account written by a man called Gerald de Barri, better known as Giraldus Cambrensis or Gerald of Wales, as a consequence of two visits which he made to the country in 1183 and 1185.[2] Gerald, a strong advocate of church reform, was partly Anglo-Norman and partly Welsh, and his family were among the first to settle in Ireland after the invasion of the late 1160s. His commentary on Ireland is therefore not an unbiased one, and in many respects resembles what a European settler in the Americas or Australia in more recent centuries would have said about the indigenous inhabitants there. It is the defence produced by an agent of an invading and conquering army to justify its actions in dispossessing the native peoples, seizing and colonizing their lands, and, if necessary, bringing their way of life to an end. There is not much room here for objectivity. Above all else, Gerald and the countless others like him through the centuries have had one task: that is, to call attention to the deficiencies of the host society and to demonstrate the benefits that will accrue to the aboriginal population as a result of their conquest. The invader, in fact, is doing that population a favour. He is sharing with them that one thing they lack – civilization.

So it is with Gerald of Wales.[3] His description of the Irish way of life has many of the characteristics common to the genre the world over. The Irish are a barbarous race. They have a primitive lifestyle. Although the island they inhabit is rich in pastures, good fishing and hunting, enjoying an excellent climate free of disease and infestation, the inhabitants are too lazy to exploit its potential. They have no interest in commerce, they have no interest in building towns, they have no interest in the hard work involved in arable farming. Their clothes, their appearance and fashions, are odd, to say the least. Their customs and practices, especially in matters sexual, are barbarous, and repugnant to all civilized people. It is a familiar picture and one which need not surprise us.

Gerald, of course, for all his Welsh blood, saw himself (at least at this stage in his career, before disillusionment set in) as an *Anglicus*, as a product of that fusion of cultures that flourished in England after the Norman conquest. He was a member of a conquering race, clearly a rung or two higher on the evolutionary ladder than the mere Irish. The Normans were, after all, renowned for their military discipline; the Irish ran, as Gerald put it, naked into battle in a disorganized rabble. The Normans were famous for their castles; the Irish, in the high Middle Ages when Gerald was writing, showed no great interest in such ostentation. The Normans had fine-tuned the business of administrative organization, financial regulation, and governmental order; the Irish did not keep administrative records, had only begun to experiment with sealed charters, and were a long way from the cult of the civil servant which was in danger, in Gerald's day, of taking root in England. Naturally, therefore, Gerald thought that they were backward and uncivilized, and a lot of what he has to say about the Irish rings true. But they can perhaps be defended from his charge of barbarism.

This accusation stems from Gerald's failure – or, more accurately, his refusal – to understand Irish society. It was, of course, a failure common to many people outside Ireland throughout the Middle Ages. As far as most were concerned, Ireland stuck out in the sea on the furthest edge of the known world: the belief was that one could go no further west without the risk of falling off. In the early eighth century the great historian of the English, Bede, described the Irish as a 'little community, isolated at the uttermost ends of the earth'.[4] He was writing before the discovery of Iceland and Greenland, but, nearly seven hundred years later, a Catalan pilgrim to St Patrick's Purgatory at Lough Derg recorded his achievement in having 'arrived at the end of the earth, in Ireland, which is the most remote province of the western world'.[5] When St Bernard of Clairvaux wrote to the fateful Leinster king Diarmait Mac Murchada, in or around 1148, to congratulate him on having founded a Cistercian abbey at Baltinglass in co. Wicklow, he felt compelled to point out that 'in our opinion it is really a great miracle that a king at the end of the earth, ruling over barbarous peoples, should undertake with great generosity such works of mercy'.[6]

All share the view that Ireland was a place apart – remote, isolated, and, inevitably therefore, different. This was understandable. It was natural to expect that people living in the furthest extremity of the earth would be wild and uncivilized – one would be surprised, perhaps disappointed, if they turned out to be anything else. The Irishman Johannes Scotus Eriugena was arguably the greatest scholar in ninth-century Europe. Yet, one can still appreciate the surprise of the papal librarian Anastasius when, having viewed Eriugena's translation of the writings of Pseudo-Dionysius, executed at the request of the Frankish king, Charles the Bald (grandson of Charlemagne), he remarked:

> It is a wonderful thing how that barbarian, living at the ends of the earth, who might be supposed to be as far removed from the knowledge of this other language [Greek] as he is from the familiar use of it, has been able to comprehend such ideas and translate them into another tongue [Latin]: I refer to Johannes Scotigena, whom I have learned by report to be in all things a holy man.[7]

It seems from this that the thing which surprised Anastasius most was that a place of such obvious isolation as Ireland could nurture a society that produced such scholarship; that it could be, in spite of its many and obvious peculiarities, part of the European mainstream, open to external influences, and capable of making an important contribution to European civilization. And yet it undoubtedly was part of the mainstream and besides producing a substantial corpus of Latin literature, it has left us the most extensive and wide-ranging body of vernacular literature in early medieval Europe. So how was this brought about, what sort of society was it, and how did it come to earn the opprobrium of men such as Gerald?

Ireland, now one of the most treeless regions in Europe, was densely forested in the Middle Ages, and woodland was heavily exploited as an economic resource, with laws to protect the forests from unauthorized use or damage.[8] Forest clearance, we know from the scientific evidence, was underway from the early historic period, a process of deforestation which continued into modern times.[9] The island had a network of roads, and the word used for a road, *slige*, meaning 'a felling', indicates that they were paths cut through the forests. For many people, travel by boat on the rivers and lakes, and navigating the seas around Ireland's shores, must have been the preferred option, though – in spite of the fact that the *Navigatio Sancti Brendani*, recounting the alleged transatlantic voyages of Brendan the Navigator, became one of the most popular works in medieval Europe – the evidence would suggest that the Irish did not enjoy a particularly strong seafaring tradition until the Viking Age, and it was only at this point that naval warfare became significant. It was in this period too that several Viking coastal settlements developed into towns, hitherto unknown in Ireland, although there were settlements of some sort around many of the larger ecclesiastical centres.[10]

While few traces survive of the lives of ordinary people, the rich and powerful inhabitants of early medieval Ireland have left behind the remnants of their civilization. The countryside is dotted with the remains of tens of thousands of ring-forts, the farmsteads of early Ireland. Ring-forts were usually constructed in places where the land was worth farming, often at or near the top of a hill with a good view of the surrounding countryside. Ringed by as many as three ditches up to two metres deep and sometimes filled with water, with banks made from the earth taken from the ditches, and perhaps a palisade on top, they had a strong defensive capacity. Such an earthen ring-fort is known as a *rath* and the area inside it where the occupants lived is a *lios*. In parts of the country where the land is stony, ring-forts are generally constructed of stone and known as a *caiseal* or *cathair*, the word *dún* usually being reserved for exceptionally large examples. The farmhouses and buildings would have been at the centre, with perhaps a milking-yard outside, a mill for the corn (if the owners were wealthy enough to afford one), and servants' huts, and stretching beyond them would have been the fields of crops and pastures for grazing animals. The lake-dwelling, or *crannóg*, is another form of habitation surviving from early medieval Ireland, though far less common than the ring-fort. Many of these are man-made islands, and thus more difficult and more expensive to build than a ring-fort, but providing better defence since they were harder of access. Being so costly to build, we can be fairly sure that they were the well-defended homes of powerful people, and some the palaces of kings.[11]

Until the late Viking Age Ireland was a coinless society where cows were a common medium of exchange (a *sét* being a unit of value equal to a heifer or half a milch cow), an indication of both their prevalence and their economic importance.[12] Land was measured in terms of the number of cows it could sustain, while fines and rents and dues were also calculated in cows. A well-off farmer was a *bóaire*, a 'lord of cows'. All the evidence from the surviving literature, both from the annals and the sagas, indicates that cattle-raiding was an everyday occurrence. It is interesting to note too that whereas elsewhere in Europe in the early Middle Ages it was common to make manuscripts from sheep-skin, in Ireland calf-skin was preferred.[13] Dairy-farming was at the heart of the Irish agricultural system. In summer it was normal to live on milk and dairy products such as butter, cheese, curds and whey, while in autumn some cattle were killed, their beef being salted to eat in winter. From what we can tell (largely as a result of archaeo-logical excavation), meat from pigs was also quite common, the latter being fed on the mast from the forests. Sheep, it would appear, were kept more for their wool than their mutton, while the native horse was small, perhaps not unlike the Connemara pony of today, and horse-meat, though occa-sionally consumed, was generally frowned upon.[14]

Some arable farming was done in all parts of Ireland, but it was generally not as important as pastoral farming; the latter, of course, was also less time-consuming and less energy-sapping and the Irish preference for it was something upon which foreign writers were wont to comment derisively. That said, the surviving written sources indicate that extensive crop-cultivation took place in early medieval Ireland, though obvi-ously the situation varied from region to region in accordance with landscape and climatic variations. Ploughing and sowing were carried out in spring, the former with oxen rather than horses, though the possession of a full plough-team of four to six animals was beyond all but the most prosperous farmers. Harvesting was done, using the sickle, by a team known as a *meitheal* and, once harvested, kilns were used to dry the newly threshed grain, though again less well-off farmers might only rent, or possess a share in, a drying kiln and a barn for storing the grain. Grain was milled in horizontal water-mills, which were elaborate affairs served by an artificially diverted mill-race, and the mill-wright was a craftsman of some stature in early Irish society. Here again, mills seem to have been jointly owned and the subject was contentious enough for a law to exist to regulate their shared use.[15] The main crops were oats, barley and wheat, used for making bread (wheaten bread being the preserve of royalty and nobility), porridge, gruel and, in the case of the barley, for brewing beer. We know that vegetable patches and apple orchards were cultivated and bees kept.[16]

It is very difficult to assess the relative prosperity of early medieval Ireland, but since the economy was largely agrarian and the population (in so far as it is possible to tell) low, the evidence would seem to suggest that conditions for many communities were prosperous, other than at times of famine and disease. If weather conditions were right and cattle were free of murrain, the food supply was guaranteed. This made for a relatively stable economy, with no undue pressure for land, and with such land as was in use being carefully husbanded and properly regulated by law. The surviving sources, and the archaeological and artifactual evidence in particular, point to the existence of a considerable amount of disposable wealth in early Christian Ireland. This is represented today by the extant vellum manuscripts, some of which, it is estimated, would have required the skins of several hundred cattle, and by the great array of precious metalwork objects which survive from the period, some of them secular (such as brooches and ring-pins), many others ecclesiastical, such as altar vessels, ornamental book-covers, bishops' crosiers, and shrines for sacred relics. These, in turn, are the relics of a society that was well organized and, in certain quarters at least, wealthy, and that must have compared favourably with other parts of western Europe.

We are not dependent on archaeologists alone to piece together this picture of early Irish economy and society. In fact, our mental picture of Ireland in, for instance, the seventh and early eighth centuries is clearer and far more detailed than that available for almost any country in Europe. This is because it was at that point that the Old Irish law texts were set down (the Brehon laws as they are often called, from the word *brithemain*, meaning 'judges'), many of which still survive in later manuscripts. These give a remarkably detailed and intricate picture of Irish society at the time of their composition. A number of caveats are necessary, however. The law tracts were composed before the Viking incursions, before the church reform of the late eleventh and early twelfth centuries, and before the English invasion, an event which, next to the introduction of Christianity, has been the most formative external influence on Irish history. Irish society changed over the course of time, and we must be careful not to present a picture of a society that is static and fossilized by falling into the trap of using texts which antedate these events to describe their aftermath. Furthermore, the law tracts present a highly schematized and symmetric picture of society; this obviously appealed to the early jurists' quest for precision but cannot frequently have matched reality. If we complement the law tracts with other sources of varying composition dates and intended to serve a different purpose – texts such as the annals, the genealogies, the Saints' Lives, the great sagas, origin-legends, praise-poetry, and so on – we get a much rounder picture, one which proves that, as in today's world, the theory of the law is often contradicted by the reality of practice.

The greatest influence on the formation and development of Irish law was the Christian church. Until quite recently, scholars believed that the Old Irish laws were collections of ancient oral and pre-Christian custom, later written down by members of a secular legal caste which, after the introduction of Christianity, adapted itself reluctantly to the new regime and became Christian and literate. One frequently reads that the Old Irish laws were the preserve of the druids, and that, in spite of their Christian veneer, we can use the laws (and the sagas) as evidence for the pre-Christian pagan past, to provide us with (to borrow from the title of one now outdated work on the subject) 'a window on the Iron Age'.[17] More recent work, however, has suggested that the writings of the period, including the law texts, were not pagan but Christian, and were not written by secular descendants of the druids but by churchmen, learned Christian jurists, who drew not just on native sources but on foreign sources, and the Old Testament in particular, in order to lay down the law proper for a Christian society.[18]

The churchmen who came to christianize Ireland in the fifth and sixth centuries brought into the country copies of the great works of learning produced by the early church fathers, men like Augustine, Gregory the Great, Jerome, Ambrose, and many others. In the late sixth and the seventh centuries the church-run schools of Ireland became great centres of learning in such Christian literature, and in time made a significant contribution to both church and society in

14

Britain and Europe. A caste of scholars emerged who were lawyers, canonists, historians, poets and grammarians, who wrote in Latin and Irish and who were very often churchmen and who functioned in a society that was predominantly ecclesiastical (though, of course, much of what we know of that society we derive from churchmen, and to a large extent we view it through their eyes). While not everyone would accept that all the lawyers and all the poets were clerics, the fact is that the environment in which they worked was ecclesiastically dominated, and the men at the upper ranks of the profession were churchmen – literate, church-trained, and in holy orders.

When these men were drawing up rules for governing society, let us say, the proper punishment for theft, they looked to the Old Testament and adopted the biblical precept as their own, adapting it perhaps to suit particular Irish circumstances. The society that they helped to mould was one that was intensely aristocratic. The leading churchmen themselves were often aristocrats. St Colum Cille, for example, is said to have been a great-grandson of Niall Noígiallach (Niall of the Nine Hostages), eponymous ancestor of the Uí Néill, the most powerful dynastic federation in early medieval Ireland. Being an aristocratic society it was by its nature hierarchical. Status and honour (*enech*, literally 'face') meant everything. To offend against a person of high status, to outrage his honour, incurred a greater penalty than a similar crime against a person of lower status. Status was measured in terms of one's 'honour-price' (*lóg n-enech*), which had to be paid, in whole or in part, in restitution for major offences against him, and these were considerably higher for a king than a cottier. Likewise, an individual could forfeit his honour-price if he broke certain rules: a king should not do manual work, default on an oath or tolerate a satire; a lord should not refuse hospitality, shelter a fugitive or eat stolen food.[19] The law made a basic distinction between those who were *nemed* ('sacred'), including kings, clerics and poets, and those who were not, and then a further distinction among the latter between those who were *sóer* ('free') and those who were *dóer* ('unfree'). But there were essentially three grades of society –

kings of one kind or another, lords of varying degrees of status, and various classifications of commoners. In the latter two groups there was a certain amount of mobility, some upward but even more downward mobility as people at the lower grades of the nobility sank over time to become high-ranking commoners. In the highly stratified and rather rigid world of the law tracts, a person's exact position in this arrangement was vital.

Ireland was a land of many kings. According to the law tracts, there were three grades of kings. At the bottom of the scale was the king of a small local kingdom or *túath*, and he was known as the *rí túaithe*. Then came the 'overking' or *ruiri* who was king not only over his own *túath* but over several other petty kingdoms. Finally, there was the 'king of overkings' or *rí ruirech*, who effectively ruled a whole province, though even his power was rooted in his own core territory.[20] The annals and sagas frequently accord individuals the title of king of Ireland, but in the law tracts a king of all Ireland, while not unheard of, is an extremely rare bird.[21] That, therefore, was the theory of it, and it may also have been the practice at the time when the classical law tracts were being put together (though some legal historians would doubt it), but the fact of the matter is that kings lower than the *rí ruirech*, the province-king, hardly mattered. Over time, many of these lesser individuals were no longer called a king (*rí*) at all. By the eleventh and twelfth centuries, the *túath*, the old tribal kingdom, was no longer a 'kingdom', and it was not ruled by a king but by a man described in Irish documents as a *toísech* (which originally may have meant a leader of a war-band) or more often by a *tigerna*, a 'lord' (indeed, from as early as the eighth century the Latin *dux* is frequently used for such people). It seems clear that the refusal to call such a man a *rí* reflects a distinct erosion in the status of petty kings subsequent to the time when the law tracts were compiled, and a corresponding increase in the power of the province-kings who came from the ranks of the dominant dynasties.[22]

If we examine the actuality of royal power, we can see the same sort of change taking place. Clearly, Irish society revolved around the figure of the king, and great symbolism was attached to his inauguration, his mating with the goddess of the land from which would come fertility to man and beast throughout his reign,[23] the alleged practices at which ceremonies earned Gerald de Barri's condemnation in a famous passage in his *Topographia*.[24] Yet, if one were to take the law tracts at face value, kings had relatively few powers. While stress was laid on a king's justice, from which flowed peace and prosperity, and from whose injustice sprang famine, plague and infertility, the king, it is clear, did not make the law and he did not enforce justice, save in exceptional circumstances. According to the text known as *Críth Gablach*, a king could pass a legal ordinance only in an emergency, such as in a time of plague, after defeat in battle, or, curiously, 'for expulsion of a foreign race, i.e. against the Saxons'.[25] But we know that, despite what the law tracts say, kings played a prominent role in enforcing ecclesiastical law and ensuring the collection of church taxes.[26] Increasingly, as time went by, they also began to raise secular taxes, one of the better-known instances being the tax of 4000 cows levied by Ruaidrí Ua Conchobair on 'the men of Ireland' in 1166 which he gave to the Hiberno-Scandinavians of Dublin in return for their acknowledgement of his claim to the high-kingship of Ireland.[27] By then too we find kings passing secular legislation. In 1040 the Munster king Donnchad, son of the great Brian Bóruma, legislated against theft, while a decade later he passed a law prohibiting injustices of any kind, while his nephew and successor Tairdelbach Ua Briain passed a law in 1068 which caused an annalist to remark that 'no better law had been enacted in Munster for a long time'.[28] Apparently, then, kings were far from powerless as legislators, particularly in this later period.

Under the law, the king was not the ultimate owner of the land of the tribal territory in a way that kings elsewhere claimed to be. These lands were owned by the free families over whom he was the chosen leader, though the king was, however, owed the loyalty of freemen, and could convene an *óenach*, or assembly. Where kings *were* granted considerable powers under the law was in the field of external relations. It was he who made peace or war on behalf of his kingdom, and he might summon his men at any time to take part in a *slógad*, or hosting, to attack a neighbouring kingdom or defend his own from attack. It was he who entered into negotiations with other kingdoms. It was he who decided if the kingdom should submit to another more powerful neighbour (which might involve the acceptance of a ceremonial gift, and the handing over of tribute and/or hostages) or if they should attempt to force a weak kingdom into submission. Technically speaking, an overkingdom had no right to annex another *túath* and to expel its dynasty, but the cold fact of life is that from quite an early period the dominant dynasties in the island were busy interfering in power struggles among their neighbours, ejecting their inferiors from kingship, and appropriating their territories to themselves.[29]

It is this activity which has given the impression that Ireland was a country where anarchy, indeed, chaos, reigned in the body politic, if we may call it that. Goddard Orpen, for instance, the great historian of Anglo-Norman Ireland, described pre-invasion Irish politics as 'a maze of inter-provincial and inter-tribal fighting'.[30] To an extent, it was that; but it was not purposeless. It goes without saying that most people in early medieval Ireland were simple land-dwellers, farmers who spent their lives peaceably, living off the produce of the land. By comparison, only small numbers lived as fighters and warriors. The problem is that we learn most of what we know about the politics of the period from the various compilations of annals, and annalists, when not simply recording church news, concentrate their writing on recounting the activities of kings and warriors, the people who did most of the fighting.

Perhaps the major weakness in the Irish body politic was that there was no definite law for choosing a king. In any kingdom, whether a tiny *túath* or a whole province, a man might make himself king so long as he was brave enough, popular enough, and powerful enough to do so. If he was the son or close relative of a previous king, his chances were all the better. However, a king during the course of his life might have several wives and many sons by each. In a short time a royal family was divided into several rival branches, with cousins and second cousins all trying to push the others out and make their leader king. It was when they did not manage to do so that they invaded the lands of another kin-group or sept and set themselves up as kings there.

The point can best be illustrated by picking one province, let us say Connacht, and comparing how it stood in the eighth century with how it stood in the twelfth. At an earlier point in history the dominant dynasty in Connacht had been the Uí Fiachrach. In common with most Irish lineage names, this is a patronymic and means, in effect, that the Uí Fiachrach either were, thought they were, or wanted others to think they were, all descended from one man, Fiachra. What happened in the course of time was that the family split up into two main branches, who fought with each other for supremacy. The Uí Fiachrach Muaide ended up, as their name suggests, in the valley of the river Moy in north-west Connacht, while the Uí Fiachrach Aidni ended up in the south of the province.

To make matters worse, the Uí Fiachrach were not only fighting themselves. They faced competition for the control of Connacht from another dynasty. These were the Uí Briúin and, as their name implies, they all claimed to have sprung from a man called Brión. About the year 700 the Uí Briúin were based around Carnfree in the modern co. Roscommon. Over the years, they too began to splinter. The first branch, the Uí Briúin Aí, stayed in the original homelands. As they grew, they also produced new segments and, after the eleventh century when the Irish septs generally resorted to the precocious device of adopting surnames, the best-known of the Uí Briúin Aí was the famous line of Uí Chonchobair (the O'Connors), kings of Connacht throughout the high and later Middle Ages. The second branch of the Uí Briúin was the Uí Briúin Seola, who were pushed out by the others and settled in new lands east of Lough Corrib. They later split up again and the famous Uí Flaithbertaig (O'Flaherty family) was their most successful branch. Finally, there were the Uí Briúin Bréifne, who moved north-east, dispossessed other weaker septs from their lands in what is now Cavan and Leitrim, and set themselves up as kings there. Later, their chief family was the Uí Ruairc (O'Rourkes).

So it went on over the centuries, one dynasty rising in power, another falling. That is what most of the fighting in native Irish society was about. As dynasties grew, they made war on their distant relatives to try to grab the kingship, and they spread out into the lands of other septs. Not everyone can be a winner, however, and in time many families faded into insignificance. Like the lesser kings they fell down the social ladder, and they let others compete for the top prize of the provincial kingship. The theory of the law books was cast aside. In the eleventh and twelfth centuries the half dozen or so great kings ruthlessly expelled whole dynasties, partitioned the weaker kingdoms and appointed either their own sons or their favourites as puppet rulers over them, and granted away sections of them to their own vassals or to the church. As a result, these province-kings were dominating huge territorial lordships, and operating within structures of power and lordship that were not very far removed from those which pertained in the so-called feudal kingdoms of Europe.

Below the rank of kings stood the noblemen, and below the nobles the commoners. A nobleman or lord (*flaith*) was obviously distinguishable from a commoner by virtue of his birth and wealth, but, in early medieval Ireland, it was the possession of clients (*céili*, literally 'companions') which conferred the status of lordship. Clientship was the Irish equivalent of the feudal bond. It was the institution which bound the lord and his dependant together in a relationship which had mutual benefits, but was, of course, more favourable to the lord. In essence, the lord granted the client a fief (*rath*) of land or stock, and in return the client bound himself to make specific payments to the lord: he might provide a food rent in the form of part of his produce, or hospitality to the lord during winter, or some such service. It was part of the duty of the lord to provide physical defence for the client and to protect his rights from outside encroachment. A lord who failed in his duty to a client could, according to the Introduction to the great legal compendium known as the

Senchas Már ('the Great Tradition'), be demoted to the rank of a commoner.[31]

There were two kinds of clients – the free client (*sóerchéile*) and the base client (*céile gíallnae*). The free client was often quite a wealthy nobleman himself and had to pay a high annual rent for his fief, and the bond with his lord (which he was free to terminate at will) seems to have involved him undertaking to perform military service, to accompany the lord on military expeditions and raids, for which he might obtain a share of the plunder. Free clientship, therefore, provided Irish lords with their military retinues. But somebody had to remain at home, to work the land, to produce transferable wealth, and this is where the base clients came in. The lord advanced the base client his fief – cows, land, farm implements, and so forth. It was a system whereby the lord could lease surplus stock to the client, and get a share of the produce that resulted. For instance, the law tracts dictate that the well-off farmer, known as the *bóaire,* paid his lord an annual food rent of a milch cow, while the less well-off *ócaire* paid a two-year-old bullock. The client could not afford the stock himself, and needed the lord to finance the deal, while the lord could not have survived without the client doing his share of the manual work, motivated, of course, by that most basic instinct, the pursuit of profit. The base client also provided hospitality for the lord and his entourage, performed military duties and, we are told, had to help in the construction of the rampart about the lord's *dún* (or fort).[32] Because of the base client's role as 'provider of food[rent]', later sources call him a *biatach*, who became in turn the *betagh* familiar to students of Anglo-Norman Ireland, native Irish manorial tenants some of whom may have had a status similar to that of an English villein, others of whom were substantial farmers.[33]

Although the clients were free men, that is not to say that early Irish society was in any sense egalitarian; quite the reverse. The family, or kin-group (*fine*), rather than the individual, was the legal unit recognized under the law. It was the family which owned property, which came into an inheritance, which was held responsible for the misdemeanours of its individual members. If a man was murdered, it was the prerogative of the family to seek revenge or to claim compensation in the form of a 'body-fine' (*éraic*) from the culprit. The family group that mattered most in the early period (to judge from its ubiquity in the law tracts) was the *derbfine* or 'true kin', made up of all those descended from a common great-grandfather in the male line. (The female line was not recognized because, when a woman married, though she retained some links with her own kin, her children were normally part of her husband's *fine*.) It seems quite likely, however, that at a relatively early point (though to date these matters is notoriously difficult) the *derbfine* was being replaced by the nuclear family as the most significant legal grouping, and was no longer the primary property-owning kindred group.[34]

Today's nuclear family would be rather surprised by its medieval equivalent. Modern Ireland, for so long a divorce-free bastion, could not be more different from its earlier self, in that, while divorce was being stamped out by reforming churchmen all over Europe, it remained commonplace in Ireland, at least among the royalty and aristocracy for whom records survive.[35] This was not in defiance of Irish law, it was part and parcel of it. Divorce was permitted in many circumstances. A full law tract survives on the subject, *Cáin Lánamna*, which concentrates on how the couple's property should be divided at the divorce. The law adopted a very severe attitude to women regarded as having left their husbands without due cause. Such a woman, the law says, has no rights in society, and cannot be harboured by anybody. With few exceptions, women could not buy or sell or make any form of contract or transaction without the consent of those who had authority over her: her father when she was a girl, her husband when she married, her son when she was a widow. This is an illustration of the way in which the claims sometimes made as to the degree of freedom and power enjoyed by women in early Irish society have been exaggerated.[36] In the sagas, it is true, women are frequently very powerful – one only has to think of Queen Medb in *Táin Bó Cúailnge*, who was the real leader of Connacht rather than her weak husband, Ailill. But in real life it was otherwise and the power of women was much more circumscribed. The annals are our primary source for politico-military history, and it is hard to find in them a single example of a female political or military leader. The image of women portrayed in 'wisdom-texts' such as 'The Triads of Ireland' is very different.[37] Here, the qualities one finds being lauded are reticence of speech, virtue, and industry in the home. Frequently too one finds that sexual promiscuity by women is condemned (admittedly by men and usually clerical men at that), as are other bad habits such as making spells, composing or commissioning illegal satires, and stealing.[38]

As might be expected, sexual promiscuity in men was not frowned upon to the same extent. Medieval Ireland was, in fact, a country in which polygamy seems to have been rife. The author of one law tract, *Bretha Crólige*, claimed that there was disagreement in Irish law as to whether polygamy was proper, but justified the practice by reference to the Old Testament, claiming that God's chosen people enjoyed a plurality of unions.[39] The laws allowed for different forms of sexual union – formal unions, which were obviously what we would call a marriage, but also less permanent arrangements where the woman would have fewer property rights and entitlements than the chief wife. However, the children of either arrangement had rights of inheritance, and this is obviously one of the most frequent causes of succession disputes, since the brothers fighting to succeed to the kingship were very often born of different mothers and lacked much in the way of personal attachment to each other. This situation was made worse by the practice of fosterage, whereby the upbringing of children was entrusted to others, normally political allies, the result being that individuals sometimes developed stronger ties with their foster-family than with their own family.

The church, of course, looked with disapproval on these multiple marriages. The most frequent causes of external complaint about Irish society in the eleventh and twelfth centuries were the irregularities in marriage law. Those commenting on Ireland, the likes of Gerald de Barri, St Bernard of Clairvaux, and more than one archbishop of Canterbury, even the popes, continually condemned Irish marriage laws and the sexual licentiousness which they believed to be rampant in Irish society. They may have exaggerated the situation. In a society where aristocrats married aristocrats, and where the pool of prospective spouses was so limited, it was inevitable that marriage would take place within what the church viewed as the forbidden degrees of consanguinity (marriage even to one's distant cousins). Irish kings and nobles in so doing were technically guilty of incest. If one adds to that the prevalence of divorce and the presence of polygamy and serial monogamy (the practice of putting several wives aside in turn and replacing them with another), there was, relatively speaking, a high proportion of half-siblings and step-siblings, and complicated personal entanglements were bound to occur. The rather severe clerics of the Gregorian reform frowned on this, needless to say. But in some respects the Irish were only doing formally what kings and nobles all over Christendom did informally, while maintaining a pretence of adherence to church law on the subject. Kings sought above all an heir. When they failed to produce one by their first wife, irrespective of what the church said, more often than not they found a method of putting her aside and trying again with a new wife. Kings, too, sought alliances. They married not out of love or desire but out of political expediency. That does not mean that they did not love or experience desire, merely that they often did so with someone other than their wife, and to these illicit sexual liaisons, and their offspring, the church usually turned a blind eye.

However, by making formal provision for the divorced wife, or the children of a second wife, or a concubine and her offspring, the Irish kings and their legal system by the late eleventh century stood condemned abroad. Archbishop Lanfranc of Canterbury, writing in 1074 to Tairdelbach Ua Briain of Munster, listed a number of what he regarded as the ills bedevilling church and society in Ireland: these included faults as serious as the improper consecration of bishops; the conferral of holy orders in return for money; and irregularities in the provision of that most basic of sacraments, baptism. However, his first, most detailed and most severe criticism was reserved for marriage practices which he described as 'a law of marriage which is rather a law of fornication'. He added that 'certain reports have reached us ... that in your kingdom a man abandons at his own discretion and without any grounds in canon law the wife who is lawfully married to him, not hesitating to form a criminal alliance ... with any other woman he pleases, either a relative of his own or of his deserted wife or a woman whom somebody else has abandoned in an equally disgraceful way'.[40] When Lanfranc's successor, Archbishop Anselm, wrote to Tairdelbach's son Muirchertach, again marriage topped his list of complaints: 'It is said that men exchange their wives as freely and publicly as a man might change his horse'.[41] Marriage practices were among the issues addressed at the first Irish reforming synod for which a record survives, that of Cashel in 1101, although apparently without much success.[42] When Bernard of Clairvaux in his 'Life of St Malachy' was depicting in colourful language the sort of challenge that faced his subject, he described how Malachy 'had been sent not to men but to beasts', adding that they 'were Christians in name, in fact pagans; there was no giving of tithes or first-fruits; no entry into lawful marriages; no making of confessions'.[43]

This unacceptable sexual laxity was something for which the Irish paid dearly, to the extent that in 1155 Pope Adrian IV gave legal sanction for an invasion of their country by a neighbouring king, Henry II of England, allegedly for the purpose of eradicating such evils. It was more than a decade before the English invasion of Ireland took place, but when Pope Alexander III wrote to Henry II in its immediate aftermath, he began his letter by expressing his joy at how Henry had

> extended your majesty's power and wonderfully and magnificently triumphed over the disordered and undisciplined Irish, a people, we have heard, the Roman rulers, conquerors of the world in their time, left unapproached, a people unmindful of the fear of God which, as if unbridled, indiscriminately turns

aside from the straight road for the depths of vice, throws off the religion of Christian faith and virtue, and destroys itself in internecine slaughter,[44]

and then added, as the first item on his list of complaints against the Irish, that they 'openly cohabit with their step-mothers and do not blush to bear children by them; a man will misuse his brother's wife while his brother is still alive; a man will live in concubinage with two sisters, and many have intercourse with daughters of mothers they have deserted'. This, then, is the justification for the invasion. When the English court chronicler Roger of Howden condemned the Irish it was because they had 'as many wives as they wished',[45] and when Ralph of Diss reported on the Irish agreement at the synod of Cashel in 1171–2 to conform to the usages of the English church, he claimed that it was 'above all else, in matters relating to marriage'.[46]

The view that the conquest of Ireland was brought about by the immorality of the Irish was not confined to outsiders. The Annals of Connacht, in recording the events of the year 1233, preserve a story to the effect that the pope offered the last high-king of Ireland, Ruaidrí Ua Conchobair, six wives and the title of high-king if he 'would renounce the sin of adultery henceforth'; but, because he would not, 'God took the rule and sovereignty from his seed for ever, in punishment for his sin'.[47] This same story is preserved in a slightly different form in the Scottish chronicle of John of Fordun:

> The kingdom of Ireland … came to an end with the lustful King Roderic (begotten, forsooth, of the stock of our own race), who would have six wives at once, not like a Christian king, and would not send them away, in spite of the loss of his kingdom – though he had often been warned by the whole church, both archbishops and bishops, and chidden with fearful threats, by all the inhabitants, both chiefs and private persons. He was therefore despised by them all; and they would never more deign to obey him – neither deign they to obey any king to this day. Besides, as thou seest, that kingdom, so renowned formerly, in our forefathers' time, is now miserably split up into thirty kingdoms or more.[48]

A version of it found its way into the text known as *Trí Biorgh-aoithe an Bháis* ('The Three Shafts of Death') written by the seventeenth-century antiquarian Geoffrey Keating, in which the fate of Ua Conchobair and of his enemy Diarmait Mac Murchada are tied together, the latter's downfall being blamed on his rape of the wife of Tigernán Ua Ruairc of Bréifne, Ua Conchobair's on his lust for all the women of his kingdom, married or single.[49] It is not the accuracy of the story that matters so much as the implication: that the Irish brought conquest upon themselves by their refusal to conform to the norms of society elsewhere in twelfth-century Europe.

2

A KINGDOM UNIQUE TO ITSELF?

Geoffrey Keating's lasting achievement is his monumental *Foras Feasa ar Éirinn* ('Foundation of Knowledge on Ireland'), compiled around 1634, one of the aims of which was to refute what he regarded as the long-standing denigration of Ireland by foreign, mainly English commentators, and to assert its right to sovereign status. Ireland is, he says, a 'kingdom unique to itself, like a little world'.[1] However sincerely he may have held that view, Keating's analysis, which has been shared by many others down through the centuries, has only served to perpetuate the notion that there was something immutable and archaic about early Irish society, an 'enduring tradition' (to borrow from the title of one recent work on the subject),[2] which merited preservation in its own right, and which prevailed in spite of the country's repeated subjection to external assault. This view does not do justice to its subject, in that it fails to recognize that Irish society was an evolving entity which was not only responsive to external stimulus but had within itself the capacity to change. One of those external stimuli, the Viking incursion, was thought by one scholar to have brought about 'the passing of the old order',[3] since he viewed the political, social, and economic changes which seemed to be taking place in its aftermath as a product of that cataclysm; it is, however, possible to argue that those changes would have

28

taken place, or were taking place, anyway, and that it was not Irish society that adapted to cope with the Vikings so much as the reverse.

That is not to say that the Vikings were not, from the Irish perspective, a pernicious force and that the Irish did not have to develop a means of surmounting the challenge they represented. The first recorded Viking raid on Ireland took place in 795. While it is wrong to paint the Vikings as mere pirates, their early raids were certainly very damaging and unquestionably the fabric of Irish society – both church and lay society – suffered greatly as a result of the destruction of property, the seizure of moveable wealth, and the increased expenditure on arms and armies which the Viking wars necessitated. There may even have been moments in the ninth century when they appeared capable of conquering the whole country. Instead, though, over a period, they became part of everyday life, just one more violent group in a society that was already very violent. A great deal has been written about the destruction of the monasteries by Viking raiders, and they did, of course, raid the church; but so too did the Irish.[4] The medieval church was an intensely political institution. In Ireland, every dynasty had its favoured church, and every province had its major ecclesiastical showpiece. Rival dynasties and the kings of neighbouring provinces had few qualms about attacking such centres, since by impoverishing an ecclesiastical settlement which was the hub of economic activity in their enemy's land, they were impoverishing the enemy himself. The Vikings acted similarly. Since 841 their main centre of power had been Dublin. If the Vikings were destroyers, pillagers of the church, the area around Dublin which they came to control should have been denuded of ecclesiastical wealth, property, and influence. However, this was anything but the case and the churches and church property at places like Clondalkin, Glasnevin, Kilmainham, Lusk, Shankill, Swords and Tallaght remained important focal points in the diocese of Dublin for centuries to come.

Dublin, and the other main Viking enclaves at Waterford, Wexford, Limerick and Cork, came to resemble other Irish kingdoms, and were open to attack from the armies of other kings. The Irish found it hard to unite against them and Irish kings often fought alongside the Vikings against other Irish dynasts. Perhaps the earliest notable example of this collaboration occurred in 850 when the Vikings, who had recently established a base at Dublin, joined their neighbouring Irish king, Cináed mac Conaing of North Brega, in despoiling the lands of the then high-king, Máel Sechnaill mac Maíl Ruanaid.[5] This form of cooperation was to become a common feature of Irish politics in the years that followed. The Vikings (or Ostmen as they called themselves) had large fleets which Irish kings hired for use against their own enemies. The economic potential of their towns and the trading networks they had established were recognized and exploited by the Irish who, by the eleventh or early twelfth century, had even established royal residences within their walls.[6]

One thing that is noticeable about the main Ostman towns is that they were all in the southern half of Ireland. The northern kings were able to prevent the growth of Viking power in the north of the country, but ultimately this may have been to their own disadvantage since, by denying themselves access to Viking trade, they were stunting their own economic development. That there was extensive Viking settlement in the southern half of Ireland is an indication of the weakness of the kings of Munster, who were unable to prevent them gaining a foothold there. From the seventh century to the mid-tenth century Munster was ruled by the Eóganacht kings: the Meic Carthaig (Mac Carthys), who were later kings of Desmond (*Desmumu*, 'south Munster'), were descended from the Eóganacht. One of the weaknesses from which the Eóganacht suffered was that the kingship of Munster tended to rotate arbitrarily between several competing branches, unlike some other provinces in which a narrow group of families retained the right to succeed to the kingship. Therefore, no one group emerged from the Eóganacht to dominate the kingship and no one centre of power developed within the dynasty. In fact, instead of Munster developing as a kingdom, with one dominant dynasty, it was really a confederation of lesser dynasties. In this period its king was not particularly powerful. He exercised little control over the lesser dynasties within Munster and, with few exceptions, played a very small part on the national stage, frequently suffering defeat at the hands of other more powerful province-kings.[7]

It was because of the weakness and fragmentation of the Eóganacht dynasty that a rival force rose to power in Munster in the tenth century. This was the Dál Cais, whose centre of power was in the basin of the lower Shannon, and whose new power stemmed partly from the fact that they controlled this strategic waterway. The first of their kings to obtain real power was Cennétig mac Lorcáin who, when he died in 951, was called in the annals *rí Tuadmuman*, king of Thomond (literally 'north Munster'), proof that Cennétig's status was such that he could with justification claim to rule not just his core territory of Dál Cais but a large part of the ancient province of Munster. He was succeeded by his son Mathgamain, who gained control over North and East Munster, including the Ostmen of Waterford, whose support he enlisted in obtaining mastery over the other most important Ostman city in Munster, Limerick. When Mathgamain was murdered in 976 he was succeeded by his brother, the illustrious Brian Bóruma.[8] Brian too asserted control over the Ostmen of Limerick and over the rival Eóganacht to make himself king of all Munster in everything but name. As king of Munster Brian was a figure of national importance because now he found himself in conflict with other province-kings; and by far the most important of these was Máel Sechnaill mac Domnaill, king of the Southern Uí Néill.

The Uí Néill were the most important royal dynasty in Ireland.[9] They dominated the northern half of the island, which was known as *Leth Cuinn* ('Conn's Half'), called after Conn Cétchathach (Conn of the Hundred Battles), from whom the province Connacht takes its name. The Uí Néill took their name from Niall Noígiallach (Niall of the Nine Hostages) who was a descendant of Conn, or so the early historians would have us believe. By tradition, some of Niall's sons settled in the north-west of Ireland. One of them, Conall, gave his name to Tír Conaill ('the land of Conall', consisting for the most part of modern co. Donegal), and the people who inhabited this area became known as Cenél Conaill ('the race of Conall'). The name of another son, Eógan, is preserved in Inis Eógain (the Inishowen peninsula). Later, descendants of Eógan spread southwards and gave their name to Tír Eógain (modern Tyrone), the people themselves being called Cenél nEógain. These two dynasties have an important place in Irish history. In later centuries, the main grouping among the Cenél Conaill was the family of O'Donnell, and the main branch of the Cenél nEógain was the line of O'Neill. Collectively, Cenél Conaill and Cenél nEógain are known to historians as the Northern Uí Néill. Other alleged descendants of Niall Noígiallach, whom historians call the Southern Uí Néill, lived in the north midlands, in what are nowadays counties Meath, Westmeath, part of Longford and part of Offaly. The most important segment among them was the Clann Cholmáin ('the family of Colmán'), descended from Colmán Már who lived in the mid-sixth century. It is to this branch that the Uí Maíl Sechnaill (O'Melaghlin) belonged, who were kings of Mide (literally meaning 'the middle [of Ireland]', which became Meath) in the eleventh and twelfth centuries.

The high-king over all the Uí Néill, Northern and Southern, was entitled to call himself *rí Temrach*, king of Tara. There is considerable debate among historians as to what precisely the kingship of Tara implied. The title itself was very ancient and it was certainly not a normal tribal kingship. While it is not true to say that to be king of Tara was to be high-king of Ireland, there was undoubtedly some special prestige attached to it, and the Uí Néill did their best to convince people that by virtue of the fact that they were kings of Tara they were *ipso facto* high-kings of Ireland. They commissioned propaganda to that effect, claiming that Tara was the ancient capital of Ireland. The learned classes fabricated a pre-history of the country which linked all the dynasties and all the various peoples inhabiting the island by descent from a common set of ancestors. This allowed the belief to take hold that the Irish were a separate nation and that Ireland was a separate country. The law tracts taught that things should be done 'according to the custom of the island of Ireland' and, of course, the best reason that such writers had for the belief that the Irish were one nation was the fact that they all spoke the same language. Hence, the idea grew that in the past the Irish had one king, one set of laws, and one capital; and in time the Uí Néill were able to convince most people that that ancient capital was Tara.[10]

Of course, the Uí Néill themselves believed this propaganda, believed that they were the rightful kings of Ireland, since they were descended from a man, Niall Noígiallach, who had been, so they thought, high-king of Ireland before the dawn of Irish history. Brian Bóruma, in their eyes, was an upstart, a man whose grandfather had been a minor chieftain in what is now east co. Clare, who belonged to a dynasty which came from nowhere in the tenth century to challenge the great Uí Néill supremacy. In a country which was so aristocratic and so conscious of rank and status, this was unheard-of presumption. It meant that Brian was heading for trouble with the reigning overking of the Uí Néill, Máel Sechnaill mac Domnaill, once he began to assert himself outside Munster in the early 980s. Máel Sechnaill invaded Brian's core kingdom, the territory of Dál Cais, and cut down the sacred tree where the kings of Dál Cais were inaugurated, an act not without its symbolism: Máel Sechnaill was clearly intent on denying Brian any claim to kingship. This, however, did little to stop Brian and the two kings spent several more years trying to get the better of each other. In 997 they held a royal meeting near Clonfert and reached an agreement whereby Máel Sechnaill would be king over the northern half of Ireland, *Leth Cuinn*, and Brian would be king over the southern half, *Leth Moga*. But the king of Munster was not content with this for long and soon restarted the war. Eventually, in 1002, Máel Sechnaill was forced to give hostages to Brian as a sign of his submission, effectively acknowledging that Brian was entitled to call himself high-king of Ireland, and in the process ending a tradition of Uí Néill claims to the high-kingship that had lasted for six centuries. Brian forced all other province-kings to submit to him as overlord and in 1005, when he made a ceremonial visit to Armagh, he had his secretary inscribe a record of the occasion in the famous *Book of Armagh*, an inscription in which he was given the unique title *Imperator Scotorum*, 'emperor of the Irish'.[11]

Historians have placed great emphasis on Brian Bóruma's achievement, and not without reason. To begin with, he ended the supremacy of the Eóganacht within Munster. Then he brought to an end the hegemony which the Uí Néill claimed to hold over the Irish body politic. They had sought to be masters of the Irish political scene, and believed the high-kingship of Ireland to be theirs by exclusive right, but by intruding himself into the high-kingship Brian brought that to an end. There was nothing illegal about this. There was no law that said that the overking of the Uí Néill *had* to be king of Ireland. It was a supremacy which depended for its continuance on the force of tradition, and it was this tradition which Brian broke. In doing so, he created a new situation. He demonstrated to the other province-kings who had been denied any claim to the high-kingship of Ireland for so long, that it was theirs for the taking, that they could make themselves master over the whole island if they were powerful enough to do so. As a result, the history of Ireland in the eleventh and twelfth centuries is one largely shaped by Brian Bóruma and is, in short, the story of the struggle between the various province-kings to realize this ambition.

Brian's achievement was obviously due to his own personal ability as a political leader and a military commander. He was also a clever manipulator of the church, whose support he won by a show of generosity and by filling the leading ecclesiastical offices with friends and relatives.[12] Brian also exploited the economic wealth and military might of the Ostman towns better than any of his predecessors. Limerick and Waterford were cities whose contingents of heavily armed and armoured soldiers were at his beck and call. He also gained control over Dublin which, ultimately, led to his downfall. However, perhaps the most important explanation for Brian's success lies in divisions among his opponents. Connacht, for instance, was prevented from offering effective opposition to Munster under Brian by the fact that two rival branches of the Uí Briúin, the Uí Chonchobair (O'Connors) of Uí Briúin Aí and the Uí Ruairc (O'Rourkes) of Uí Briúin Bréifne were too preoccupied with fighting each other to unite in opposition to the king of Munster. The same was true in Leinster, where Brian was able to exploit internecine divisions for his own purposes. Most important of all, however, since it was they whom he toppled from the high-kingship of Ireland, were divisions among the Uí Néill. Time and geography had driven the Northern and the Southern Uí Néill so far apart from each other that the days were well and truly over when they might be able to unite in defence of their prerogative of retaining the kingship in Uí Néill hands. Not only that, but the Northern Uí Néill were split, as already mentioned, between the Cenél nEógain and the Cenél Conaill. These two branches opposed each other more than their common enemies and waged war so vehemently against one another that to join forces against Munster was ordinarily out of the question. Similar divisions were to be found among the Southern Uí Néill, to such an extent that Máel Sechnaill, who had once been high-king of Ireland himself, became, when Brian reigned supreme, just one of his subordinate allies.

Máel Sechnaill stayed loyal to Brian when a revolt broke out against him in Leinster in 1012. The Ostmen of Dublin, who were often closely aligned with the Leinstermen, joined this revolt. Brian led his armies to invade Leinster, and laid Dublin under a siege that is said to have lasted for three months, until Christmas 1013. At that point Brian and his men returned home, but the Leinstermen and the Ostmen of Dublin took the opportunity to send messengers to the Isle of Man and the Scottish Isles, and gathered together a vast Viking fleet, ready for Brian's next move. On Good Friday 1014 they fought Brian's forces in perhaps the most famous battle in Irish history. By normal standards Clontarf was a long and bloody battle, and it ended in the defeat of Dublin and Leinster, though in the hour of victory Brian himself was assassinated.[13] The Vikings, of course, who had been called to fight Brian, then sailed off to their homes, but the Ostmen of Dublin stayed on as rulers there. It is true that within a few generations legend had it that Clontarf was a contest to see whether the Vikings or the Irish would rule Ireland, and that the Vikings lost; and this is a view which has persisted. However, that is not really what Clontarf was all about. Rather, this battle was the last episode in Brian Bóruma's attempt to force all the other province-kings and all of his lesser rivals to acknowledge him as high-king. It was successful to the extent that his forces won the battle and vanquished the Leinster–Ostman alliance, but because Brian lost his own life, ultimately his dynasty lost out and it was to be another half century or more before the Dál Cais achieved dominance again in the person of Brian's grandson, Tairdelbach – by then sporting with pride the surname Ua Briain ('descendant of Brian', literally 'grandson').

After the death of Brian, Máel Sechnaill was able to regain the kingship of Ireland, and he died in 1022. It is at this point that the real sea-change in Irish politics occurred, because, for a full half-century after 1022, there was no recognized high-king of Ireland, none of the province-kings being dominant enough to impose his rule. Brian's son Donnchad liked to think of himself as king but he never managed to fill his father's boots, and could not even overcome internal opposition within the Dál Cais.[14] In fact, for much of the mid-eleventh century the most powerful king in Ireland was another upstart in the same mould as Brian Bóruma. His name was Diarmait mac Maíl na mBó and he was a Leinsterman.[15] Just as the Dál Cais to which Brian belonged were newcomers to power in Munster, Diarmait mac Maíl na mBó's dynasty, the Uí Chennselaig, had been excluded from the kingship of Leinster for three centuries until he came along. The Uí Chennselaig were from south Leinster and had their capital at Ferns in co. Wexford, whereas the other reigning Leinster dynasties dominated the area from co. Kildare eastwards to south co. Dublin and north Wicklow. These north Leinster dynasts were suffering from the attacks of the Uí Néill in Mide, and from the growing power of the Ostmen of Dublin, and it was this weakness which Diarmait mac Maíl na mBó exploited. Furthermore, so far as we can tell, his dynasty, the Uí Chennselaig, had complete control over the Ostman town of Wexford. Wexford had important trading connections across the Irish Sea and Diarmait mac Maíl na mBó was proba- bly able to harness the economic wealth that this trade gener- ated in order to finance his own expansion.

In 1052 Diarmait even managed to do what Brian Bóruma and Máel Sechnaill had failed to accomplish: he seized Dublin and made himself king.[16] Shortly afterwards he bestowed Dublin on his eldest or most favoured son, Murchad, ancestor of the famous line of the Meic Murchada (Mac Murroughs). It seems that at that time the ruling Ostman dynasty of Dublin also controlled the Isle of Man and, to a lesser extent perhaps, the Western Isles of Scotland. This is a region which Irish sources call *Inse Gall* ('the islands of the foreigners'), and it is where Echmarcach, the exiled Ostman ruler of Dublin, took refuge after his expulsion by the Leinstermen in 1052. Gaining control of Dublin, one of the most important trading centres in western Europe, meant an enormous increase of the power of King Diarmait and his son Murchad. But they were not content with it, and in 1061 Murchad invaded the Isle of Man, defeated Echmarcach in battle, and took *cáin* or tribute from the inhabitants as a sign of his overlordship. From then until his death in 1070 this Leinster prince reigned as both king of Dublin and of the Isle of Man, and when Diarmait himself was killed two years later at the head of an army that included many hundreds of Ostman warriors, among the titles he was given by an annalist was 'king of the Isles (*rí Indsi Gall*)'.[17]

That same set of annals describes Diarmait as 'king of Wales'. This, of course, is a gross exaggeration, but it is worth noting that the Welsh chronicles accord him an unusually long obituary notice, saying that he was 'the most praiseworthy and bravest king of the Irish – terrible towards his foes and kind towards the poor and gentle towards pilgrims'.[18] This is evidence of a very elevated status and probably indicates that he had close contacts with Wales. Most probably this is connected with the control he had over Dublin from 1052 onwards since many of the Irish contacts with Wales in this period were channelled through Dublin.[19] The Ostmen had a powerful fleet and were in the habit of raiding and trading in Wales. The most famous king of Dublin in the eleventh century was Sitriuc Silkenbeard, and when his son was captured in 1029, Sitriuc paid for his release by handing over a ransom of 120 Welsh horses. As to raids by the Dubliners on Wales, there was one in the very next year. Furthermore, when Sitriuc was banished from Dublin in 1036, he almost certainly took refuge in Wales, since the next entry in the annals records that Sitriuc's son was murdered in Wales by another member of the family.[20]

The Ostmen had, in fact, a very close involvement in Welsh affairs. Cynan ab Iago, the would-be prince of Gwynedd or North Wales, married a member of Sitriuc's family and took refuge in Dublin when he was forced into exile in the mid-eleventh century. From Dublin he made several attempts to recover power in Wales, but was always unsuccessful. However, his son was more fortunate. A remarkable and unique biography of Gruffudd ap Cynan, which may have been written within a generation of his death in 1137, still survives.[21] It describes a quite extraordinary story. Gruffudd ap Cynan ruled Gwynedd for over half a century, yet he was born near Dublin, and was reared in Swords in north co. Dublin. When he grew to manhood he enlisted Irish support, invaded Anglesey, and conquered North Wales from his enemies. From time to time he got into difficulty in Wales, whether at the hands of Welsh enemies or of the Normans, who were gradually starting to penetrate Wales from England, and on each occasion, according to the evidence of his biography and of the Welsh chronicles, he took refuge in Ireland, enlisted Irish and Ostman support, and managed to recover his grip on Gwynedd. His life-story is a remarkable tale of constant to-ing and fro-ing across the Irish Sea, and if even part of it is true, then the relationship between Ireland and Wales in the eleventh and early twelfth centuries was one of the utmost intimacy.

Diarmait mac Maíl na mBó played a part in fostering that relationship most probably, as already noted, because of his association with Dublin and of the presence there of the exiled Cynan ab Iago. We know that the Anglo-Saxon earl of Wessex, Harold Godwinesson, spent the winter of 1051–2 in Ireland with Diarmait 'under the king's protection', and that after the battle of Hastings Harold's sons again fled to Diarmait. He then supplied them with a fleet of sixty-six ships for one of their unsuccessful attempts to overturn the Norman conquest of England, one source commenting that the failure of this invasion 'filled Ireland with mourning'.[22] Diarmait mac Maíl na mBó was thus a man who offered protection to exiled dynasts from Britain and who provided them with military and naval support in the attempt to secure their reinstatement. Therefore, after he gained control of Dublin, he presumably became the protector of the exiled Cynan ab Iago of Gwynedd and sponsored his unsuccessful attempts to recover North Wales, in return for some acknowledgement of suzerainty. Presumably this lies behind the generous words of his Welsh obituarist and the colourful claim of the Irish annals that he was entitled to call himself 'king of Wales'.

From this newly won position of power, Diarmait mac Maíl na mBó supported Tairdelbach Ua Briain against his uncle Donnchad, and eventually in 1064 Donnchad was forced to abdicate, by going on pilgrimage to Rome, where he died. When Diarmait mac Maíl na mBó himself died in battle in 1072, he was described, admittedly by the partisan *Book of Leinster*, as *rí hErend co fressabra*, 'king of Ireland with opposition', and that is not far off the mark. It is an important title which gained currency in this period to describe these men who were claimants to the kingship of Ireland and generally regarded as such, but who were never, or hardly ever, entirely unopposed (*cen fressabra*, 'without opposition'). The phrase *rí hErend co fressabra* is thus used in the annals to describe an individual who styled himself high-king of Ireland, and who had managed to get most of the other province-kings to acknowledge him as such, but for whom there were always one or two who simply refused to do so, or who did so only under duress. The eleventh and twelfth centuries were, therefore, a period that witnessed great warfare in Ireland, but not senseless violence. What we find is that the man who was high-king of Ireland *with* opposition was trying to become king *without* opposition, by forcing all the other province-kings to acknowledge his claim to the kingship. These have been called 'the wars of the circuits', because kings found themselves locked into a circuit of campaigns, moving from province to province, each forcing his rivals into submission, taking hostages from them to try to ensure their future good behaviour, then going on to the next province and repeating the exercise there, all the time keeping a weather-eye on the situation back home, since his rivals within his own province (and his own family) often took advantage of his absence on campaign to instigate a revolt.

Diarmait mac Maíl na mBó was succeeded as the most dominant province-king by his protégé Tairdelbach Ua Briain of Munster, grandson of Brian Bóruma, who died in 1086. Ua Briain was a man of very considerable stature both within Ireland and abroad. He corresponded with one of the greatest of the medieval popes, Gregory VII, and with Lanfranc, one of the most illustrious of Canterbury's archbishops. He also established his capital in the wealthy trading city of Limerick. What is more, in 1072, as part of his campaign to get all other province-kings to acknowledge his claim to be high-king of Ireland, Tairdelbach marched his armies on Dublin and accepted the kingship of the city-state from the inhabitants.[23] That he did so is an indication of the way in which the assertion of power over Dublin was becoming part and parcel of the race for the high-kingship. A year later two unidentified kinsmen of Tairdelbach were killed in the Isle of Man, proof that in gaining power in Dublin the Uí Briain royal house, like the Leinstermen before them, were keen to assert their dominance in the Irish Sea region as a whole. Then in 1075 Tairdelbach followed the precedent set by Diarmait mac Maíl na mBó and appointed his son and successor, Muirchertach, as king of Dublin. Tairdelbach too involved himself in Welsh politics, and assisted in the succession to power of his own Welsh allies in both the kingdom of North Wales and the kingdom of South Wales. It may have been as a result of this Welsh activity that he got himself into trouble with the new Norman king of England, William the Conqueror: the latter died in 1087, and the *Anglo-Saxon Chronicle* says that had he lived a short while longer he would have conquered Ireland without any weapons.[24] We cannot be certain what this refers to, but it serves to emphasize the point that as the kings of Ireland grew in stature and in international reputation in the eleventh and twelfth centuries they got sucked into the international arena.

This is true to an even greater extent in the case of Muirchertach Ua Briain, who succeeded his father in 1086. This man's career is a microcosm of all that was good and bad in Irish politics in the period.[25] If Muirchertach's control of Dublin – a town with which he was to be associated for forty years, where he most likely had one of his royal palaces, and whose military might and economic wealth he exploited to great personal benefit – was an indication of all that was 'good', all that was progressive and innovative in Irish politics, the events of 1086, following the death of his father Tairdelbach, were all too typically damaging, negative and self-destructive. Tairdelbach Ua Briain left three sons: Muirchertach, Tadc and Diarmait. All three sought power, and Munster was divided between them. Tadc died at this point but his sons carried on the struggle to get their share of power, while the other brother, Diarmait, was to be a thorn in Muirchertach's side for the rest of his life. In spite of the considerable concessions that Muirchertach made to him – he appears, for instance, to have been appointed governor of the important Ostman town of Waterford – Diarmait consistently tried to undermine his brother and eventually, after Muirchertach's death, it was Diarmait's children who reaped the reward: they inherited the kingdom of Thomond, and the descendants of the great Muirchertach ended up as petty chieftains in West Clare.

This succession dispute illustrates all that was 'bad' about the Irish polity. Power was very much a personal thing; it withered away very quickly at a king's death if he did not leave an heir strong enough to beat off the challenge of near relatives and enemies. Because there was no fixed law of dynastic succession, the path to kingship in Ireland was potentially wide open.[26] A person had to have ability and charisma and needed to command authority, and while royal blood helped it could always be invented: it was probably Muirchertach Ua Briain who commissioned the marvellous piece of pseudo-history known as *Cogad Gaedel re Gallaib* ('The war of the Irish with the foreigners') in order to convince contemporaries of his entitlement to rule Ireland by virtue of the fact that his great-grandfather, Brian Bóruma, had, almost single-handedly (so the *Cogad* claims) saved the country from Viking oppression.[27] More so than anything else, what paved the way to power in eleventh- and twelfth-century Ireland, however, was not personal virtue, and not blue blood, but access to the levers of power – to manpower, resources and arms. To be a king's eldest or favourite son was a help, of course, because such a person had the opportunity during his father's lifetime to build up a powerbase, ready to ease himself into the succession when his father died. But arms and armies were not exclusively the possession of any one man: hence the ubiquitous power struggles; hence the fact that the enmity within dynasties was often as great as that between them; and hence the opposition that Muirchertach Ua Briain faced from his brothers and his brothers' sons.

Owing to this opposition, Muirchertach hardly set foot outside Munster for several years after 1086. During this period he lost control of Dublin and it was taken over by an Islesman called Godred Crovan (Gofraid Méránach), the founder of a dynasty that ruled over Man and the Isles, in whole or in part, for the next two centuries. His seizure of Dublin from his base on the Isle of Man is further proof that Dublin and Man were treated by contemporaries as a single political entity: the ruler of one was entitled to seek to add the other to his domain. Godred died in 1095, having been banished from Dublin by Muirchertach Ua Briain in the previous year, and then, according to the *Chronicle of the Kings of Man*, the chieftains of the Isles sent an embassy to Ua Briain, asking him to provide a regent to govern their kingdom until Godred's young son came of age.[28] Muirchertach willingly complied, appointing his nephew, Domnall mac Taidc, to rule over them. This story sounds somewhat fanciful, but we know from the Irish annals that Domnall's brother Amlaíb (Olaf) was killed in the Isle of Man in 1096,[29] presumably in pursuit of Domnall's ambitions there. This is another indication of how rapidly Irish kings began to dominate the Irish Sea region once they laid hands on Dublin.

This new Irish hegemony was not, however, to everyone's liking and the famous Norse king, Magnus Barelegs, the last great Viking warlord, led two western expeditions in 1098 and 1102 to stop it in its tracks.[30] Magnus based himself in the Isle of Man and during the second campaign Dublin was his target, and there is evidence to suggest that he gained control of the city.[31] This put him at loggerheads with Muirchertach Ua Briain, but they compromised by arranging a marriage between Muirchertach's daughter and Magnus's young son Sigurd, who was to rule as king of the Isles with Muirchertach's blessing after King Magnus's return to Norway. The whole project collapsed, however, when Magnus was unexpectedly killed raiding in Ulster in 1103, whereupon Sigurd cast aside his child-bride and returned to Norway. Dublin, and perhaps the Isles, then passed back into Munster control, but in 1111 Domnall mac Taidc forcibly seized the Isles against his uncle's wishes and Muirchertach came to Dublin and, as reported in the annals, spent three months in the town, presumably to ensure that it did not fall into Domnall's hands. The fact that the king of Munster could leave his own province and spend a quarter of a year in residence in Dublin says much about the degree of control which the Munstermen had over the city, about the importance they attached to it as a satellite possession, and about the place of Dublin in the Irish polity – it was becoming a home away from home for ambitious Irish dynasts. Not only that, but

Muirchertach continued the policy adopted by his father and by Diarmait mac Maíl na mBó: he appointed his own son and heir as king over the town.[32]

Like his father before him too Muirchertach had involvements further afield. The two leading Welsh allies of Tairdelbach Ua Briain appear to have been Gruffudd ap Cynan of Gwynedd (North Wales) and Rhys ap Tewdwr, the king of Deheubarth (South Wales). They both won back their kingdoms together in 1081 thanks to an army supplied by the Uí Briain royal house of Munster. In 1093 Rhys ap Tewdwr was killed by the Normans who were then just beginning to settle in South Wales. His heir was his son, Gruffudd ap Rhys. We can get no better reminder of the dimness of our understanding of the inter-dynastic connections between Ireland and Wales at this point than from contemplating what happened next. This young boy, Gruffudd ap Rhys, fled to Ireland, and there he spent, probably at Muirchertach Ua Briain's court in Limerick, the next twenty-two years. He did not return to Wales until 1115, and his long enforced exile in Ireland does not appear to have done him much harm, because, even though the Normans had established a permanent base in South Wales by then, he was able to rouse the Welsh to back him, and he recovered at least part of his ancestral kingdom of Deheubarth. When he was expelled by the Normans in 1127, he returned again to Ireland.[33]

The Normans who forced Gruffudd ap Rhys to flee to Ireland were the de Montgomery brothers, and soon afterwards they themselves got into trouble by rebelling against the new king of England, Henry I. To try to resist Henry, they needed allies. Therefore in 1101 they sent an embassy to Ireland, to Muirchertach Ua Briain, looking for his help. The man whom they sent was the steward of Pembroke, Gerald of Windsor, a very important man in Irish history since it is from him that the Irish Geraldines are descended. As a result of Gerald's embassy, Muirchertach Ua Briain agreed that his daughter would marry one of the de Montgomerys, Arnulf, and she was duly sent off to Wales, along with a fleet of armed ships. The Welsh chronicler's account of the alliance is interesting: it says that Arnulf

> thought to make peace with the Irish and to obtain help from them. And he sent messengers to Ireland, that is Gerald the Steward and many others, to ask for the daughter of King Murtart for his wife. And that he easily obtained; and the messengers came joyfully to their land. And Murtart sent his daughter and many armed ships along with her to his aid. And when the earls [the de Montgomery brothers] had exalted themselves with pride because of those events, they refused to accept any peace from the king [Henry I].[34]

It is interesting that the Normans' alliance is here interpreted as an attempt 'to make peace' with the Irish. It is interesting too that they were perceived as becoming 'exalted with pride' because of the marriage alliance, after their emissaries 'came joyfully' with the news, and then refused to accept peace with Henry I on the strength of it, a reminder of the importance of the Irish input into Welsh warfare at this point. King Henry responded by placing a trade embargo on Ireland and choking off all commercial contacts between the ports of Ireland and England. This had the desired effect. A contemporary English chronicler, William of Malmesbury, speaking probably of these events, tells us that Ua Briain's 'insolence soon subsided, for of what value would Ireland be if deprived of the merchandise of England?'.[35]

After the revolt collapsed, Arnulf, according to the chronicler Orderic Vitalis, fled to his new father-in-law in Ireland, and hoped that he might succeed to Ua Briain's kingdom of Munster. That may seem a bit far-fetched, but Arnulf de Montgomery was lord of Pembroke: sixty-five years later the new ruler of Pembroke was Richard fitz Gilbert de Clare, better known in Ireland as Strongbow, and he succeeded to *his* father-in-law's kingdom by marrying the daughter of Diarmait Mac Murchada, king of Leinster. If Arnulf did flee to Ireland (we know that Ua Briain wrote a letter to the archbishop of Canterbury on his behalf)[36] he did not last long there.

Orderic claims that the Irish used the Normans to ward off the aggression of Magnus Barelegs. Then,

> when the Irish had tasted blood by killing King Magnus and his companions they grew more unruly and suddenly turned to kill the Normans. Their king took his daughter away from Arnulf and gave the wanton girl in an unlawful marriage to one of his cousins. He resolved to murder Arnulf himself as a reward for his alliance, but the latter, learning of the execrable plots of this barbarous race, fled to his own people and lived for twenty years afterwards with no fixed abode.[37]

It is impossible to know how much reliance, if any, to place on this story, but it does at least raise the intriguing possibility that there were contingents of Anglo-Normans participating in Irish warfare two-thirds of a century before they began arriving there *en masse*, and even if Orderic is mistaken, his condemnation of the mores of Irish society, particularly their marriage practices, is in keeping with what we know of contemporary opinion.

These events are a measure of the stature of Muirchertach Ua Briain at the height of his power. He changed the face of Irish politics in other ways too. In 1089, the same year in which he regained control of Dublin, Muirchertach took advantage of internal warfare in Leinster to take temporary control of that province also. Here he was not doing as Irish kings of the past had done, forcing other province-kings to submit to his overlordship: he was actually seeking to replace them. In 1093 he went to Connacht and expelled the heads of the reigning dynasty, driving them all the way north to Tír Eógain, giving their lands to a minor local chieftain whom he supported, and making this man, from nothing, king of Connacht.[38] Although the tactic did not succeed for long, it indicates how ruthlessly innovative he was. He performed a similar deed in the following year when he marched to Mide (Meath) and banished the ruling dynasty into Bréifne. To that extent he simply repeated what he had tried in Connacht, but he was even more thorough on this occasion, because he partitioned Meath in two and appointed two minor local lords to rule the divided province under his authority. By the mid-1090s, therefore, Muirchertach Ua Briain, after a decade's struggle, controlled Munster and Leinster and the Hiberno-Scandinavian towns; he had also intervened to good effect in Connacht and Meath. The next twenty years of his life were spent trying to extend his control even further north, in particular, to get the northern king, Domnall Mac Lochlainn of Cenél nEógain, to submit to him as overking.

In Mac Lochlainn, however, Muirchertach had met his match, and the northern king may well have learned from the innovations which Muirchertach introduced. For instance, as already mentioned, along with the Cenél nEógain the other major sept comprising the Northern Uí Néill was the Cenél Conaill, for long now distinct dynasties with distinct ruling families. But in 1112 Domnall Mac Lochlainn of Cenél nEógain appointed his own son as king of Cenél Conaill. This move was doomed to failure, but is nevertheless a prime example of the way in which the practices of kingship were changing in this period and the niceties of politics were being abandoned in favour of more ruthless methods. Tír Conaill lay to the west of Tír Eógain; to the east lay the kingdom of the Ulaid. This kingdom, which had anciently covered all of Ulster, had long since been reduced to what are nowadays counties Down and Antrim, and was ruled by a dynasty very proud of its ancient glory, who were very reluctant vassals of the Cenél nEógain. They often sided with Ua Briain and the men of Munster in their efforts to force Mac Lochlainn into submission. In 1113, therefore, Domnall Mac Lochlainn marched into Ulaid, defeated their forces, expelled their king, and did exactly as Ua Briain had done in Meath, partitioned the kingdom. Not only that, but he took a large slice of the kingdom for himself. This again was innovation. What was happening here was the annexation of land. Domnall Mac Lochlainn was acting as a lord, a *dominus terre*, exercising authority not simply over the peoples who inhabited particular areas, but over areas inhabited by particular peoples. That is what is significant about the politics of this age, and about

Muirchertach Ua Briain's contribution to it, since he largely started this trend. In doing so he was not simply aping the developments that were taking place in feudal society abroad, but his foreign connections were such that he was undoubtedly influenced and impressed by the power of kings elsewhere, and was anxious to push his own powers of lordship to their elastic limit.

Muirchertach's involvement with the church was a manifestation of the same aggrandizing policy. In the late eleventh and early twelfth centuries the influence of the reform movement which had been sweeping the European church for some decades began to be felt in Ireland. There is occasionally a tendency to assume that it was as a result of this movement, which came to be known as the Gregorian reform, that Ireland came into contact with the European church, and that this movement brought Ireland into the European mainstream in a way that had never previously been the case. This assumption ignores the earlier achievements of the Irish church during its Golden Age, when Ireland made a not inconsiderable contribution to the civilization of Europe, which reflected itself in great learning, in beautiful works of art, and in a widely held perception that it was a place of great sanctity, an *insula sanctorum*. The fact is that the Irish church had always been open to external influence. It had always been open to receive scholars from abroad to study in its schools, and this was as true in the eleventh century, when the great Welsh scholar, Sulien, bishop of St Davids, spent at least thirteen years studying there, as it was in the seventh century of which Bede later wrote that 'there were many English nobles and lesser folk in Ireland who had left their own land … either to pursue religious studies or to lead a life of stricter discipline; some of these soon devoted themselves to the monastic life, while others preferred to travel, studying under various teachers in turn; the Irish welcomed them all kindly, and, without asking for any payment, provided them with daily food, books, and instruction'.[39]

The flow in the other direction was even heavier, to such an extent that it is now nearly twelve hundred years since

Walafrid Strabo, based in the monastery of Reichenau on Lake Constance on the modern Swiss-German border, commented on 'the Irish people, with whom the custom of travelling to foreign lands has become almost second nature'.[40] He was referring to those *Scoti vagantes*, the wandering Irish, who were part of a vast *peregrinatio* movement to the Continent. They consisted of priests and monks who evangelized parts of Europe which were without pastoral care, scholars who went to teach or to study, and pilgrims visiting the great shrines and pilgrimage centres of Europe. In the ninth century Irish churchmen and scholars appear throughout Europe, particularly in the Carolingian empire. In the tenth, they still turn up in great numbers all over the Frankish empire, in the Low Countries in places like Ghent, Liège, and Metz; in the valley of the Main, at centres like Würzburg, Mainz and Fulda; in Bavaria, at Regensburg (Ratisbon) and Salzburg; then in the Alpine region at St Gall (named, of course, after an Irish missionary), and Reichenau – this is to name but a few cities and abbeys where Irish influence was strong, and where it remained strong. In 1067, Muiredach mac Robartaig (or Marianus Scotus) left his native Tír Conaill and founded the priory of St Peter at Regensburg. Another Irish abbey, St James's, was founded in the same place in 1111; then came Würzburg (1134), Nüremberg (1140), Constance (1142), Erfurt (1150), Vienna (1155), and Eichstadt (1183). This last house was founded after the English invasion of Ireland. In some respects, therefore, the Irish church remained expansionist and outward-looking right up to the late twelfth century. It was not so cut off from the rest of Christendom as one might imagine, and it was not so decayed and ridden with abuse that it was incapable of making a contribution to the Christian church on the European mainland.[41]

The Irish church also had a long tradition of contact with the church in Anglo-Saxon England, with places like Worcester, Winchester, Winchcombe, Glastonbury, and Canterbury.[42] The pace of reform in the English church increased rapidly in the aftermath of the Norman conquest in 1066. If these religious centres became vehicles for reform

in the church in England, and there were Irishman in training for priestly orders there, it followed that when they
returned to Ireland they brought these ideas with them. We
get the first evidence of this wind of change only eight years
after the Norman conquest. In 1074 the Ostmen of Dublin
chose as their bishop a man called Gilla Pátraic, and he was
sent to the new reform-minded archbishop of Canterbury,
Lanfranc, who canonically examined him, and, when he
proved satisfactory, consecrated him as bishop. Gilla Pátraic
then swore canonical obedience to Lanfranc. The archbishop of Canterbury was, therefore, the metropolitan, the
provincial superior, of the bishop of Dublin. This procedure
was repeated for each of Gilla Pátraic's successors at Dublin
over the next half century, and when Waterford got a bishop
in 1096 he too was consecrated by the archbishop of
Canterbury and swore obedience to him, as did one of the
bishops of Limerick. Another of Limerick's bishops, Gilla
Espaic, author of an important treatise on church organization, known as *De Statu Ecclesiae* ('Concerning church
order'), was an acquaintance and correspondent of
Archbishop Anselm of Canterbury.[43]

These were, of course, Ostman dioceses, which may have
chosen to affiliate themselves with Canterbury in order to
emphasize their distinctiveness from the rest of the Irish
church. In 1121, for instance, during a dispute over the succession to the diocese of Dublin, a letter was sent to the archbishop of Canterbury from 'all the burgesses of Dublin, and
the whole assembly of the clergy', stating that 'the bishops of
Ireland are very jealous of us, and especially that bishop who
lives in Armagh, because we are unwilling to submit to their
ordination but wish always to be under your rule'.[44] Gilla
Pátraic, before he became bishop of Dublin, had been a
monk at Worcester. His successor as bishop was Donngus,
who had been a monk at Canterbury, who was succeeded in
turn by his nephew Samuel who had studied at St Albans,
and the first bishop of Waterford, Máel Ísu, was a monk of
Winchester. Since these bishops received their training in
England, they may, therefore, have been out of step with the

rest of the Irish church. But, although they were appointed to the Ostman dioceses and studied in England, all these bishops were native Irishmen, products of the Irish church, not outsiders trying to force this new regime on reluctant natives. Furthermore, the appointment of Gilla Pátraic to Dublin in 1074 had the backing, not only of the Ostman underking of the city, but of the city's new overlord, Tairdelbach Ua Briain. When Máel Ísu was chosen as bishop of Waterford in 1096, a letter was sent to Archbishop Anselm asking him to perform the consecration, among the signatories to which was Muirchertach Ua Briain and his brother Diarmait. And when the Dubliners chose a new bishop in 1121, their new Irish overlord, Tairdelbach Ua Conchobair of Connacht, supported their selection. Therefore, when, during this period, the inhabitants of the Ostman towns decided that they needed a bishop, and that they would send the candidate to Canterbury for consecration, they had the full support of the Irish kings. It was not, as it is sometimes portrayed, an imperialist gesture on Canterbury's part; turning to Canterbury was clearly something of which the Irish kings approved.

Evidently, the Irish kings recognized that these new Ostman dioceses would have to meet the standards now becoming common throughout the Western church, standards for which the Irish church in general was not yet ready. The most basic standard of all was that bishops should be consecrated by canonically qualified superiors, and within the Irish church at that point there was nobody qualified to do this. To have such superiors the Irish church needed considerable reorganization, so that it acquired a structured, territorially based, diocesan system, which it as yet did not have. In this movement towards reform Muirchertach Ua Briain took the lead. The first reforming synod, whose decrees we still have, took place under his direction at Cashel in 1101. His motives were, no doubt, mixed. It would be wrong to cast doubt on the sincerity of his actions, but as high-king of Ireland, Muirchertach presumably had no wish to preside over a country out of step with the rest of Europe, whose church was viewed as backward. To a certain extent, his own international image and reputation depended upon the perceived status of the Irish church. The council that he convened at Cashel, therefore, concerned itself with the sort of issues synods throughout Europe were dealing with at that time. It dealt with the laws on marriage, with securing various clerical privileges, and with establishing the freedom of the church from lay exactions. It also made an effort to improve the quality of churchmen by insisting on them taking holy orders, and on being celibate, and it tried to eradicate abuses like simony. The proposed reforms were quite sweeping. If the Irish church was lagging behind the church in the rest of Europe, these provisions were designed to help it catch up. In theory, they brought it into line with the church elsewhere, with one major exception: the absence as yet of a proper diocesan structure, and this was very success-fully provided for at the synod of Ráith Bressail in 1111, again under the auspices of Muirchertach Ua Briain. The structure arrived at was one which respected the traditional division of the country into two halves. Two ecclesiastical provinces were established, the headship of the northern half (*Leth Cuinn*) going to Armagh, and that of the southern half (*Leth Moga*) to Cashel, each province being divided into twelve dioceses, Armagh having the primacy. This system was later modified. To reflect the growing power of Connacht (and its ecclesiasti-cal capital at Tuam), and to bring Dublin into the ambit of the Irish church (since the issue had not been dealt with at Ráith Bressail), the country was divided into four ecclesiastical provinces at the synod of Kells-Mellifont in 1152, when the papal legate, Cardinal John Paparo, conferred pallia, the symbols of archiepiscopal jurisdiction, on the new archbishops of Armagh, Cashel, Dublin and Tuam (the archbishop of Armagh retaining primacy over all Ireland), a structure which has lasted to this day.

The increasing power of Connacht to which the synod of Kells-Mellifont gave expression was first felt in the aftermath of 1114, when Muirchertach Ua Briain was taken seriously ill and fell from power. Thereafter, the balance of power in the country shifted northwards and his place as the most powerful king in Ireland was soon taken by Tairdelbach Ua Conchobair, who had been king of Connacht since 1106. As part of his bid for power Ua Conchobair marched on Dublin in 1118 and made himself king.[45] The symbolism is significant. The high-kingship of Ireland was now vacant and Ua Conchobair made good his bid for it by marching his armies on Dublin and accepting its kingship from the populace: without Dublin, his claim to the high-kingship of Ireland would ring hollow. Then in 1126 he performed an equally significant act: Tairdelbach became the fourth successive claimant to the kingship of Ireland to appoint his intended heir (his son Conchobar) as king of Dublin. Tairdelbach Ua Conchobair was a remarkable military commander and his reign is notable for the use he made of naval forces and for the construction of castles and bridges.[46] Like Muirchertach Ua Briain before him, he deposed other province-kings, partitioned their kingdoms, and his favourite son Conchobar was at various stages appointed king not only over Dublin but over Leinster and Meath as well. He gravely weakened the status of the Ua Briain kings of Thomond by setting up as rivals a branch of the Eóganacht who bore the surname Mac Carthaig (Mac Carthy), whom he allowed to rule the kingdom of Desmond. Munster never recovered from this division, a collapse made all the greater by the slaughter of the forces of Tairdelbach Ua Briain at the battle of Móin Mór in 1151 which shattered Uí Briain power; thereafter Munster tended to remain divided in two, and easily fell victim to English assault after 1169. When his son Conchobar was killed in Meath in 1144 Tairdelbach Ua Conchobair allowed a member of the Uí Maíl Sechnaill dynasty to continue ruling in the west of the province, but divided east Meath between Tigernán Ua Ruairc of Bréifne and Diarmait Mac Murchada of Leinster. Meath was now so weak that it was a cockpit of warfare between these and other competing kings and again fell with barely a whimper into the hands of the ambitious English warrior-baron, Hugh de Lacy, in 1172.

By the mid-1140s Ua Conchobair's place as king of Ireland was coming under threat from the northern king,

Muirchertach Mac Lochlainn, who had succeeded to the king-ship of Cenél nEógain following the death of his uncle Conchobar in 1136.[47] His first major victory outside Tír Eógain came in 1147 when he was victorious in battle over the east Ulster kingdom of Ulaid. Within a year he had obtained the hostages of his western neighbours, the Cenél Conaill, and of the Airgialla of south Ulster. This gesture of submission was performed at a formal assembly at Armagh, and made him the paramount king throughout the north of Ireland. In 1149 he led a cavalry march south and took hostages from Bréifne and Meath, and went to Dublin where he received the submission of the Ostmen and of their overlord, Diarmait Mac Murchada of Leinster. It was this success that made him a challenger for the high-kingship of Ireland and there followed several years of robust rivalry between him and Tairdelbach Ua Conchobair. In 1153 Mac Lochlainn routed the forces of Tairdelbach's son Ruaidrí, while in the following year the Connacht fleet scored only a limited success in a major naval confrontation off the Inishowen coast, partly because Mac Lochlainn had, in anticipation of the assault, hired a fleet from as far afield as Galloway, Kintyre and Man. In its after-math, Muirchertach paraded his armies over Connacht and Bréifne, and came to Dublin, where the Ostmen proclaimed him as king and he gave them twelve hundred cows as *tuarastal* or wages, a sign of his overlordship.[48] Although the kingship of Tara had held (or was believed by contemporaries to have held) a special place in the Irish body politic, the myth became hard to square with reality when the province of Meath lost its former greatness and Tara became the scene of petty local squabbles. At the same time, Dublin was rising in importance both economically and symbolically. Implicitly, therefore, Muirchertach Mac Lochlainn's march on Dublin in 1154 secured him the high-kingship of Ireland. He demon-strated his new status by flexing his muscles further afield, by invading Osraige (Ossory) in 1156, in alliance with Diarmait Mac Murchada of Leinster, and by partitioning Munster in the following year, where he laid siege to Limerick and was granted its kingship by the Ostmen.

Since the great Tairdelbach Ua Conchobair died in 1156, his son Ruaidrí now emerged to challenge Mac Lochlainn, and invaded Tír Eógain in 1157 and 1158, though Ruaidrí and his allies, Ua Ruairc of Bréifne and Ua Briain of Thomond, were defeated by Mac Lochlainn in the battle of Ardee in 1159. In 1161, when he took the hostages of Bréifne and received the formal submission of Ruaidrí Ua Conchobair and Diarmait Mac Murchada, Muirchertach was styled in the annals 'king of Ireland without opposition'. When he attended the consecration of the Cistercian abbey church of Mellifont, co. Louth, in 1157, he granted the monks lands in the kingdom of Meath, and when he issued a charter at about the same time to the Cistercian house of Newry, co. Down, styling himself '*Rex totius Hibernie*', he handed over lands in the vicinity of this house too. The significance of both land grants is that they were outside his own kingdom of Tír Eógain, and he was therefore assuming a proprietary right to the estates of those who had become his vassals. Therefore, Muirchertach Mac Lochlainn was not content with military overlordship, with receiving submissions and exacting hostages from his rivals, with compelling them to perform military service in his army, and deposing those who did not meet with his approval. He sought something akin to territorial lordship of the lands he conquered. He charged for the privilege of accession to kingship: an Ua Maíl Sechnaill dynast paid one hundred ounces of gold for the kingship of western Meath in 1163. When Muirchertach invaded Ulaid in 1165, not only did he temporarily banish its king, Eochaid Mac Duinnsléibe, but he gave away lands in the kingdom to the church of Saul, co. Down, and to Donnchad Ua Cerbaill of Airgialla. In the following year, however, he treacherously blinded Eochaid, and this led to Muirchertach's own downfall. Tír Eógain was invaded by the united forces of Airgialla and Bréifne, and, in a battle in south co. Armagh, Muirchertach was slain. His death gravely weakened the Mac Lochlainn family and ultimately paved the way for the restoration of the O'Neills to power in the north. More importantly, Muirchertach's ally Diarmait Mac

Murchada was left exposed by his death and shortly afterwards took flight overseas, so that, in a very real sense, the death of Muirchertach Mac Lochlainn precipitated the English invasion of Ireland.

3

ADVENTUS ANGLORUM

In the mid-1830s the great Irish scholar John O'Donovan toured the country gathering local traditions on behalf of the Ordnance Survey, and when he visited the townland of Ballynagran, co. Wicklow, he was informed that the ruined structure there, known locally as Mac Dermot's castle, was the place to which Diarmait Mac Murchada had brought Derbforgaill, the wife of Tigernán Ua Ruairc, when he abducted her in 1152.[1] The story has little to recommend it since the castle may postdate the event by as much as a century, but, if it tells us anything, it is that one should not underestimate the force of tradition. The so-called 'rape of Dervorgilla' may be just a line in a set of annals, but at some point it entered the public imagination. Historians, anxious not to allow undue weight to personal animus, tend to play down the importance of events such as these as motivating forces, but in this case they may be wrong. When, during a raid on Bréifne in 1152, Diarmait Mac Murchada made off with the wife of Tigernán Ua Ruairc, he made an enemy for life; and it was an outrage for which, as we shall see, Tigernán later sought harsh vengeance.

In the middle years of the twelfth century Mac Murchada of Leinster and Ua Ruairc of Bréifne were rivals for supremacy over the declining kingdom of Meath, and by and large Ua Ruairc got the upper hand, though in 1156 Mac Murchada

severely routed his forces there.[2] What advances Mac
Murchada made (when, for example, he gained control of
Dublin in 1162) he made through association with
Muirchertach Mac Lochlainn, king of Tír Eógain, but when
the latter fell on the battlefield in 1166 Mac Murchada was
defenceless. The new king of Ireland was Ruaidrí Ua
Conchobair, ally of Ua Ruairc. Together, in the same year, they
marched on Dublin, where the Ostmen acknowledged Ua
Conchobair as king, who was then 'inaugurated king as hon-
ourably as any king of the Irish was ever inaugurated, and he
presented their *tuarastal* [ceremonial stipend] to the Ostmen
in many cows, for he levied a tax of four thousand cows upon
the men of Ireland for them'.[3] Soon afterwards they turned
their attention southwards, to Mac Murchada. On their
approach Diarmait burned Ferns, for fear of what the Four
Masters call 'his castle and his house' falling into enemy
hands. Ua Conchobair, however, was content to leave Diarmait
in power, provided he gained his submission, which he duly
did. Not so Tigernán Ua Ruairc. He joined forces with the
Ostmen of Dublin and some of Mac Murchada's own rebellious Leinster vassals, and together they came after him,
marched on his core territory of Uí Chennselaig, demolished
his castle at Ferns and forced Diarmait to flee. Without an ally
in Ireland, on 1 August 1166, Mac Murchada, his wife and
daughter and a small group of followers, set sail for Bristol,
causing the scribe of the *Book of Leinster* to exclaim 'O king of
heaven, awful the deed done in Ireland today, the kalends of
August, that is, the expulsion overseas, by the men of Ireland,
of Diarmait son of Donnchad Mac Murchada, king of Leinster
and the Ostmen. Alas, alas, what shall I do?'[4] The exiled king
was received by the reeve of Bristol, Robert fitz Harding, a
confidant of Henry II of England, and from that moment on
his fortunes never looked back. Within a year he was back in
Ireland, back in power, and Ireland was facing invasion.

Historians who study the invasion of Ireland that took place
in the late 1160s are aware that there is no contemporary
depiction of it as Anglo-Norman or Cambro-Norman, or, for
that matter, Anglo-French or Anglo-Continental. Such terms

are modern concoctions, convenient shorthands, which serve to emphasize the undoubted fact that those who began to settle in Ireland at this point were not of any one national or ethnic origin, but included people whose backgrounds lay scattered throughout Britain, northern France and the Low Countries. The difficulty, of course, with all of these terms is that they fly in the face of the overwhelming contemporary view that what these years witnessed was, to use Gerald de Barri's phrase, *adventus Anglorum*, 'the arrival of the English'.[5] Most reasonably well-informed contemporaries, Gerald included, must have known that this was hardly a satisfactory encapsulation of the invaders' origins, and yet it is employed with remarkable consistency (except in charters, where the nationality of all the various parties addressed is, presumably for legal reasons, spelt out). Its ubiquity must reflect a contemporary perception that the essential dynamic of the invasion was supplied from England, and that the invasion was, for all intents and purposes, especially after the intervention of the king of England, an English affair.[6]

The invasion is sometimes portrayed as an unforeseen accident, but if one examines Diarmait Mac Murchada's actions in the summer of 1166, when he was ejected from his kingdom and sailed into exile, it seems that he did not simply go abroad in pursuit of mercenaries – hired hands to help him recover his kingdom, who would go back whence they came, their pockets filled with pay, once that task had been completed. To view the invasion in those terms is to ignore the evidence of the two most important and most detailed contemporary accounts of the invasion, the Norman-French *chanson de geste* to which Goddard Orpen gave the title *The Song of Dermot and the Earl,* and Gerald de Barri's great history of the invasion, entitled *Expugnatio Hibernica* ('The Irish conquest'). One does, of course, have to be careful in using these texts, since both were written with the benefit of considerable hindsight, both describe events from the invaders' perspective, and both seek to justify the English conquest. Nevertheless, though independent of each other both accounts are quite consistent in their portrayal of events and, where they can be checked against other sources, remarkably accurate. To deal with the *Song of Dermot* first: it specifically states that Diarmait Mac Murchada went to Aquitaine in pursuit of a meeting with the king of England and, when he caught up with him, offered to become his liege-man, his vassal, and to hold his kingdom as a fief of the crown of England. Diarmait is made to exclaim:

> 'Hear, noble king, whence I was born, of what country.
> Of Ireland I was born a lord, in Ireland acknowledged king;
> But wrongfully my own people have cast me out of my kingdom.
> To you I come to make plaint, good sire,
> In the presence of the barons of your empire.
> Your liege-man I shall become henceforth all the days of my life,
> On condition that you be my helper so that I do not lose at all:
> You I shall acknowledge as sire and lord,
> In the presence of your barons and earls.'
> Then the King promised him, the powerful king of England,
> That willingly would he help him as soon as he should be able.[7]

It would be hard to find a plainer statement of the situation. Diarmait has become the liege-man of Henry II. He has done fealty to him. Henry is to be his sire and lord, with the duty of protecting him from his enemies. Gerald goes one step further. According to him, Diarmait did not merely swear an oath of fealty, he performed homage for his kingdom:

> His ship ploughed the waves, the wind was favourable, and he came to Henry II, king of England, intending to make an urgent plea for his help ... When he [Henry] had duly heard the reason for his exile and arrival at the court, and had received from him the bond of submission and the oath of fealty, he granted him letters patent in the following terms: 'Henry king of England, duke of Normandy and Aquitaine, and count of Anjou, gives his greeting to all his faithful subjects ... When you receive this present letter, be advised that we have admitted to our most intimate grace and favour Diarmait, prince of Leinster. Wherefore, if any person from within our wide dominions wishes to help in restoring him, as having done us fealty and homage, let him know that he has our goodwill and permission to do this.'[8]

Whatever the precise differences between these two accounts
– one talks about Mac Murchada doing fealty, the other
about fealty and homage – the essential point is that if these
two near-contemporary sources are to be believed, Mac
Murchada, in going abroad in 1166, intended to enlist the
support of Henry II to win back his kingdom of Leinster, and
had decided that the means by which he would gain Henry's
support, win back his kingdom, and hold onto it, was by
becoming Henry's vassal. Therefore, the invasion was no
accident. If these accounts are to be believed, Diarmait Mac
Murchada foresaw the consequences of his action in appeal-
ing to Henry II for help, and equally he planned to win that
help by becoming Henry's liegeman, thus establishing a
feudal bond between Leinster and the kingdom of England.

After Henry accepted Diarmait's oath of fealty and issued
him, as we have seen, with letters authorizing his vassals
throughout his many lands to come to Mac Murchada's aid,
Diarmait went to South Wales. This was a very natural place to
go in view of the long-standing closeness in the relationship
throughout history between Wales and the southern half of
Ireland. But the question here again is: was Diarmait simply
seeking temporary military aid in Wales? The *Song of Dermot*
claims otherwise:

> King Dermot then sent word by letter and by messenger,
> He sent over Maurice Regan, his own interpreter.
> To Wales this man crossed over [bearing]...
> The letters of King Dermot which the king sent in all directions.
> To earls, barons, knights, squires, sergeants, common soldiers,
> Horsemen and foot, in all directions the king sent word:

And the *Song* claims to quote what the letter said:

> 'Whoever shall wish for land or pence, horses, armour, or
>   chargers,
> Gold and silver, I shall give them ample pay;
> Whoever shall wish for soil or sod richly shall I enfeoff them'.
> He would also give them sufficient farm-stock and a handsome
>   fief.[9]

According to the *Song*, therefore, Mac Murchada offered land in Ireland to those who would come to his aid.

Diarmait came back to Ireland in August 1167 with a small band of people of Flemish origin who had settled in Pembrokeshire at the south-western tip of Wales; they were led by Richard fitz Godebert, ancestor of the Roche family in Ireland, and with their help he won back the core of his kingdom, his ancestral lands of Uí Chennselaig. At this moment Ruaidrí Ua Conchobair was presiding over a great national conference at Athboy in Meath, which 'passed many good resolutions respecting veneration for churches and clerics, and control of tribes and territories, so that women used to traverse Ireland alone'.[10] Having done that, Ua Conchobair and Ua Ruairc marched to oppose Mac Murchada, and fought two battles, one in which some of the Connacht forces were routed and one in which the army of Bréifne defeated Mac Murchada's troops, causing the death of 'the son of the king of Wales, who was the battle-prop of the island of Britain, who had come across the sea in the army of Mac Murchada', presumably a son of the lord Rhys ap Gruffudd, prince of Deheubarth.[11] After this defeat Diarmait came to Ua Conchobair and handed over hostages in return for his kingdom of Uí Chennselaig and, significantly, he was forced to give one hundred ounces of gold to Tigernán Ua Ruairc for his *enech*, his 'honour', in reparation, that is, for the offence of abducting Derbforgaill fifteen years earlier.[12] Both the *Expugnatio* and the *Song* ascribe great importance to this grudge which Ua Ruairc bore. Gerald says that Tigernán 'was stirred to extreme anger on two counts, of which however the disgrace, rather than the loss of his wife, grieved him more deeply, and he vented all the venom of his fury with a view to revenge', and he, therefore, was the one inciting Ruaidrí Ua Conchobair to suppress Mac Murchada.[13] Similarly, the *Song* has Ua Ruairc complaining to King Ruaidrí of the manner in which Mac Murchada

> Took his wife by force from him, and placed her at Ferns for her abode.

To the king of Connaught of the outrage bitterly he complains,
And of the injury; very earnestly he besought him to make ready
   for him
Some of his household and of his men so that he could avenge
   his shame.[14]

By making reparation for his offence Mac Murchada had
now purchased his reinstatement in Uí Chennselaig, but the
kingdom of all Leinster was still denied him, and this is what
he sought to recover when, about 1 May 1169, the main body
of his foreign allies arrived. They landed in three ships at
Bannow Bay in co. Wexford – 30 knights, 60 men-at-arms,
and 300 foot-archers. They were led by Robert fitz Stephen,
uncle of Gerald de Barri, and they included in their ranks
Gerald's brother, Robert de Barri, the first of the Barry
family in Ireland (to be joined the next day by Maurice de
Prendergast, a Pembrokeshire Fleming with two shiploads of
men-at-arms and archers). Because of his intimate connection with them, when Gerald describes these men's actions –
under what circumstances they came to Ireland, and what
they expected to gain – no one could be better placed to do
so. Gerald tells us that before Robert fitz Stephen ever set
foot in Ireland 'a firm guarantee' (*firma sponsio*) was given by
Mac Murchada that if Robert fitz Stephen came to Ireland
and helped Diarmait recover his kingdom, Diarmait would
grant Robert and his half-brother Maurice fitz Gerald (the
founder of the Irish Geraldines), the town of Wexford and
the adjoining territory.[15] Sure enough, this is precisely what
happened. After they landed at Bannow Bay, they proceeded
to attack the Ostmen of Wexford, conquered the town, and
Mac Murchada granted it to fitz Stephen and fitz Gerald.
According to Gerald, Robert fitz Stephen then told his followers that Diarmait Mac Murchada 'loves our race; he is
encouraging our race to come here, and has decided to
settle them in this island and give them permanent roots
there. Perhaps the outcome of this present action will be that
the five divisions of the island will be reduced to one, and
sovereignty over the whole kingdom will devolve upon our
race for the future.'[16] If we accept this at face value (and it

must always be borne in mind that we have only Gerald's word for it), the invaders believed that Mac Murchada had decided that the best way of restoring himself to power in Ireland was by enlisting foreign support, but he did not envisage a temporary arrangement; he planned that a colony would be established in Ireland, and that these men would be granted land to hold by military tenure, and that, in return for their new acquisitions, the settlers would provide Diarmait with military service (just what he needed if his army was to be tough enough to withstand his enemies).

Granting away the town of Wexford was one thing. It was run by the Ostmen, not by Diarmait himself. It was therefore semi-autonomous, and Mac Murchada in effect merely swapped one set of errant vassals for another set of potentially errant vassals. However, granting away the succession to the kingdom of Leinster was another matter altogether. This Diarmait did to the lord of Pembroke and Strigoil, Richard fitz Gilbert de Clare, better known as Strongbow. According to both the *Expugnatio* and the *Song of Dermot*, Mac Murchada met Strongbow in Wales, sometime in 1166–7, and they too made a deal. Here is how the *Song* puts it:

> King Dermot then, you must know, goes everywhere seeking aid:
> Aid everywhere he seeks in Wales and in England.
> So far did he ask for aid up and down in this kingdom
> That he had an interview, so says the geste, with Earl Richard [Strongbow].
> He was a brave earl, courteous, generous and lavish.
> Very earnestly the king besought him, very courteously,
> To give him some succour, or that he himself should come
> To conquer his kingdom, from which he had been wrongfully cast out.
> To the Earl he told plainly how he had been betrayed by his people:
> How his people had betrayed him, and driven him out, and put him to flight.
> His daughter he offered him to wife, the thing in the world that he most loved:

> That he would let him have her to wife, and would give Leinster
>   to him,
> On condition that he would aid him so that he should be able
>   to subdue it.[17]

Here, then, assuming the accuracy of this source, we have Diarmait promising his daughter, the famous Aífe, in marriage to Strongbow, together with the succession to his kingdom after Diarmait's own death. This prompts the question: did Diarmait Mac Murchada really intend that Strongbow would succeed him as king of Leinster, or was it just an empty promise? Was it the case that since he wanted Strongbow's aid, he was prepared to offer him anything to get it, without necessarily having considered how Strongbow would get a return on the investment? Of course, it is impossible to be certain just what Diarmait had in mind, but there are, perhaps, grounds for accepting the view that Mac Murchada may well have contemplated having Strongbow succeed him as king of Leinster.[18] Irish historians have been reluctant to accept this, for a number of reasons. To start with, if Strongbow did succeed to Leinster, the pretext under which he would do so is that he was Diarmait's heir, but he does not appear to have been Diarmait's heir, either under the terms of Irish Brehon law or English common law. Under the common law of England, the oldest surviving son inherited property and title, and if there was no son, the property was divided between the daughters. But Diarmait Mac Murchada had several sons, and had other daughters besides Aífe. The only way in which Strongbow could have inherited Leinster through marriage with Aífe is if all Diarmait's other children were deceased or were regarded as illegitimate, since illegitimate children, in theory at least, could not inherit property. This is probably how Strongbow's succession was justified. Diarmait Mac Murchada had married more than once. Aífe seems to have been a child of his last union. The church, anxious, as we have already seen, to stamp out irregularities in Irish marriage practices, may have recognized this as canonical and Aífe therefore became Diarmait's only legitimate heir. Of course, this must remain a suggestion; it cannot be proven.

However, even if the English could attempt to claim that Strongbow succeeded by right through English law, he had no right to do so in accordance with Irish convention, and therefore when Diarmait offered Strongbow the kingship of Leinster, he was offering something which was not within his powers, for two reasons. Firstly, in Ireland, technically speaking at least, succession to kingship was elective. A king did not choose his successor, a broader kin-group was meant to have this role. Therefore, even if Diarmait wanted Strongbow to succeed, he could not insist on it. Secondly, in any case, kingship was exclusive to the male descendants of previous kings; it could not be passed on through the female line. Be that as it may, whatever the theory of regnal succession, the practice in eleventh- and twelfth-century Ireland was such that the rules of kingship, and succession to kingship, were breaking down. Kings of one province were imposing themselves or a near relative or an ally as king over another province, without any regard for the fact that these people had no ancestral connection with that kingdom. Except for the fact that he was not even an Irishman, Strongbow was no different from one of these 'strangers in sovereignty'.

Strongbow also had the full support of Diarmait's most powerful son, Domnall Cáemánach. Domnall might have expected to succeed his father as king of Leinster, but instead he supported Strongbow, his sister's husband, or half-sister's husband. Why should he be willing to do that? Perhaps the answer lies in the fact that both Diarmait Mac Murchada and his son Domnall Cáemánach felt that the best or only chance of them retaining any power in Leinster was through Strongbow: without him they had no hope at all; with him, they had some chance. And so it was to prove. After the death of Diarmait in 1171 and of Domnall Cáemánach in 1175, the Mac Murchada dynasty remained quiescent for several generations. Although there were rival branches of the family, none of these stood the test of time, and a century later, in the 1270s, when the English colony in Leinster started to go into decline, and the Irish began to recover the position of power they had lost earlier, they were led by Domnall Cáemánach's great-grandson, and hence they became known as the MacMurrough Kavanaghs: this is Mac Murchada Cáemánach, the surname deriving from Domnall Cáemánach's nickname. In that sense, Diarmait Mac Murchada's dynasty was a success, and his descendants survived as kings of Leinster until the sixteenth century.[19]

Strongbow did not go to Ireland until August 1170, though his uncle Hervey de Montmorency had arrived in the main fleet in 1169, and was granted by Mac Murchada two cantreds between Wexford and Waterford. With these knights, and especially their forces of archers, Mac Murchada had sufficient resources to set about the recovery of Leinster. Although the Irish still, according to the annals, 'set little store by' them,[20] Ruaidrí Ua Conchobair responded to this new challenge by leading an army to Leinster, where he accepted Mac Murchada's submission, and – rather too leniently, it would appear – allowed him to remain as king of Leinster, in return for the receipt of Diarmait's son as a hostage, and an undertaking to send back his foreign allies as soon as all Leinster had again been subdued. It is doubtful, of course, whether Mac Murchada had any such intention and, indeed, according to Gerald, he was now beginning to set his sights on the high-kingship of Ireland. Contingents of reinforcements were still arriving periodically. At Baginbun, co. Wexford, early in May 1170, another of the Geraldines, Raymond le Gros, arrived with fresh troops, to be followed on 23 August by Strongbow himself with as many as two hundred knights and a thousand troops. They took Waterford, and there Strongbow married Aífe as planned.

In September 1170, Strongbow, Mac Murchada and all the might of the English military machine advanced on Dublin. Ruaidrí Ua Conchobair assembled the armies of his allies and marched to meet them.[21] He camped at Clondalkin and blocked all the main approach routes to the town from the south. According to the *Song*, those which were afforested on either side had trees felled to block access, while others were entrenched, but Strongbow's army outflanked him by traversing the Wicklow and Dublin mountains and approaching the town by way of Rathfarnham.[22] While both sides were engaged in negotiations, some of the more impetuous of the English forces, under Raymond le Gros and Miles de Cogan, 'eager for battle and plunder' as Gerald puts it, 'made an enthusiastic assault on the walls, were immediately victorious, and valiantly overran the city, with considerable slaughter of the inhabitants'.[23] According to the Four Masters, the Ostmen were slaughtered 'in the middle of their fortress', by the English, 'who carried off their cattle and goods'. Gerald claims that the greater part of the inhabitants of Dublin escaped the slaughter by boarding ship and heading for the Isles, bringing their most precious belongings with them. It is possible that many of them never returned, though the refugees were led by their king, Ascall Mac Turcaill, and within weeks of the death of Diarmait Mac Murchada about May Day 1171, Ascall launched an invasion of Dublin in the hope of ousting its English garrison. He had somewhere between sixty and one hundred shiploads of warriors and they proceeded to an assault on the eastern gate of the town, but a sortie out of the south gate by some of the garrison caught them by surprise in the rear, and the invading army was heavily defeated; Ascall Mac Turcaill was captured at the seashore as he fled to his ship, and was later beheaded in the town.

It was after this disaster that Ruaidrí Ua Conchobair instigated his famous siege of Dublin. The *Song* says that Ua Conchobair himself camped his forces at Castleknock, that his northern ally, Mac Duinn Sléibe of Ulaid, set up camp at Clontarf, Ua Briain of Thomond at Kilmainham, and Murchad Mac Murchada (the late King Diarmait's brother, an opponent of Strongbow) at Dalkey, while Gerald says that thirty shiploads of warriors from the Isles sailed into the harbour of the Liffey and blockaded it. The siege is said to have lasted about two months, with the English forces being confined within the walls, without access to provisions by either land or sea. Negotiations then ensued, with Strongbow, rather remarkably, offering to swear an oath of fealty to King Ruaidrí if he could retain Leinster under Ua Conchobair's overlordship. But Ua Conchobair would compromise only to the extent of allowing the English to hold the three Ostman towns of Dublin, Wexford and Waterford.[24] It was after the collapse of the negotiations on this sticking-point that the besieged garrison decided to make a sortie, caught Ruaidrí's forces unawares (he himself was bathing, apparently in the Liffey), 'killed a multitude of their rabble, and carried off their provisions, their armour, and their sumpter-horses',[25] the *Song* noting that 'so much provision did they find, corn, meal and bacon, that for a year in the city they had victuals in abundance'.

The humiliation of King Ruaidrí Ua Conchobair at Dublin proved to be a turning point in its history, and a landmark in the English conquest of Ireland. Gerald, in recounting these events, describes Dublin as 'the capital of the kingdom (*regni caput*)', and this by then it undoubtedly was.[26] But Strongbow's possession of it was now secure, and Diarmait Mac Murchada was dead. Strongbow had married his daughter with the widely publicized intention of succeeding to the kingdom of Leinster in her right, and was now putting it into effect. This was, undoubtedly, a major development in English politics. He was an important tenant of the crown, not just in the south Welsh marches, but in England and Normandy, and was now the heir to a kingdom and controller of Dublin and Waterford, the two most important trading ports in Ireland. There were, therefore, severe implications for Henry II's authority involved in Strongbow's rapid ascent to power in Ireland. And hence Henry now made plans to come to Ireland himself to take control of the situation. Aware of his impending expedition, Strongbow sailed to meet the king and to assuage his anger. As a sign of his good faith he handed over to Henry, Dublin and the adjacent cantreds, as well as the other 'coastal towns' and all castles.[27]

Historians have rightly stressed that when Henry came to Ireland himself in 1171, he did so more to bring the pioneers there back into line than to conquer the Irish.[28] That said, one should not lose sight of the fact that coming to Ireland (the first king of England ever to do so), having the Irish province-kings submit to him, adding Ireland to the already long list of his dominions, alongside England, Normandy, Aquitaine and Anjou, and adopting the title 'lord of Ireland', was not something Henry II reluctantly embraced. Though it may not have topped his list of priorities, no king, certainly no king as ambitious, domineering and 'relentlessly expansionist' as Henry fitz Empress,[29] reluctantly extends his overlordship over a neighbouring kingdom. And no man who came to dominate so much of north-western Europe, from the Scottish border in the north to the Pyrenees in the south, in the manner that Henry did, in the process becoming western Europe's most powerful ruler, could but look longingly at Ireland and hope to bring it within his grasp.

In 1155, shortly after his accession to the throne, Henry had discussed plans for an invasion of Ireland. If the papal document *Laudabiliter* is genuine, it was obtained at this point from the English pope, Adrian IV, to provide justification for such an invasion (though Henry may have been acting at the behest of Archbishop Theobald, anxious to re-assert Canterbury's waning influence over the Irish church).[30] According to the archbishop's secretary, John of Salisbury, a usually reliable source, such a privilege was obtained, and John himself was instructed by the pope to give to Henry 'a golden ring, adorned by a fine emerald, in token of his investiture with the government of Ireland; and this ring is still, by the king's command, preserved in the public treasury'.[31] The plans were, however, shelved at this point. It was only when Diarmait Mac Murchada came to him in Aquitaine that the plan was resurrected. Even if Henry had no great immediate interest in Ireland, he did accept Mac Murchada's oath of fealty, and thereby showed himself willing to become the overlord of a dispossessed Irish province-king, with, of course, the concomitant duty to protect him from his enemies. Thus, there hardly seems reason to doubt that the arrival of Diarmait Mac Murchada at the court of Henry II provided an opportunity which Henry was happy to embrace. And if the king of England saw opportunities opening up for himself in Ireland, it would be naive to imagine that those opportunities would not come at the expense of others.

When Henry II landed in Ireland he did not have to do battle with the native rulers (a Welsh chronicler says that he 'stayed that winter without doing any harm to the Irish'),[32] and during his brief stay there, which lasted from mid-October 1171 to mid-April of the following year, several of the more important Irish kings, and quite a few of lesser importance, voluntarily submitted to him. Of course, they did not have a great deal of choice. Henry brought with him an army of about 500 knights and anything up to 4000 archers. In the field, these would have made quick work of any Irish resistance. It is true to say that several Irish kings who felt themselves under threat from the aggressive expansionism of Strongbow and the other settlers probably thought that the arrival of Henry was good news, since he came to Ireland, after all, primarily because he was worried about the rapid gains the freelance operators were making. The Irish kings hoped that he would be a restraining influence on the more aggressive of the new arrivals (indeed, one English chronicler claims that Henry had come to Ireland in the first place because of 'the call of the Irish to be defended against Richard [Strongbow]'),[33] and to some extent this hope proved justified. Henry did not stop the conquest, but he did slow up the pace. Henceforth, if the settlers were to seize more lands, their operations, in theory at least, had to be licensed by Henry. Therefore, the hope of securing Henry's protection against the aggression of the colonists may have motivated some Irish kings to submit to him, and to make oaths of fealty to him.

There is one other consideration here that should not be forgotten. In 1171, when Henry II arrived in Ireland, Ruaidrí Ua Conchobair was high-king. He had become king simply by compelling the other province-kings to acknowledge him as such. Many of them did so reluctantly. They would have been only too happy to throw off their allegiance and transfer it to another – in this case, the king of England. It may be that the submission by the Irish kings was a temporary expedient, into which too much should not be read. By submitting to Henry they bought some time; they knew that he would not stay in

Ireland long, and hoped, perhaps, that the *status quo ante* would return after his departure.

The response of the Irish church leaders to the invasion was similarly complex. It was not dictated by 'patriotism', by anti-Englishness, or by a desire to defend their flock from foreign assault. There are few contemporary signs of any such sentiment, and no reason why one should expect otherwise. The one overriding consideration that coloured their response was the question of whether or not the English assertion of lordship over Ireland would help or hinder the process of reform then underway in the Irish church. From what we can tell, it was the unanimous view of the Irish hierarchy that such an assertion of lordship would prove beneficial. In 1171–2 the Irish prelates, the bishops and leading abbots, submitted to Henry without hesitation, swore fealty to him, and accepted him and his heirs as their lord and king. They then sent letters to Pope Alexander III explaining why they did so, and the benefits which they hoped would accrue to the Irish church and people as a result. We do not have the texts of those letters, but we do have Pope Alexander's reply to the Irish bishops, in which he says that:

> '... *Your letters* ... have informed us how great are the enormities of vice with which the Irish people is contaminated and how they have put aside the fear of God and the faith of the Christian religion to put their salvation in jeopardy. We have further learnt from *your letters* that our dearest son in Christ, Henry noble king of the English, prompted by God, has, with his assembled forces, subjected to his rule that barbarous and uncivilised people, ignorant of divine law, and that what was unlawfully being practised in your country is already, with God's help, beginning to decrease, and we are overjoyed.'[34]

The cause of the pope's joy was his belief that King Henry and the English presence in Ireland in general would be instruments of reform in the Irish church, and if he got his information from the Irish bishops, then they too believed this. They, the Irish bishops, also believed that the process of reform in Irish church-life and society, which had been underway for three-quarters of a century or more, was far from complete, that there were forces within Irish society which were hindering the process of *self*-reform, and that external aid was necessary to bring it about. What they sought becomes clear from Pope Alexander's letter written to Henry II at this same time, in which he lists four specific abuses among the Irish which need addressing, and presumably it was the Irish bishops who supplied the information. The first concerns lax marriage practices, the second, the eating of meat during Lent, the third, that they were not paying tithes to the church, and the fourth, that they were showing insufficient respect for church property and for clerics themselves.[35]

These last two were significant and had been among the first things addressed in the reform movement throughout Europe during the preceding century. Tithes were a vital source of income for the church; the system of tithes, whereby a proportion, strictly speaking a tenth, of income was paid to the local church for its maintenance, was the very basis of the parochial system throughout the Western church. Under the synodal reforms introduced in Ireland in the early twelfth century, the country was divided up into thirty or so dioceses, but the process of dividing the dioceses in turn into parishes, each with a parish church, a parish priest, and parishioners paying for their upkeep, was as yet in its infancy, and the Irish church leaders who supported the English invasion obviously believed that this would be greatly accelerated by such intervention. And their expectations were not misplaced. Those parts of Ireland which were conquered by the English were carved up into fiefs and at a local level manors were erected for the better exploitation of the land. Hand in hand with the creation of a manor-based economy went the development of a parochial system, so that their boundaries were often one and the same. Therefore, if the development of parishes and the exaction of tithes was a major desideratum on the part of the Irish bishops, then there is every reason to think that they favoured the introduction of the 'feudal' system of land-tenure because it would facilitate that aim.

Likewise, if they complained to the pope that church property and churchmen themselves were not sufficiently respected by the Irish, they were making the same sort of complaint that continental churchmen had been making throughout the previous century: laymen should not interfere unduly in church affairs, they should not have the primary role in choosing who should succeed to ecclesiastical office, and the church should be exempt from excessive secular taxation. These were common complaints. In England, church and state had arrived at a compromise that worked well, by and large, whereby the king would not appoint bishops, but the church did need to obtain his permission before proceeding with the appointment of a new bishop and, while a bishopric was unoccupied, the property of the diocese (what was known as the temporalities) belonged to the king. This orderly, reasonable *modus vivendi* between church and state was presumably what the Irish bishops wished to see in operation in Ireland and it explains why, when the second synod of Cashel was held in 1171–2, it passed legislation to do with marriage, the payment of tithes, the freedom of the church from lay control, and the safeguarding of clerical privileges. Furthermore, in order to ensure that these provisions would take effect, it announced the principle that henceforth the Irish church was to be brought into line, and to operate in conformity, with the English church. The Irish church as it had existed for 700 years since the time of Patrick was to be no more, and it was to be no more by its own volition.

As already stated, there was nothing 'unpatriotic' about the adoption of this policy or about the way in which the Irish kings flocked to the court of the king of England to swear their allegiance to him. Neither was there anything treacherous about Diarmait Mac Murchada's actions in inviting English assistance. That is not to say that contemporaries did not condemn him for his deeds. There may be some doubt over the reliability of the obituary of Mac Murchada that occurs in the seventeenth-century Annals of the Four Masters, which has it that

> Diarmait Mac Murchada, king of Leinster, by whom a trembling sod was made of all Ireland – after having brought over Saxons,

after having done extensive injuries to the Irish, after plundering many churches, Kells, Clonard, etc. – died before the end of the year of an insufferable and unknown disease, for he became putrid while living, through the miracles of God, Colum Cille, and Finnian and the other saints of Ireland, whose churches he had profaned and burned some time before; and he died at Ferns, without [making] a will, without penance, without the body of Christ, without unction, as his evil deeds deserved.[36]

This has to be set against the polite account of his passing that occurs in the (admittedly biased) *Book of Leinster*, which simply says that he 'died at Ferns after victory of extreme unction and penance in his sixty-first year'. However, it is worth pointing out the next line in the same text: 'Thereafter the English wretchedly rule'. This is a source one would have expected to be sympathetic to Diarmait and supportive of his actions. But it is quite clear that the author was no supporter of the English invasion; and his statement about the English wretchedly ruling is not very far removed from the comment by the author of the annals of 'Tigernach', a contemporary chronicle compiled in Connacht, which describes the arrival of Robert fitz Stephen as 'the start of Ireland's woe'. It should be pointed out too that elsewhere in the *Book of Leinster* there is a set of annals which sums up the invasion in these words: 'The English came into Ireland and Ireland was destroyed by them'.[37]

Diarmait Mac Murchada's fiercest foe was, as already noted, Tigernán Ua Ruairc of Bréifne, and both men died within a year of each other. As far as Gerald was concerned, to judge from what he has to say in the *Expugnatio*, Tigernán's death was regarded at the time as a major breakthrough in the conquest, and he describes how his head was cut off and sent to Henry II as a trophy: that is an indication of its significance.[38] But according to the Irish annals, Ua Ruairc was assassinated by the English in treachery, and his head was hoisted over the gate of the fortress at Dublin. The annalist describes this as 'a sore and miserable sight for the Irish'. Then the annalist tells us that the rest of the body, in an act of extraordinary vindictiveness, was hung, feet upwards, at another place on the north side of the town. There is a huge contrast between the obituaries of both men. Whereas the annals of 'Tigernach' say that Mac Murchada was 'a man who troubled and destroyed Ireland', who died 'after mustering the foreigners and ruining the Irish, after plundering and razing churches and territories', the same annals call Ua Ruairc 'the deedful leopard of the Irish, Leth Cuinn's man of battle and lasting defence … surpasser of all the Irish in might and abundance'. Hence, by contrasting both men in this way the authors, consciously or otherwise, are expressing a contemporary perception of the reprehensible nature of Mac Murchada's actions in enlisting English aid, and of general Irish disapproval of the deed.

Gerald de Barri has the most detailed account of the invasion, and because he is usually very critical of the Irish, one should pay special attention when he occasionally shows sympathy for them. He, of course, sees the invasion as divine punishment for the sins of the Irish, and claims that a national council of all the Irish church, meeting at Armagh in the immediate aftermath of the invasion, admitted as much (God's punishment of the Irish for their practice of carrying off English people into slavery); but it is worth pointing out that he concedes that the assembled clerics regarded the invasion as 'a disaster which had befallen them'.[39] Again, Gerald puts into Ruaidrí Ua Conchobair's mouth a speech warning that the English are 'a race most hostile to ours, a race which has long been eager to rule us all alike … a race moreover which asserts that by the Fate's decree they are entitled to jurisdiction over our land'.[40] Now, one does not have to believe that these are the exact words Ruaidrí uttered; one does not even have to believe that Ruaidrí made the speech at all. What Gerald is telling us here is that it was his understanding of Ruaidrí Ua Conchobair's view, and of the view held by the Irish in general, that they suspected the English of having long held hostile intentions towards Ireland, and that the Irish disputed the legality of the English claim to Ireland. According to Gerald, Ua Conchobair sent messages to Robert fitz Stephen to persuade him 'to leave peacefully and with mutual goodwill this country in which he could claim for himself no right of jurisdiction'.[41] So says Gerald, Robert's own nephew; there seems little reason for doubting what he has to say on the point, since it reflects poorly on fitz Stephen and the whole English enterprise. Clearly this is simply Gerald's way of stating that, right from the very start, the Irish, led by their king, disputed the legitimacy of the English title.

Gerald goes so far as to admit that there were problems about the legality of some of the invaders' conquests in Ireland. He has no doubt that Strongbow was entitled to claim Leinster by virtue of his marriage to Mac Murchada's daughter, but then he adds: 'as regards Waterford, Desmond, Thomond, and Meath, all of which were seized unlawfully, I make no excuses for the Earl'.[42] He quotes what he claims is the text of a message sent by Ua Conchobair to Diarmait Mac Murchada, as follows:

> 'Contrary to the conditions of our treaty you have invited into this island a large number of foreigners. Yet we put up with this with a good grace while you confined yourself within your province of Leinster. But now, since you are unmindful of your oath and without feelings of pity for the hostage you have given [Diarmait's son, Conchobar], and have arrogantly trespassed beyond the stipulated limits and your ancestral boundaries, you must either restrain the forays of your foreign troops for the future, or else we will send you without fail the severed head of your son.'[43]

This may, of course, have been concocted by Gerald, but it is at least an indication of the way he *expected* Ruaidrí to feel. Gerald is conscious of the need to rebut criticism of the invasion. At one stage he refers to 'vociferous complaints that the kings of England hold Ireland unlawfully'.[44] Who were making these complaints? Hardly the English themselves. Gerald also states:

> [Robert] fitz Stephen and the Earl cannot in any sense be classed as mere robbers, as far as Leinster is concerned. Both rest their claims on the same legal position, for they both acted within the law in restoring Diarmait to his lands, the one because he had taken an oath of allegiance to him, and the

other because he had married his daughter ... The remaining princes of Ireland immediately made a voluntary submission to Henry, and thus conferred a legal claim that is beyond dispute. So ... it must be clear from the above that in entering Ireland the English were not guilty of injustice such as is foolishly attributed to them by the ill-informed.[45]

This last statement is the important point: somebody, by the mid-1180s when Gerald was writing, was of the view that the English invasion of Ireland was unjust.

If, therefore, a sense of injustice was felt by the native Irish as early as the 1180s, it must have found a political, and hence a military, expression. For this reason, it is wrong to think that the conquest proceeded smoothly in this first generation. The *Expugnatio* records a speech said to have been made by Strongbow's uncle, Hervey de Montmorency, in which he declares:

'... the whole population of Ireland has joined in plotting our destruction, not without good reason ... We are surrounded on all sides by external hazards ... Countless numbers without, and many within, are trying to accomplish our total destruction. What happens if these men free themselves from the bonds with which they are but lightly tied and make a sudden rush to seize our arms? ... We must choose one of two policies. Either we must vigorously pursue that end for which we have come here, and with the aid of our armed might and our valour subdue with a strong arm this rebellious people, completely casting aside all pretence of clemency; or ... turn our ships around and leave this people which so deserves our pity to enjoy their country and ancestral lands in peace.'[46]

According to Hervey, therefore, 'the whole population of Ireland' was engaged in a plot to overturn the conquest. That plot found its opportunity in the summer of 1173, when Henry II's eldest son, the young king Henry, rebelled against his father, in league with Louis of France. In order to subdue the rebels, large numbers of the new settlers in Ireland, including their leaders Strongbow and Hugh de Lacy, went to Normandy to fight alongside their lord, Henry II. This was the signal for an Irish revolt. Gerald says: 'The Irish had got to hear of the serious disturbances which had lately broken out in the lands beyond the sea, and, as they are a race consistent only in their fickleness ... [the Earl, on his return] found almost all the princes of that country in open revolt against the king and himself'.[47] Sure enough, we know that in 1173 Domnall Mór Ua Briain attacked Strongbow's garrison in Waterford, and that a disinherited grandson of Diarmait Mac Murchada revolted against his new uncle by doing battle with the English settlers in Leinster.[48]

This revolt in Ireland was matched by a rebellion in Wales. These disturbances took place in the south-east marches of Wales, the area between Glamorgan and Gwent, led by the local Welsh princeling, Iorwerth ab Owain. What is most interesting is that the target of this revolt too was Strongbow and the high point of the rebellion was reached in mid-August 1173 when the rebels swept as far as the very walls of Chepstow castle, the *caput* of Strongbow's lordship.[49] Here we have two rebellions taking place against Strongbow in the same summer – one in Ireland, the other in Wales. We have no evidence that the organizers collaborated in any way, but we can imagine that both sides knew well what was going on on the other side of the Irish Sea. The same set of circumstances applied on both sides. First, both Irish and Welsh had the same target – Strongbow. Second, he, being with the king in Normandy, was conveniently absent from both arenas, which meant that the defensive strength of the colonists was considerably weakened. And third, both the Irish and the Welsh had a common grievance, a common experience of colonial harassment and dispossession. It was that common grievance that led to these simultaneous revolts breaking out on both sides of the Irish Sea in 1173; and for the next hundred and fifty years, right the way through to the period of the Bruce invasion, they were to become a continual occurrence.

Resistance to the conquest was, therefore, present from the start, though it is undoubtedly true that perennial political fissures among the Irish militated against it. It was also the case that the attempt at conquering the whole country got bogged down quite early on. When the Anglo-Irish annals compiled in Dublin describe the death of Hugh de Lacy in 1186, they add the curious comment: 'There ended the conquest'.[50] Gerald of Wales makes a very similar point:

> This island ... would long since have been successfully and effectively subdued from one end to the other ... had not the further influx of fresh troops been cut off by royal decree ... For when our people arrived there first, the Irish were paralysed and panic-stricken by the sheer novelty of the event ... But thanks to the half-hearted dragging out of the conquest over a long period ... the natives gradually became skilled and versed in handling arrows and other arms ... Consequently this people, which to begin with could have been easily routed, recovered its morale and military strength, and was enabled to put up a stronger resistance.[51]

This passage was written in the 1180s. As far as Gerald was concerned, and we have no reason to doubt him, the Irish rally was well and truly under way. All the signs were there to indicate that the English invasion of Ireland was not going to lead to a complete conquest.

4

FROM KINGDOM TO LORDSHIP

Beginning in the late 1160s, and in the space of a few short years, the face of Ireland was transformed and the course of Irish history irrevocably changed. The English invasion effected a revolutionary metamorphosis on the landscape of Ireland, bringing enormous changes in patterns of land-holding and methods of land exploitation; there followed an agricultural and economic transformation, and the introduction of a whole new social system affecting everything from the laws people used, to the homes they lived in, to the food they put on the table. Of course, it was by no means the case that all of Ireland felt the impact of these developments. Change was confined to those parts of the country successfully exposed to English colonization, which, as we shall see, never affected the entire island. Furthermore, while the events of the late twelfth century were clearly momentous, it would be wrong to underestimate the degree to which there was some form of continuity from the pre-invasion period. This expressed itself in very visible ways in, for instance, the re-use by the settlers of sites (both church sites and centres of secular power) formerly occupied by the Irish, but it can also be seen in the manner in which the new settlement was dictated by pre-existing political and territorial structures. Sometimes, it is true, existing territorial divisions were ignored in the carve-up that followed the invasion, but in many instances they were respected and simply adapted for use by their new lords.

Therefore, when Strongbow succeeded to Leinster he inherited the kingdom built up by Diarmait Mac Murchada and his predecessors (less those towns and lands, including Dublin and its hinterland, which Henry II insisted, as a precautionary measure and because of their great wealth, on taking into his own hands). But, for Strongbow and his like, gaining such a sizeable territorial lordship was only a first step, and was worthless if he could not secure possession of it. To do so he needed to defend it from those who might seek to challenge his claim or rebel against his authority, and, since the defence of an entire Irish provincial kingdom was a task beyond the capacity of any one man, the method to which he had recourse was that which lay at the basis of 'feudal' society elsewhere: the division of his new lordship into manageable estates, and the apportioning of this land to family, friends and followers, who might in turn subdivide their new acquisitions, in a process known to historians as subinfeudation. Thus, as the pyramid of lordship began to take shape, Strongbow, the tenant-in-chief of the crown, had his own tenants and sub-tenants, and just as he owed military service to the king for Leinster (to a total of one hundred knights), so those who held part of Leinster under him owed him military service or annual rents.

The same process was repeated elsewhere in the country. Hugh de Lacy, one of the largest landholders in Herefordshire, was granted by Henry II the province of Meath (which consisted of the modern counties of Meath and Westmeath, and parts of Longford and Offaly). Hugh held Meath for the service of fifty knights, and made a reality of his new acquisition by parcelling out his lordship to adherents of his own, some of whom had followed him from his home base in Herefordshire (though, of course, like Strongbow, he kept some of the best land and most desirable locations as his own seigneurial estates). Several of Hugh's followers were granted fiefs that amounted to entire baronies, which were then further subdivided into manors, and we can recover the boundaries of some of these manors by comparison with parish boundaries, since the two were often coterminous.[1]

Hugh's sub-tenants were charged with the responsibility of defending Meath from Irish attack and they did so, in conjunction with de Lacy himself, by a process of incastellation.[2] The earliest efforts at castle construction, both in Meath and elsewhere, involved the erection of earthen mottes or mounds (many, no doubt, adaptations of existing features), sometimes with a bailey (an earthwork enclosure) attached. The greatest density of mottes lies, as might be expected from the pattern of settlement in the colony, in the eastern half of the island, and their construction was confined to the early decades of the conquest, the late twelfth and early thirteenth centuries.[3] In other parts of the island which were settled relatively early – for instance, in parts of counties Waterford, Cork, and Limerick – mottes are conspicuous by their absence, and here the settlers may have constructed military ringworks (though these are present too in areas of motte construction) which, unlike the motte, relied not on their elevation but on a palisaded bank and ditch, and perhaps a fortified gatehouse, though the remains of these structures are so similar to pre-invasion ring-forts that they are difficult to identify.[4]

When a motte or other earthwork castle had been constructed – or a stone castle in the case of the great lords – military control was, it would appear, quickly established, the sites, of course, having been carefully chosen with defence and ease of communications in mind. Domination of the surrounding countryside thus secure, the next step involved the conversion of the military outpost into manageable agricultural units usually organized in the form of a manor (though some mottes and ringworks were undoubtedly just temporary campaign fortifications), since without tenants land was useless and incapable of yielding a profit, and without an effective occupation of the newly won territory such conquests would quickly evaporate. An inducement to settlement involved the establishment of boroughs throughout the lordship, which were given the elements of an urban constitution, although some were undoubtedly no more than agricultural villages. Divided up into burgage plots held by burgesses on favourable terms, and with their own court, borough status and the tenurial advantages it brought, must have encouraged many to make a new home for themselves in Ireland.[5] Therefore, although our evidence for it is patchy and in many cases neglected, there followed in the years immediately succeeding the initial invasion, and for much of the next century, the immigration into Ireland of large numbers of settlers from the neighbouring island – peasant farmers, parish priests, merchants, craftsmen, and labourers. We cannot, of course, put a number on the level of immigration, but it was substantial enough to change permanently the complexion of many of those parts of the island which were comprehensively colonized, and to introduce into Ireland a nucleus of people whose loyalties lay elsewhere and whose culture remained that of their transmarine homeland.

This process of settlement was part of a much wider movement of colonization that affected many of the peripheral regions of Europe in this age. Prior to and concomitant with the English movement into Ireland there was a seepage of population from England into Wales and Scotland, similar in some respects to the way in which immigrants from Germany colonized eastern Europe, Christian Spain expanded its boundaries at the expense of Islam, and crusaders and colonists tried their fortunes in the eastern Mediterranean and the Holy Land. The High Middle Ages, especially the period from, let us say, 1000 to 1300 AD, were an age of rapid economic growth, territorial aggrandizement, and profound social and cultural change. There was a great vitality in western European society, a rising population, improved methods of agricultural production and an increase in the area of land under cultivation, as well as a growth in commercial activity and a rapid urbanization. As the author of one recent influential work on the subject put it:

> Everywhere in Europe in the twelfth and thirteenth centuries trees were being felled, roots laboriously grubbed out, ditches delved to drain waterlogged land. Recruiting agents travelled in the overpopulated parts of Europe collecting emigrants; wagons full of anxious new settlers creaked their way across the continent; busy ports sent off ships full of colonists to alien

and distant destinations; bands of knights hacked out new lordships.

As much as anywhere else on the European periphery this was to be the experience of Ireland in the late twelfth and the thirteenth centuries. The 1169 invasion, so often viewed in isolation as a turning point in Anglo-Irish relations, was certainly that, but it was much more besides. It was an episode in European history and a manifestation of that process of 'conquest, colonization and cultural change' that this epoch witnessed and that contributed to 'the making of Europe' as we know it.[6]

For the political historian, what is interesting is the way in which these changes came about, and did so, in many respects, imperceptibly. The kingdom of Ireland almost drifted into being a lordship attached to the English crown. And the contemporary Irish sources are proof that one can live through a revolution and barely notice it, because if one were dependent on the Irish annals alone one would be virtually unaware that this extraordinary transformation was taking place. For instance, there is one set of Irish annals which is certainly contemporaneous with the invasion – the Munster chronicle known as the Annals of Inisfallen. Arguably, Henry II's expedition was the single most important turning point in Irish history, but this annalist devotes a mere one sentence to it. He tells us that Henry came to Ireland, landed at Waterford, where the two Munster kings, Ua Briain of Thomond and Mac Carthaig of Desmond, submitted to him; then he went to Dublin, where he spent the winter. That is the full extent of the account, just one brief sentence, and no mention at all of the enormous consequences of the event.

The reason that the annals fail to describe the physical manifestations of the transformation then taking place in Irish society is not that the Irish failed to grasp the significance of recent events. To expect this kind of detail in annals is to misunderstand their nature and purpose. Annals are like front-page newspaper headlines: usually they deal with high politics. In the 1170s, therefore, although the countryside, culture and society of Ireland were being convulsed by change, the annals tend to confine comment to the latest negotiations between the new overlord of Ireland, Henry II, and the high-king of Ireland, Ruaidrí Ua Conchobair, or the details of the last atrocity committed by one side on the other.

When we talk about Irish politics in the 1170s, broadly speaking there are two themes: the attempt by Henry II to sort out some kind of working relationship with Ruaidrí Ua Conchobair, and then the continuing and relentless expansion of the colony outwards from its base in Leinster. Henry II's brief expedition to Ireland in the winter of 1171–2 was a highly successful one from his point of view (although a Welsh chronicler claims that 'mortality befell those who had gone with the king to Ireland because of the novelty of the unaccustomed foods, and also because the ships had not been able to sail with merchandise in winter, on account of the fury of the Irish Sea').[7] His biggest worry was that Strongbow might grow too powerful in Ireland and become a threat, so that a primary consideration of his policy was to regularize Strongbow's position in Ireland. He had no intention of removing Strongbow from power; it was simply a matter of demonstrating his own superiority and establishing a set of ground-rules, and a means of ensuring that Strongbow complied with them. Therefore, Henry took Dublin, Wexford, and Waterford into his own hands, and, as already noted, left Strongbow holding the rest of Leinster, for the service of one hundred knights.

As already discussed, it had been a feature of the enmity between Diarmait Mac Murchada and Tigernán Ua Ruairc that both had their eyes set on annexing the same piece of territory: the vulnerable kingdom of Meath that separated their kingdoms of Leinster and Bréifne. Now that Strongbow held Leinster, there was obviously a worry that he might seek to continue Mac Murchada's policy of pushing northwards into Meath, and thus Henry introduced a mechanism for preventing it. He granted Meath, as we have seen, to Hugh de Lacy, who was new to Ireland, not being one of Diarmait Mac Murchada's original recruits. He was a man intentionally set up in Meath as a rival of Strongbow, to counterbalance the latter's growing power in the lordship. Also, Meath was a crucial border zone between the new colony in Dublin and Leinster and Ruaidrí Ua Conchobair's kingdom of Connacht. Hence, it is not surprising that the 1170s saw widespread warfare in Meath as Hugh de Lacy set about subinfeudating his new acquisition, parcelling it out among those who had taken the gamble in following him to Ireland. As de Lacy and his tenants carved out manors for themselves, with a motte-and-bailey timber castle at their centre to protect them from attack, so they were bound to meet with Irish opposition. Indeed, Tigernán Ua Ruairc met his death in a confrontation with de Lacy's men in Meath. Ruaidrí Ua Conchobair was not happy about this English presence on his doorstep, and he led an invasion of Meath in 1174. We gain some idea of the extent of the power Ua Conchobair could still muster, and the seriousness with which the Irish viewed the English expansion into Meath, from the range of those who joined this campaign: Ruaidrí was supported, not just by his own vassals, the sub-kings of Connacht, but by the dispossessed Irish king of Meath, Magnus Ua Maíl Sechnaill, the kings of Breífne, Airgialla, and Ulaid, and also by the kings of Cenél nEógain and Cenél Conaill – in other words, by the whole of *Leth Cuinn* (the northern half of Ireland). The targets of the assault were the castles de Lacy and his men had built at Trim and Duleek, which they destroyed. They then marched all the way to the outskirts of Dublin, and although they turned back rather than assault the city, had they done so, this campaign might well have brought the conquest to a standstill.[8] As it was, the settlers responded to it by redoubling their efforts. They reinforced their castles: the origins of the massive fortress at Trim can be traced to these years, and it was at Trim that they hanged the man whom Hugh de Lacy had dispossessed from the kingship of Meath, Magnus Ua Maíl Sechnaill.

Strongbow was having an equally difficult time of it in Leinster. As we have already seen, in 1173 he had gone off to the Continent to help Henry II and, according to Gerald, the Irish took advantage of his absence to rebel. When he returned, he found, as Gerald put it, 'almost all the princes of that country in open revolt against the king and himself'. It is widely reported in contemporary sources that Domnall Mór Ua Briain, king of Thomond, joined by Ruaidrí Ua Conchobair's son, led an army into Ossory which forced Strongbow's garrison in Kilkenny to abandon the town and retreat to Waterford. Then in the following year, 1174, the colonists made another attempt to push out from Leinster into Munster. The annals of Tigernach say that Strongbow wanted to destroy Munster but that Ruaidrí Ua Conchobair came to help it. When Strongbow heard that Ruaidrí was marching to oppose him, he sent to Dublin for reinforcements, which arrived at Thurles. There they did battle with Domnall Mór Ua Briain and the Munstermen, assisted by the army of Connacht (except for those troops left behind to protect King Ruaidrí), and in that battle at Thurles the earl and his men were defeated, the annals of Tigernach saying that 1700 of them were slain. Strongbow then retreated to Waterford; Ua Briain returned safely to Thomond, 'and the king of Ireland with his armies marched into Connacht after the triumphant victory of that battle'.

It was because of the continuing vulnerability of the lordship, the upper hand which Ruaidrí Ua Conchobair was beginning to obtain, and the need, therefore, to reach a *modus vivendi* with him, that in October 1175 Henry II and Ruaidrí agreed to the so-called Treaty of Windsor. It is fairly clear what Henry II wanted out of the treaty with Ua Conchobair. He sought to safeguard whatever gains had already been made in Ireland. This meant compromising with Ruaidrí, buying his compliance, and striking a deal with him that had sufficient attraction for Ua Conchobair to make him accept the *status quo*. Ruaidrí, for his part, was prepared to acknowledge that Henry was his overlord (though he was not called upon to deliver a declaration of fealty in person), and agreed to hand over an annual tribute amounting to one hide out of every ten animals slaughtered, 'save that he shall not meddle with those lands which the lord king has retained in his lordship and in the lordship of his barons'. These the treaty lists: Meath,

Dublin, Wexford and all Leinster, and that part of Munster from Waterford to Dungarvan. Ruaidrí does not appear to have had to swallow too much pride to accept this because, in return, Henry acknowledged his position as king of Connacht and stated that 'he shall hold his land [of Connacht] as fully and as peacefully as he held it before the lord king entered Ireland'.[9] Furthermore, the treaty includes the provision that if any of the province-kings 'shall be rebels to the king of England *and to Ruaidrí* and shall refuse to pay the tribute ... he, Ruaidrí, shall judge them and remove them'. Here Ruaidrí Ua Conchobair is getting a legal entitlement to remove from power anyone who rebels against him. What is more, the treaty also says that 'the constable of the king of England in that land [Ireland] shall, when called upon by [Ruaidrí], aid him to do what is necessary'. Thus, instead of being at the receiving end of the colonists' aggression, Ruaidrí is being given a promise of military aid by them against his enemies.

The Treaty of Windsor was, therefore, a solid achievement by Ruaidrí Ua Conchobair, but for that very reason it is not surprising that the colonists in Ireland had no interest in making it work. In setting out the extent of the lands held by the settlers in Ireland, the treaty implicitly drew a line on the map of Ireland, and dictated that the conquest stop there. But it was all very well for Henry II to make a gentleman's agreement with Ruaidrí Ua Conchobair; it was another matter to get the frontiersmen to abide by it. The great weakness of the agreement was that there was no effective enforcement clause. The bounds of the colony were to stay as they were on the day that the agreement was made, but should the colonists go on the offensive and try to make further inroads, there was nothing in the Treaty of Windsor to stop them. On the other hand, if Ruaidrí Ua Conchobair was to try to push back the frontiers of the colony (to invade Meath, for instance, as he had done in 1174), he would be acting in contravention of the agreement because, under its terms, he was king only for as long 'as he shall faithfully serve' the king of England. To launch a hostile attack on men who were tenants-in-chief of the king of England, who held their lands by charter directly of the king, was to repudiate his oath of fealty and for it Ruaidrí could forfeit his kingship.

There were, therefore, weaknesses in Ruaidrí's position. Who decided whether he was faithful to his oath of fealty? It was clearly in the interests of the colonists to provoke Ruaidrí into repudiating his fealty so that the treaty could be rendered void, and this seems to have been what happened. The colonists were extending the area under their control outwards from the area allowed under the treaty, but there was no one to prevent them. They were fully intent, for instance, on annexing Ua Briain's kingdom of Thomond and Mac Carthaig's kingdom of Desmond, in particular their respective capitals at Limerick and Cork, and there was little or nothing Ruaidrí could do about this. Now, some would hold that since the Uí Chonchobair kings of Connacht and the Uí Briain kings of Thomond were traditional rivals, Ruaidrí might have had no great objection to Ua Briain's displacement by the English – they might, in fact, have been doing him a favour in ridding him of a long-standing thorn in his side. Likewise, in the early weeks of 1177 John de Courcy set off from Dublin with a contingent of men from the garrison there and after three days arrived at Downpatrick, the capital of the kingdom of the Ulaid, which he overran, forcing its king to flee and thereby winning for himself a kingdom. Of this, one authority on the subject has said that Ruaidrí 'is unlikely to have been perturbed unduly by the fate of a region that was well beyond his control in any case'.[10] And this may be right: there *were* petty provincial rivalries involved. Ruaidrí Ua Conchobair was very much king of Connacht first and high-king of Ireland second, a very poor second. Nevertheless, the lesson of Irish history in the previous 150 years or so is that these kings believed in making the kingship of Ireland a reality. Ruaidrí Ua Conchobair believed that he was high-king of Ireland and that there were certain prerogatives that were his as a result. One of these was that the major issues of the day – the invasion of province-kingdoms, the annexation of territory, the displacement of royal dynasties – were matters for the king of Ireland. That is the whole key to the Treaty of Windsor as far as Ruaidrí was concerned: it acknowledged that this was his role, and doubtless his envoys had negotiated hard and long to ensure its inclusion in the text of the treaty.

It is far from certain, therefore, that Ruaidrí acquiesced in the infringements of the treaty which were taking place within weeks of its agreement.[11] These changes – the enlargement of the bounds of the English lordship – were not in his interest, because whatever hope he had of exercising overlordship of native Irish kings, he had little or no say once these areas came into the hands of English feudatories, who carved them up among their followers and brought over little communities of peasant farmers and artisans from England and Wales to settle them. It was, it seems, the English settlers who caused the abandonment of the treaty on the grounds that Henry had struck a deal too favourable to Ruaidrí Ua Conchobair. Thus, in May 1177, Henry held a council at Oxford at which he dropped all pretence of abiding by the Treaty of Windsor. He took the cities of Cork and Limerick into his own hands, and granted Mac Carthaig's kingdom of Desmond to Robert fitz Stephen and Miles de Cogan, and gave Ua Briain's kingdom of Thomond to Philip de Briouze.[12]

That was not the most important decision made at Oxford. Henry had four legitimate sons. The youngest was the nine-year-old John, and at the council of Oxford Henry announced his intention of making John king of Ireland. Had things turned out as Henry planned, Ireland would have descended in a cadet line of the Plantagenets. That, though, was never to be, because John's three older brothers predeceased him, and the lord of Ireland became king of England, thereby reattaching Ireland firmly to the English crown. Henry II requested the pope in 1177 to provide young John with a crown. This request may have arisen from the contemporary belief that the papacy had sovereignty over islands – the privilege which had empowered the papacy, under the terms of the alleged papal document *Laudabiliter*, to authorize the English invasion of Ireland in the first place – though it should be pointed out that one late Irish source claims that the crown of Ireland had been brought to Rome in 1064 by Brian Bóruma's son,

Donnchad mac Briain, and 'remained with the Popes untill Pope Adrean gave the same to King Henry the second that conquered Ireland'.[13] As Henry had given up on his earlier plan of ruling Ireland through the intermediary power of Ruaidrí Ua Conchobair, he may have sought a papal grant of a crown as a means of neutralizing Irish opposition: if the pope approved of it, Ua Conchobair would find it hard to oppose. As it happened, the reigning pope refused to grant John a crown. According to one chronicler, he 'strongly resisted' the move, and it may be the case that Ua Conchobair intervened with Rome to prevent it. We know that the archbishop of Dublin, Lorcán Ua Tuathail, acted as a representative of Ruaidrí in negotiations at this time. He was present at the Third Lateran Council in 1179, and was appointed papal legate to Ireland. After his return to Ireland, King Ruaidrí sent him off on an embassy to Henry II.[14] According to a *Life* of St Lorcán written soon after his death, his mission arose because of a sudden and violent quarrel that had broken out between the two kings.[15] Henry may have been unhappy with Ruaidrí, who perhaps had reneged on the payments of tribute due under the terms of the Treaty of Windsor, but if anyone was unhappy about the way the treaty was being flouted, it was Ruaidrí. He was still trying to make it work: according to one English chronicler, when he sent Archbishop Lorcán off to negotiate with Henry in 1180, he also sent one of his sons as a pledge of his good faith as regards the payment of overdue tribute.[16]

But Ua Conchobair was also trying to secure his rights under the treaty, still trying to cling on to the advantages it gave him, and was no doubt opposed to Henry's plan to make his nine-year-old son king of Ireland, a position he himself claimed. We can perhaps see an example of Ruaidrí's ambitions in this regard in the election of his nephew Tommaltach Ua Conchobair as archbishop of Armagh. Kings throughout Christendom assumed the right to present churchmen of their choosing to important ecclesiastical office, but obviously only within their own territory. If the king of Connacht interfered in the election of an archbishop of Armagh, he was asserting a right outside his own province, just the sort of privilege of which Ruaidrí had been assured under the terms of the Treaty of Windsor. Ruaidrí was, however, in a difficult position in that, not only was he trying to forestall English aggression, but he faced opposition even within his own family. In 1177, for example, an army of the settlers left Dublin and invaded Connacht while Ruaidrí was off elsewhere. They caused a great deal of destruction and made off with considerable booty, but they managed to find their way around Connacht, from target to target, because one of Ruaidrí's own sons acted as their guide.[17] As punishment, Ruaidrí burned his eyes out, but the opposition he faced from other members of his large family was such that in 1183 he abdicated and retired to the Augustinian abbey of Cong.

At this point the Treaty of Windsor was definitely dead, because it was a personal arrangement between King Henry and Ruaidrí and was not intended to outlive either party. Ruaidrí's abdication may have changed matters also as far as the papacy was concerned because the pope did eventually agree to grant young John a crown and, according to the testimony of at least three English chroniclers, papal legates arrived in England at Christmas 1186 bearing the crown of Ireland.[18] But John was never crowned king of Ireland. He always remained 'lord of Ireland', and although the practice of referring to Ireland as a kingdom persisted intermittently throughout his reign, increasingly the preference was for 'the land of Ireland' or what historians call (though it was not in contemporary usage) 'the lordship of Ireland'.

It is difficult to know why Henry changed his mind about making John king, and it may have had as much to do with the politics of his Angevin 'empire' as with Irish affairs. If it was to do with Irish politics, there is one likely explanation. After the death of Strongbow in 1176, the most important of the resident barons in Ireland was the lord of Meath, Hugh de Lacy, who, in or around the year 1180, married Ruaidrí Ua Conchobair's daughter. There is no reason to think that he believed that he might thereby inherit Ruaidrí's kingdom of Connacht, let alone the kingship of Ireland, but that did

not stop gossip going around to that effect. English chroniclers were of the view that de Lacy aspired to be king; one
even goes so far as to say that he had procured a crown for
himself.[19] Gerald de Barri refers to 'the suspicion which
arose concerning him due to his excessive friendliness
towards the Irish', adding that 'there were more and more
rumours of Hugh's suspected disloyalty', and that 'he was
strongly suspected of wanting to throw off his allegiance and
usurp the government of the kingdom, and with it the crown
and sceptre'.[20] These rumours were presumably unfounded,
but after Hugh married Ruaidrí's daughter he was removed
from the position of justiciar (chief governor of Ireland)
and, although he was subsequently reappointed, the suspi-
cions remained. Thus, in August 1184, when the Lord John
was sixteen, he was knighted, and preparations were set in
train for him to lead his own expedition to Ireland to take
charge of the country in person. When John arrived in
Ireland in 1185, de Lacy was less than keen on the development. The Irish annals say that he persuaded the Irish rulers
not to swear fealty to John or to give him hostages. They add,
'for it was Hugh de Lacy who was king of Ireland when the
son of the king of the Saxons arrived'.[21] That, of course, was
a ludicrous exaggeration, but it illustrates the extent of Hugh
de Lacy's power in Ireland, and it illustrates too the vast
power that individual English barons, free of royal interference, could accumulate in Ireland, and the threat that they
could pose to royal power there.

It was partly to counter this growing power, and to stamp his
own seal on the development of the lordship, that the Lord
John came to Ireland in 1185.[22] The Irish annals say that he
'came to assume the sovereignty of Ireland'. He brought quite
a large army with him and, more importantly, some of Henry
II's most experienced administrators and officials. The real
work, and the most successful work of the expedition, was
done by these men. We have very few administrative and legal
records dating from the early days after the English invasion of
Ireland – it is the turn of the century before these begin to
appear in more abundance – but when records start to survive,

covering the period after John's accession to the throne of England in 1199, they show clearly that the machinery of both local and central government had been well established in the lordship, and the normal civil law procedures that functioned in England had been transferred to Ireland and functioned there too, and some of these were probably set up during John's 1185 expedition. The apparatus of government was by no means as cumbersome and all-embracing in the late twelfth century as it is now, but, in its own way, it was comprehensive, efficient, and far-reaching. The English lordship of Ireland needed a legal system, a government, a county-by-county system for the government of localities, and a fiscal system to provide the revenues to make these work. These, from what we can tell, were partly the product of John's 1185 sojourn in his lordship of Ireland, and, to that extent, we must rate it a success.

From the earliest days of the lordship the English king was represented in Ireland by a deputy usually known as the justiciar (though by the late fourteenth century he generally bore the title of lieutenant). The justiciar, as his name implies, was the lordship's supreme judge, head of the civil administration, and chief military commander.[23] He had power to make war on the king's enemies by proclaiming royal service, in other words, summoning the tenants-in-chief of the crown to a campaign, and had an armed retinue of his own at his disposal. The office of justiciar was an itinerant one, that is to say that he asserted his authority by travelling around the lordship, administering justice as he went. The chief governor was advised on matters of policy and on day-to-day government business by a council made up of senior ministers and some of the great resident magnates of the lordship (indeed, it was part of the feudal duty of a tenant-in-chief to provide such counsel). The council was at first an informal affair only gradually gaining a fixed structure as the thirteenth century wore on, at which point too the practice emerged of holding parliaments, which began in effect as specially enlarged meetings of the council, though by the end of the century they were judicial and legislative assemblies at which not only individuals but communities were represented (who were needed if consent was to be obtained for the imposition of new taxes).[24]

Such taxes and other revenues – for example, fines and other profits of justice, and monies received from the administration of the king's demesne lands in Ireland (including royal manors and certain towns) – were accounted for at the exchequer in Dublin, perhaps the oldest of the various departments of state in the lordship. The chief clerk of the exchequer was the treasurer, who in the early years of the lordship was second only in importance to the justiciar, and under whom were the chamberlains, the chancellor, the barons of the exchequer, who did the actual auditing of accounts, and the remembrancers, who kept a record of receipts and expenditure in various rolls, among them, as their name indicates, the memoranda rolls.[25] Over the course of time the treasurer was gradually superseded in status by the chancellor whose office, the chancery, was the letter-writing office of government and the place where copies of official correspondence were maintained in various rolls including the patent and close rolls. The chancellor had custody of the great seal by which the government authenticated its documentation, and therefore, unlike the treasurer, he itinerated with the justiciar, and in a very practical sense the business of government could not be conducted without him.[26]

Neither could the business of government operate without an effective system of local government which would extend the authority of the central administration into the localities. This was done by the adoption in Ireland of the system of local government that already pertained in England, based on the shire and the office of sheriff, who was the principal local agent of the crown.[27] In England shires were divided into hundreds, while the shire's Irish equivalent, the county, was divided into cantreds (later, and to this day, called baronies). The development of a scheme of counties in Ireland was protracted, and never extended to the entire island in the Middle Ages, for several reasons, but principally because large areas of the island remained in Irish hands and because much of the country, like, for instance, Ulster, Wexford,

Kilkenny, and that portion of Meath centred on Trim, was exempt from day-to-day governmental interference, being held by their lords as what were called liberties. The great liberties, the numbers of which fluctuated but which at any one time must have made up about half of the area of the medieval lordship, were not entirely exempt from government control; the king's writ did run there, but the latter delegated some of his rights to their lords, and on a routine basis they operated free of much interference from central government, almost like miniature versions of it, with seneschals exercising the functions that sheriffs exercised in the royal counties.

The first of the counties for which we have evidence is Dublin, and we hear in the early thirteenth century of a sheriff administering Cork and Waterford jointly, then Munster, later divided into Limerick and Tipperary, then Louth (usually called Uriel), then Kerry, Connacht, Roscommon, Kildare, Carlow, and that portion of Meath centred on Kells (though Carlow, Kilkenny and Tipperary subsequently became liberties). Each was administered by a sheriff, who was responsible for collecting the bulk of the ordinary revenues due to the crown from the localities, and who had to account for them at the exchequer, allowance being made for his legitimate expenses. The sheriff also had important judicial powers. He held a biannual 'tourn' at which he dealt as judge with lesser offences, and presided over the county court, though as chief administrator rather than judge. When the justiciar held his court there, the sheriff of the county had the task of ensuring that all persons charged to appear before it did so; he had custody of prisoners, he had the task of recovering debts, and he executed writs. And, because of the unsettled conditions that affected so much of the colony throughout the Middle Ages, the Irish sheriff also had considerable military functions, more so than his counterpart in England.

Just as these organs of local and central government were extended from England to Ireland from the late 1160s onwards, so too the system of law that functioned in England

97

was applied to Ireland: the common law of England became the law of the lordship of Ireland.[28] English statutes applied in the courts of Ireland (though, increasingly, in the thirteenth century, legislation peculiar to Ireland was promulgated in Irish parliaments and councils). The most senior court was that of the justiciar, from whose judgments appeal could be made to the king in England. Later, another central court of justice emerged which, unlike the justiciar's bench, was not itinerant but sat in Dublin, being known as the common bench or court of common pleas (and which dealt with civil cases). In addition, there were itinerant justices who went 'on eyre' through the lordship.

Over the course of time, however, differences emerged between England and the lordship of Ireland in terms of the administration of justice and the application of law. These were differences of scale – justice was more intimate in Ireland because the Irish judicial infrastructure was smaller, and the king's deputy could exert more personal control – but they were also different in terms of the law of the land itself. In some respects Irish law was old-fashioned, fossilized as it was at the time of its introduction to Ireland. In the process what came to be called 'the customs of the land of Ireland' emerged, local variations on English customary law, some of which (and the tenacity with which they were adhered to by the colonists in Ireland) later became the subject of dispute between the king of England and his liegemen of Ireland. Nevertheless, in the late twelfth and thirteenth centuries Ireland gained a system of government which radically altered the future course of its history. This period saw the genesis of a parliamentary tradition in Ireland which lasted uninterrupted until the Act of Union in 1800; it saw the establishment of a system of local government based on the county which has likewise endured; and it gained a common law inheritance which has lain at the basis of the Irish legal system to this day.

To the extent that the origins of this superstructure can be traced back to the lordship of John, credit must be given to him. In terms of colonial expansion too, there were successes which flowed from his 1185 expedition. In the march between

Leinster, the heartland of the lordship, and the Irish kingdom of Desmond, lay what is nowadays co. Waterford; and one of John's first actions was to build castles in the area to protect this vital march. North of Waterford lay what is now co. Tipperary and, again, to provide security here for the borders of Leinster, and to reduce Leinster's vulnerability to attack from Munster, he granted vast estates in the area to his trusted vassals, among them William de Burgh, ancestor of the famous Burke family, and Theobald Walter, ancestor of the Butlers. Whether John's actions were part of an overall 'plan' is a matter of opinion,[29] but, intentionally or otherwise, what he was doing here was providing a buffer-zone between the English settlers in Leinster and the native kings of Munster. It may have been hard on the native rulers of the area, who lost their lands and were reduced to the status of tenants or were driven out to the badlands in the mountains and bogs, but from John's point of view as would-be master of Ireland, and from the point of view of the settlers, it made sound political and economic sense, and it is proof that the claim that John's first expedition was an unmitigated disaster is quite an over-statement.

What John did on the march of south Leinster he did also at the northern end of the province. He granted much of what is now co. Louth to two of his chief officials and advisers, Bertram de Verdon and Gilbert Pipard. With Louth (or Uriel) in their hands, with Meath in de Lacy's hands, and with Tipperary and Waterford in the hands of other new arrivals, it only remained to link the two by establishing a royal presence in the centre, and, therefore, a little later we find a royal base being estab-lished at Athlone where the Shannon divided Connacht from the lordship. In other words, from Louth, through Meath, Athlone, Tipperary and Waterford, a defensive arc was created to protect Leinster and above all Dublin, the heart of the lord-ship, from Irish assault. Again, whether this was all part of a preconceived plan is another matter, but, on paper at least, it was an intelligent arrangement for protecting what gains the English had already made in Ireland and for providing the bridgehead for a gradual forward expansion, which was clearly intended, ultimately, to encompass the whole island. Gone were the days of half-hearted conquest, gone were any thoughts (such as had been behind the Treaty of Windsor) of freezing the colony and arriving at a *modus vivendi* with the native rulers. Henceforth, there seems little reason to doubt that it would be royal policy gradually to erode the position of the native kings, and to expand the boundaries of the lordship correspondingly.

In spite of this, as already noted, John's first expedition has sometimes been dubbed a disaster. This is partly the effect of hindsight. The infamous King John, as he was later to become, was never popular, and commentators then as now have been only too willing to see failure in his every move. Gerald de Barri was in Ireland with John, and was not an admirer, but his stance was to some extent dictated by family bias. John, we have seen, established a new generation of adventurers in Ireland and brought with him to Ireland a team of top-class officials who instituted legal and administrative changes. Some of the pioneers who had been in Ireland from the earliest days of the conquest (including Gerald's relatives) resented John's attempt to impose these newcomers and this new restrictive authority on them. Thus, Gerald sarcastically remarks of John's time in Ireland that the colonists 'were so beset by litigation that they were harassed less by the enemy without the gates than by the legal business within'.[30]

As to the new arrivals, it is clear that those who had been in Ireland for fifteen years or so at that stage, and had paved the way, resented their easy acquisition of estates, and wondered why they were not being rewarded for their pioneering work. What we are seeing here is the start of what was to become a classic feature of the Anglo-Irish colony in generations to come: a resentment felt by those already settled in the lordship against newcomers from abroad. This development was somewhat ironic, in that at no stage during the Middle Ages did the Anglo-Irish colonists come to regard themselves as Irish; they were constantly at pains to point out that, no matter how long they had been settled in Ireland, they were English, they were 'the English of the land of Ireland', and yet when new men arrived from England, or English officials were sent over to take charge of the Dublin administration, they would have none of it. In the course of time, therefore, differences emerged between the English born in Ireland and the English born in England, and we can see from the reaction of the established frontiersmen in the lordship to those who came over in John's wake that this was a feature of life in Ireland from the lordship's earliest days. It is best summed up in a now famous speech which is said by Gerald to have been uttered by his uncle Maurice fitz Gerald soon after his arrival in Ireland:

> 'What are we waiting for? Surely we are not looking to our own people for help? Because we are now constrained in our actions by this circumstance, that just as we are English as far as the Irish are concerned, likewise to the English we are Irish, and the inhabitants of this island and of the other assail us with an equal degree of hatred.'[31]

This is the siege mentality which accounts for some of the opposition which John encountered while in Ireland.

However, John also alienated the native Irish. Several of the Irish province-kings had willingly submitted to Henry II when he came to Ireland in 1171. They did so for a variety of reasons, but partly at least because they believed that he would act as their protector against the aggression of the English barons. In the interval between 1171 and 1185 the Irish had become all the more aware of the need to find themselves a protector, because the expansion of the colony was proceeding apace and their status was being rapidly undermined. Following the abdication of Ruaidrí Ua Conchobair there was no recognized high-king of Ireland. For many of them, perhaps, John appeared their last chance. When John landed at Waterford, this, according to Gerald (an eye-witness), is what happened:

> As soon as the king's son arrived in Ireland, there came to meet him at Waterford the Irish of those parts, men of some note, who had hitherto been loyal to the English and peacefully disposed. They greeted him as their lord and received him with

101

the kiss of peace. But [John and his entourage] treated them with contempt and derision, and showing them scant respect, pulled some of them about by their beards, which were large and flowing according to the native custom. For their part, as soon as they had regained their freedom, they removed themselves and all their belongings to a safe distance, and made for the court of the king of Limerick [Ua Briain]. They gave him, and also the prince of Cork [Mac Carthaig], and Ruaidrí of Connacht a full account of all their experiences at the king's son's court ... They held out no hope of mature counsels or stable government in that quarter, and no hope of any security for the Irish ... They deduced that these small injustices would be followed by greater ones, and debated among themselves how the English must intend to act against the overweening and rebellious, when men of goodwill, who had kept the peace, received this treatment. So with one accord they plotted to resist, and to guard the privileges of their ancient freedom even at the risk of their own lives. In order that they might be more effective in fulfilling this aim, they made pacts with each other throughout the country, and those who had previously been enemies became friends for the first time.[32]

It is perhaps the case that too much weight should not be attached to this account since we know that Gerald was not enamoured of John, and would have happily tried to discredit him, but for what it is worth it does at least reflect Gerald's view that the policy adopted by John pushed into rebellion even those who had earlier been willing to compromise. This is confirmed by another chronicler who says that John 'lost most of his army in numerous conflicts with the Irish',[33] and was forced to return to England when the money ran out. By comparison, therefore, with his father, who had brought a vast army to Ireland but did not have to face any opposition, John was in trouble. The Irish did resist him and he had difficulty enforcing his authority. Not only did he face Irish opposition but, as previously noted, opposition from within the lordship itself, led by Hugh de Lacy, the lord of Meath. Hugh's influence and reputation were such that John's advisers probably cautioned the lord of Ireland against openly standing up to him. But by not doing so, and by scurrying off home after only eight months in residence in his new lordship, John did his reputation grave damage. If his first duty as lord of Ireland was to impose his will there, he had failed; and the rest of his life was spent trying to recover the ground lost in 1185.

The circumstances in which John made his second expedition to Ireland, in the summer of 1210, were quite different, if not altogether so, from his first. Just as his earlier campaign has been spoken of as a complete disaster, so this second campaign tends to be regarded as an unqualified success and, as one might expect, neither is the case. The 1210 campaign was of very great importance for the new English lordship in Ireland.[34] During his brief stay (he was only in Ireland for about nine weeks in that summer) John took steps to reorganize the government, sought to reach a working relationship with the Irish kings, and finally overthrew several of his more rebellious barons, including Hugh de Lacy's son, also called Hugh. Unfortunately, we do not know a great deal about the detail of John's actions while in Ireland. If we piece together the English chroniclers' accounts, we can gather that he again landed at Waterford, came to Dublin where he instituted something in the way of a government reshuffle, strengthened English laws, regulated the coinage and such matters, received the submissions of some (though not all) of the Irish, seized lands and castles from his baronial enemies – Carrickfergus in particular – expelled the de Lacy and de Briouze families, punishing the inhabitants of the Isle of Man for helping them, and returned victorious to England in late August.

The Irish annals concentrate on John's dealings with the native Irish kings, and an examination of the evidence reveals that John, who had set much store on establishing good relations with them (especially now that he had fallen out with so many of the Anglo-Irish), left Ireland on bad terms with two of the most powerful, the northern king Áed Ua Néill, and the Connacht king Cathal Crobderg Ua Conchobair, brother of the late Ruaidrí. Within a year of his expedition, John's government in Ireland had to undertake invasions of both Connacht and Ulster in an attempt to bring both kings to heel. What had happened was that John had initially shown favour to Ua Conchobair, who then joined his army on its march north to Carrickfergus. John, rather heavy-handedly, insisted on obtaining as a hostage Cathal's eldest son and intended heir. This the Connacht king was not prepared to accept. Likewise, when John asked for hostages from Ua Néill, the latter too refused to comply. Both kings were willing to hand over tribute to John – a few hundred head of cattle was a small price to pay for being left in peace – but neither was prepared to trust the capricious King John with the life of his intended heir. And this is why, in this respect, even the 1210 campaign was a failure. It did not produce a settlement. The negotiations collapsed and John left Ireland to the warfare that had consumed the country before his arrival. It was nearly two hundred years before another royal expedition took place.

As will appear from the above, King John enjoyed a chequered career as lord of Ireland, at least so far as matters of state are concerned. It is, however, worth recording that on the whole he had a better record in dealing with the Irish church. The changes proposed as a result of the second synod of Cashel (1171–2), though intended to apply to the whole country, were for the most part effective only in those parts of Ireland which were in the process of being, or soon to be, colonized. Elsewhere in the country change was less marked, the development of parishes was slower and social behaviour, sexual morals, marriage practices, and so on, remained in some respects unchanged in the unconquered parts of Ireland throughout the Middle Ages, so that Elizabethan commentators on Ireland complained about the prevalence of much the same sort of vices as had Gerald de Barri four centuries earlier.

In the conquered parts of Ireland things were very different, and change came rapidly. The last native Irishman to become archbishop of Dublin, St Lorcán Ua Tuathail, died in 1180, whereupon Henry II made use of divisions within the cathedral chapter to secure the election of his clerk, John Cumin. From this point onwards, Dublin's archbishops were either born in England or born in Ireland of English extraction. Frequently, because Dublin was the wealthiest Irish diocese, the archbishops were royal officials appointed in return for their service to the king as a bureaucrat, a diplomat or a judge, and by the late thirteenth century they were sometimes absentees who never set foot in the diocese, but lived off its revenues. Those revenues were, in theory, very substantial. The archbishop was by far the greatest landholder in co. Dublin. Of the county's 222 000 statute acres, it is estimated that the church in the Middle Ages held 104 000; and, of this, the archbishop held 53 200 (the rest were held by the two cathedrals, Christ Church and St Patrick's, and the religious houses, the most important of which were St Mary's Cistercian abbey, the Augustinian abbey of St Thomas, the Augustinian priory of All Hallows, and the hospital of St John the Baptist).[35] To exploit his lands to the full the archbishop organized them in the same way as a lay baron would, in the form of manors. The principal archiepiscopal manors of medieval Dublin were at Lusk, Portrane, Swords, Finglas, Rathcoole, Tallaght, Clondalkin, Shankill and St Sepulchre, the latter being the most important, because it was the chief manor of the archbishop, the manor-house or palace itself being located close to St Patrick's cathedral in Kevin's Street.

Another potential source of revenue for the archdiocese arose when Dublin succeeded in getting papal approval to subsume the diocese of Glendalough, so that the archdiocese stretched not just over co. Dublin but to co. Wicklow and parts of adjoining counties as well. The campaign to secure the absorption of Glendalough was a protracted one in which the church authorities had the full support of the civil power, who did so partly because Glendalough was closely tied into local north Leinster dynastic politics. The Irish lords of the Wicklow mountains opposed the move, no doubt resenting their church losing its status as a bishopric. This was not just a matter of sentiment or prestige. The English archbishops of Dublin were in almost every respect an instrument of English government in Ireland. Henry of London, for instance, who was archbishop of Dublin from 1213 to 1228, was also the justiciar from 1213 to 1215 and from 1221 to 1224. The distinction between his actions as lord archbishop and as chief governor was a fine one. It was during his episcopacy that papal approval was finally obtained to make the diocese of Glendalough part of the archdiocese of Dublin, but the inhabitants of the Wicklow mountains could be forgiven for seeing this as an attempt to bring their area within the ambit of government control. This, indeed, was to happen. The archbishop established a manor for himself at Castlekevin, in Annamoe, co. Wicklow, which, as well as being an archiepiscopal manor, was the base from which military campaigns to subdue the Irish of the Wicklow mountains were frequently launched and controlled.[36]

As a result of its annexation to the archdiocese the great monastic centre of Glendalough all but passed out of the pages of history. We have an account of what life at Glendalough was like in its dying days. The question of its amalgamation with Dublin was raised at the Fourth Lateran Council in 1215, where the archbishop of Tuam told Pope Innocent III that:

> '… Although that holy church in the mountains was from early times held in great reverence on account of St Kevin who lived there as a hermit, it is now so deserted and desolate, and has been for forty years, that from being a church it has become a den of thieves and a pit of robbers, and because it is a deserted and desolate wilderness there are more murders committed in that valley than in any other part of Ireland.'[37]

It must be said that this picture of decay does not match what we know of continued building activity and learning at Glendalough in this period, and there are grounds for doubting it.[38] The archbishop in question was Felix Ua Ruadháin, an Irishman, but he did not oppose the amalgamation of Dublin and Glendalough. He informed the pope, in fact, that when Henry II and John had taken steps to join the two dioceses they had done so in a perfectly legal manner. Ironically, this Irishman laid the blame for the dispute that arose over the merger of the two sees on, as he puts it, 'the arrogance of the Irish who then had power in the area', and who tried to resist the move. However, Archbishop Felix's testimony needs to be taken with a pinch of salt since he himself had been imposed on Tuam, from which he was subsequently expelled, and was being maintained at the expense of the king's exchequer.[39] Nevertheless, the fact that this Irish bishop should adopt this stance on the issue is an indication of the folly of seeing the history of the Irish church in this period as nothing but a reflection of a racial dispute between the Irish and the English: it was a good deal more complicated than that.

That said, a change in attitudes to the church did occur following the death of King John in 1216. His son, Henry III, was just a child, and there followed a long regency period during which control of the English government and therefore the direction of royal policy towards Ireland, was in the hands of royal ministers who had their own particular axes to grind. There is little evidence that either Henry II or John displayed anti-Irish prejudice when it came to the church. Of course, with a see as important as Dublin or Armagh, they would have liked to see someone in office who was favourable to their own position: no king anywhere in Christendom acted otherwise. It helped, therefore, if the important positions in the Irish church were filled by Englishmen, but they did not have to be. Both Henry and John worked quite happily with Irish bishops, and neither insisted on the absolute exclusion of Irishmen from the episcopate. But after John's death, the regent of England, the real power behind the throne during the minority of Henry III, was William Marshal, the lord of Leinster. The Marshal was keen on expanding the boundaries of the lordship of Ireland, and in 1216 found himself in dispute with the Irish bishop of Ferns (co. Wexford) who accused him of misappropriating lands which rightfully belonged to the diocese. As a result the bishop excommunicated him. He also, incidentally, is said to have placed a curse on the Marshal: when each of his five sons in turn succeeded to the lordship of Leinster, none leaving a son to succeed him, and Leinster was, as a result, eventually divided up between heiresses, it was widely believed that the curse of the bishop of Ferns had been responsible.[40]

In any case, in January 1217, the Marshal sent an order to the justiciar of Ireland in the king's name, stating the following:

'... Since the peace of our land of Ireland has been disturbed more frequently through the elections there of Irishmen, we command you, in virtue of the faith which holds you to us, that you should not in the future allow any Irishman in our land of Ireland to be elected or promoted in any cathedral. With the advice of our venerable father, Henry, lord archbishop of Dublin, and your own, you will by every means obtain that our clerks and other honourable Englishmen necessary to us and our kingdom be elected and promoted to bishoprics and dignities as they become vacant.'[41]

By this ruling, therefore, Irishmen would have been excluded from becoming bishops in Ireland: the wording is quite unambiguous. Obviously, the view was that they could not be trusted and that the expansion of the lordship would be facilitated if Englishmen occupied all the important positions in the Irish church.

That indicates how central the church was to the political sphere, and why governments interfered so much in its affairs. We can see the way this worked in practice if we examine the 1217 mandate in the context of one episcopal election dispute then raging. The mandate was addressed by William Marshal to the justiciar, Geoffrey de Marisco. Ten years earlier, the Marshal and de Marisco had attempted to build a castle in the cathedral city of Killaloe, a diocese which was an important frontier zone straddling the lower Shannon basin. In the same week in which the 1217 mandate was sent to Ireland a royal licence was given for the election as bishop of Killaloe of Robert Travers, the nephew of Geoffrey de Marisco. Therefore, the new policy which the government had introduced of excluding Irishmen from episcopal office was an instrument of colonial expansion, nothing more. As it happened, the cathedral chapter of Killaloe was composed mostly of Irishmen who instead elected to the position one of their own, who was then sent off to Rome to plead his case. In response, the pope stated that he had received bitter complaints from the Irish that the English were grievously oppressing them, and Henry of London, the archbishop of Dublin, was forbidden from showing favour to Robert Travers or any others of his own nation who were guilty of acts of aggression against the Irish. Then in 1220, the pope, Honorius III, dismissed Henry of London from his post as papal legate in Ireland, and appointed a new legate whom he sent to Ireland with this mandate:

> '... It has come to our ears that certain Englishmen, with unheard-of temerity, have ordered that no cleric from Ireland, no matter how educated or good-living, shall be promoted to any ecclesiastical office. Not wishing to turn deaf ears to an abuse of such audacity and evil, we order you by authority of this letter to make public denunciation of this order as void and to prohibit these English from maintaining it or attempting anything similar in future. Irish clergy should be freely admitted to ecclesiastical offices if their learning and conduct are fitting and their election canonical.'[42]

This papal pronouncement was not entirely successful. There were further instances of election disputes in which rival Irish and English candidates sought the same ecclesiastical office and the Irish government, by seeking to deny the royal licence for the Irishman's election, tried to secure the English churchman in the position. As time went on, though, and as the lordship expanded, the cathedral chapters in many dioceses, the body with responsibility for choosing the bishop, tended to have a majority of English extraction, and managed to secure the election of one from among their own ranks. In those areas which were not so heavily settled, and where an Irish majority pertained in the chapter-house, it was still necessary to obtain the king's licence for an election, and provided that the king did not feel that the particular Irishman in question represented a political risk, he was usually prepared to allow his consecration to proceed.

Some dioceses were split down the middle. The archdiocese of Armagh extends to this day from Tyrone to the Boyne. Although, therefore, most of it remained in Irish hands throughout the Middle Ages, it included co. Louth, one of the most heavily settled and anglicized parts of Ireland. This caused a major problem, because there was one diocese but, in effect, two nations, the English of Louth frequently being at enmity with the Irish of Armagh and Tyrone. The last native Irishman to occupy the primatial see was Nicholas Mac Maíl Ísu who died in 1306. Before and after him the archbishops tended to be English or Anglo-Irish and therefore the cathedral city of Armagh was in hostile territory. So, in practice, the diocese became split in two. There was an *ecclesia inter Anglicos*, a church among the English, and an *ecclesia inter Hibernicos*, a church among the Irish. Anglo-Irish archbishops lived in the *ecclesia inter Anglicos* on one of the archiepiscopal manors in co. Louth, usually Termonfeckin, while that part of the diocese that remained *inter Hibernicos* was governed by an archdeacon of Irish extraction living at Armagh. Nothing typified more the disunion and divided loyalties that afflicted the inhabitants of Ireland in the later Middle Ages.

5

COLONIAL DOMINATION AND NATIVE SURVIVAL

Henry III succeeded his father, King John, as king of England and lord of Ireland in 1216, while still a young boy. In certain respects, throughout the thirteenth century, but especially during the period of over half a century in which Henry III was to reign, the English lordship of Ireland continued to expand and to prosper. The process of territorial conquest and colonization showed few signs of faltering. Land was being taken from the Irish; it was being planted with peasant settlers from England, from Wales and even from southern Scotland; it was being divided up into manors; and the methods of agricultural cultivation practised in England were being widely introduced. In each manor, typically, part of the land was held by the lord in demesne, and part divided into open fields held by the tenants. These great fields in turn would have been subdivided into strips in such a way that each tenant would have a holding scattered among them, having a share of both good and bad land. While part of the land fed stock, sheep in particular, much was under cultivation, with a three-course rotation of crops, part going towards the cultivation of winter corn (principally oats, wheat, barley and rye), part spring corn, and part lying fallow to give the land time to recover its fertility.[1] As a result, the appearance of the very countryside was different, filled as it was with such new manors and farms, and with new towns, castles, mills, churches and religious houses, peopled now with a fairly high density of immigrant communities, speaking a different language from the native population, and paying their taxes to a different master. In the newly settled areas, in the first century or so after the initial invasion, the countryside must have teemed with life, and fairs and markets sprang up all over the place to bring together the supply of and demand for the agricultural surplus then being produced.[2]

For most of this first century of its history the Anglo-Irish colony was doing well, and it was continuing to expand. In fact, although these things are hard to calculate, it was not until about the year 1300 that the area under English control began to contract. There was, however, a difference between the expansion taking place in the lordship in the thirteenth century and that which took place in the early days of the invasion; and it may well have been this difference that ultimately undermined it. In the period from 1169 to, let us say, roughly 1220, those men from the island of Britain who conquered land for themselves on the island of Ireland brought with them literally hundreds of soldiers, servants, farmers, craftsmen, labourers and priests – everything that was needed to establish a little England beyond the sea – and it proved very successful, so that the east coast of Ireland from Carrickfergus to Cork was heavily anglicized, thickly settled, and substantially changed, and with few exceptions, permanently so. This place became the focal point of the lordship, and it remained that way throughout the later Middle Ages.

However, the expansion that took place in Ireland after 1220 or thereabouts was ordinarily undertaken by people who were not new to Ireland. It was by men who were sons and grandsons of those first pioneers. The latter were usually substantial landholders in England or Wales, and they did not have too much difficulty enticing their tenants to take the gamble on settling in Ireland. But when their sons and grandsons started to push west in the second phase of the conquest – from Cork into Kerry, from Limerick into Clare, from Meath into Galway, Roscommon and up into Sligo, from Louth into

Armagh and from Antrim into Derry – they did not have access to the same numbers of English peasants. Perhaps there was not the same population surplus in England to provide a pool of new tenants, perhaps Ireland was no longer an attractive destination, perhaps some Anglo-Irish barons had severed their links with England to such an extent that they did not have tenants in England whom they could press-gang into coming into Ireland. Whatever the reason, the fact is that even though the Anglo-Irish colony continued to expand throughout the fifty-six years of Henry III's reign, the expansion was often only superficial. On the ground, more often than not, there was not the same programme of colonization and without that it was bound to fail. The landscape was not transformed to anything like the same extent that it had been earlier in places like Leinster and Meath. The Englishness that must have characterized the little settler communities of eastern Ireland throughout the rest of the Middle Ages did not take root in the north and west. The conquerors of this area gained a military dominance over the inhabitants, but they did not replace them with newcomers. And whereas the newcomers who had settled in the east were there to stay, were a lasting testimony to the success of the initial invasion, the military dominance obtained during this second phase of expansion soon faltered.

We find this pattern repeating itself throughout Ireland. For example, the kingdom of Ulaid (comprising modern cos Down and Antrim) was one of the first parts of Ireland outside Leinster and Meath to be conquered. It was ruled by a dynasty which in the twelfth century bore the surname Mac Duinn Sléibe, who were based at Downpatrick, but whose ancestors at the dawn of Irish history had dominated all of the north of Ireland from their capital at Emain Macha (Navan Fort, near Armagh); it is their hero, Cú Chulainn, whose epic exploits are recorded in the body of tales that includes *Táin Bó Cúailgne*. Yet, this dynasty was vanquished by John de Courcy in the space of a few short years after 1177. In effect, de Courcy took the place of the Meic Duinn Sléibe kings. He was by no means an average Anglo-Irish baron. His background seems to have been in Cumbria, an area which already had close links with the north-east of Ireland, and it is men from this area whom he brought across the North Channel to Ulster.[3] He ruled Ulster in a semi-independent fashion and contemporaries gave him the title *princeps*, 'prince'. In fact, he married a princess, Affreca, daughter of the king of the Isle of Man. Because he was different from most other English settlers, perhaps because he committed himself fully to his new principality and accommodated himself to the Irish scene (becoming a devotee of the Irish saints, especially Patrick), perhaps because he did so fully immerse himself in his Ulster heartland, de Courcy gained a certain status in Irish eyes. He ruled Ulster, first from Downpatrick and later from his fortresses at Dundrum and Carrickfergus, for more than a quarter-century, and he was not without Irish support in doing so. In fact, when de Courcy finally fell from power in 1204, it was not the Irish who toppled him. He was defeated, in open battle, by another Anglo-Irishman, Hugh de Lacy II. It would seem that in doing battle with de Courcy, defeating him, expelling him and seizing his estate, de Lacy was breaking the law, and that de Courcy was entitled to seek legal redress and protection from his lord, King John. But this he did not receive. King John allowed Hugh de Lacy to hold onto his new conquest – in fact, he even created an earldom for him, giving him the title 'earl of Ulster' – and then, in 1210, circumstances and political groupings having altered, changed his mind, came to Ireland, expelled de Lacy, and took Ulster into his own hands.

Perhaps the most interesting feature of the toppling of John de Courcy by Hugh de Lacy II is that in it we are witnessing a clash of generations. John de Courcy was a man of the first generation of conquistadores, who conquered Ulster only a few years after Hugh de Lacy I conquered Meath. Hugh II was then only a child, and he was his father's younger son; his older brother Walter succeeded to Meath after their father's death in 1186. When, in 1204, the younger Hugh invaded Ulster, it was a relatively new development in the history of the lordship. As a younger son, with little or no land of his own, but lots of energy and ambition, Hugh was in a difficult position. A generation earlier he could have carved out a niche for himself in Ireland by invading the territory of some faltering Irish petty kingdom. But, a generation on, there were not so many easy pickings. The weaker Irish kingdoms had already been overrun. Such kingdoms either no longer existed or had lost to the English the more economically attractive territories under their control, the Irish making do with the less fertile areas which the settlers were content to leave in their hands. There were still some Irish kingdoms which remained intact, in the west and north of the country, but these were inhospitable regions where the balance between profitable and unprofitable land was less favourable than in the south and east. When, therefore, a young man like Hugh de Lacy came of age, and cast his eye about for land, he found that the most vulnerable prey was not an Irish dynasty but an ageing English baron, John de Courcy. With this development we are witnessing something new. We begin to find jostling taking place between the descendants of the original conquerors. In the process, the Anglo-Irish barons became their own worst enemies, and ultimately the architects of their own downfall, because, in their anxiety to compete for paramountcy with each other, they gave a breathing-space to the Irish, and the Irish used it to stage a recovery.

This happened in Ulster. In his heyday, John de Courcy was a man with whom no Irish king could compete. Yet he was brought to his knees by the Anglo-Irish of Meath fighting under the banner of Hugh de Lacy; and de Lacy in turn was brought down by King John. Ultimately, the winners in this contest were not the Anglo-Irish, and neither were they the original Meic Duinn Sléibe kings of Ulster, who never recovered from de Courcy's onslaught. The winners were the Uí Néill (the O'Neills), cousins of the Meic Lochlainn family which had ruled in mid-Ulster in the eleventh and twelfth centuries, who were soon to become, and to remain for the rest of the Middle Ages, the most powerful kings in Ireland. The first of them to emerge from obscurity was Áed Méith Ua Néill, the man who is said to have replied to King John's request for hostages in 1210: 'Depart, O foreigners, you shall have no hostages from me.'[4] When Hugh de Lacy returned to Ulster after King John's death, to try to win back his earldom, Áed Méith joined him and together in 1223–4 they waged a war that was so successful that eventually the government decided to give Hugh back his earldom, which he ruled until his death in 1242. This picture of Ua Néill and de Lacy together defies the stereotype that has stubbornly lingered on, that of native versus newcomer, Gael versus Gall. It is proof that thirteenth-century Ireland was certainly not black and white, and, as in the case of Ua Néill, some Irish were able, if not to benefit from the English presence, at least to exploit the disturbance it caused to keep their own fortunes intact.

That is not to say that there were not dangers for Ua Néill and for the Irish of the north of Ireland generally once Hugh de Lacy was restored to a position of power. Hugh was closely allied to Maurice fitz Gerald, the baron of Offaly, ancestor of the great Geraldine earls of Kildare. From 1232 until 1245 Maurice was justiciar of Ireland, and during this period he unashamedly used the forces of the crown to forward the territorial interests of the English barons in Ireland. As well as pushing into Galway and Mayo, Maurice fitz Gerald was granted by Hugh de Lacy the greater part of the modern co. Sligo. Then Hugh gave him a speculative grant of Tír Conaill (roughly equivalent to modern co. Donegal). Later, Maurice also claimed to own all Fermanagh, and in 1252 he built a castle at Cáel Uisce, near Beleek on the river Erne. It was in order to make a reality of these speculative grants that Maurice used government resources. Now, the Uí Néill might for a time have turned a blind eye to this, because the native inhabitants of Donegal, Sligo and Fermanagh were, more often than not, their enemies, but the fact is that they were being caught in a pincer grip. If these areas were conquered and settled by the English, sooner or later the Uí Néill's own territory of Tír Eógain would fall prey to the same expansionism.

Sure enough, after Áed Ua Néill's death in 1230, Hugh de Lacy and Maurice fitz Gerald encouraged a succession dispute in Tír Eógain between the Uí Néill and the Meic Lochlainn family. In 1238 Maurice and Hugh invaded Tír Eógain, and installed their own chosen candidate as king. Unfortunately for them, the man they picked, Brian Ua Néill, was no puppet and he was later to wage a lengthy war against colonial expansion in the north. Because of this war that expansion slackened. The earldom of Ulster survived but the effort to move into the north-west proved unsuccessful. One of Brian Ua Néill's allies was the king of Tír Conaill, Máel Sechnaill Ua Domnaill, and it is worth noting that when the latter was killed in 1247 in battle with Maurice fitz Gerald, at his side fell an unidentified Mac Somurli of Argyll, quite possibly Domnall, eponymous ancestor of the Clan Donald of Scotland and Ulster, who was presumably employed by Ua Domnaill to help stiffen his defences against fitz Gerald's attempted annexation. This is one of the earliest instances of the deployment of Hebridean mercenaries in post-invasion Ireland, the men who later became known as galloglasses, and who contributed considerably, especially in the north and west of the country, to the native struggle against colonial domination in the late thirteenth and the fourteenth centuries. As well as his castle at Beleek, Maurice fitz Gerald had built what is today the town of Sligo, but, after his death in 1257, the castle at Beleek was destroyed and Sligo was razed to the ground by the then king of Tír Conaill, Gofraid Ua Domnaill. That marked the effective end of English expansion into the north-west.

Any expansion into the north-west would have been prohibited if the arrangements for the government of Ireland envisaged under the Treaty of Windsor had held. Under its terms Ruaidrí Ua Conchobair's special position of eminence above the other Irish kings was recognized, and, although it had proved inoperative, the English crown and the Dublin government continued to regard the Uí Chonchobair kings of Connacht as special, and from time to time showed themselves willing to make concessions to them that they would not make to other Irish kings.[5] However, it was not all carrot; the stick was also employed. One of the best examples of this policy took place in 1215. The reigning king of Connacht was

Ruaidrí's brother Cathal Crobderg. Cathal was an intelligent, moderate, pragmatic individual. He recognized the vulnerability of his position in Connacht without security of tenure in the eyes of the English crown, the sort of secure tenure which even the most belligerent and aggressive of the colonists could not ignore. In effect, he wanted the right to hand Connacht on to his chosen heir, his son Áed. This would ensure that his core lands would not continue to be eroded by the forward thrust of colonial expansion. But equally importantly (and this shows that Cathal Crobderg was an innovator, willing to work within the new system), if the crown guaranteed to his own son the succession to Connacht, this would prevent others – brothers, cousins, nephews, other members of the sprawling Uí Chonchobair dynasty – disputing the succession and staking their claim. Therefore, Cathal was seeking the advantages which English rules of succession gave over Irish convention, in the matter of securing the undisputed succession of an eldest son to an inheritance.

To secure that, he was willing to make compromises along the way, and to make gesture after gesture of good faith, with the single aim of obtaining from the English king a charter that would confirm him in his kingdom and, most importantly, give him the right to hand it on to his son Áed when he died. In September 1215 Cathal did indeed get his charter. He was granted Connacht, except Athlone, where King John had built a castle to guard the Shannon crossing; he was to hold it to himself and his heirs – and that is the important point – for an annual payment of 300 marks (a mark equals two thirds of a pound). The charter, however, had limited value. Cathal's son Áed was not specifically mentioned, leaving open the question of who Cathal's heir was and who was going to determine it. This ambiguity only invited trouble, in the form of a succession dispute. The other weakness in the charter was that it specifically stated that Cathal would hold Connacht 'during his good service', in other words, while he remained loyal. But who was to determine whether Cathal and his successors were being loyal or disloyal? Also, the fact that he had to pay a high rent for his kingdom meant that if he ever got into arrears he could be regarded as having forfeited his kingship. Ironically, therefore, having a charter for Connacht had as many draw-backs as advantages. It tied the Uí Chonchobair kings into the feudal system. They could not ignore the distant pronounce-ments of the Dublin government as other Irish kings could, who were not similarly enmeshed. They had to accept the limi-tations which their new situation imposed upon them, and that meant paying an exorbitant rent for a kingdom they regarded as theirs by hereditary right, and it meant being very careful lest any action on their part could be misconstrued as rebellion, whatever the provocation.

It seems clear that King John knew this when he gave Cathal Crobderg his charter for Connacht, because, on the very same day, he drew up another charter, also for Connacht, this time granting it instead to Richard de Burgh. The charter was not actually executed at this point; but the message was plain. Cathal Crobderg would hold Connacht only for as long as he continued, as far as the English government was concerned, to behave himself. If he did not, the charter to Richard de Burgh would be given legal force, and Cathal would forfeit his kingdom.

The dangers inherent in the position became apparent after Cathal's death in 1224. Arrears of rent had indeed built up, and there was no difficulty in interpreting some of Áed Ua Conchobair's actions as contravening the 'good service' rule under which he held his province. King Henry III wrote to the Irish justiciar in 1226 ordering him 'to cause Áed son of Cathal, late king of Connacht, to appear before the justiciar in the king's court [at Dublin] to surrender the land of Connacht, which he ought no longer to hold on account of his and his father's forfeiture [because], by the charter of King John granted to Cathal, he held that land only so long as he should faithfully serve the king'. Soon afterwards a new charter was issued to Richard de Burgh, granting Connacht to him, except for the five cantreds near Athlone which the English king kept for himself.[6] Áed Ua Conchobair responded by burning down the royal castle at Athlone, and the Annals of Loch Cé, a chronicle written in Connacht at that point, say that he did so, 'remembering the treachery and deception practised against him'. Richard de Burgh and the Dublin government then set about the conquest of Connacht with a vengeance, carving the province up into estates for de Burgh's allies and stirring up fratricidal strife between the sons of the late King Ruaidrí Ua Conchobair and the sons of Cathal Crobderg. Eventually, Cathal's son Feidlim proved successful in out-manoeuvring his cousins and becoming a claimant to the kingship of Connacht, but in reality the days of the great Uí Chonchobair kings of Connacht were over. To placate Feidlim, the five cantreds which the king had retained in his own hands (part of modern co. Roscommon) were leased out to him at an annual rent of £400, but Connacht as a whole belonged to Richard de Burgh.

Before he gained possession of Connacht, de Burgh had had powerful landed interests in Limerick and Tipperary. (He was also, it is important to note, the nephew of Hubert de Burgh, virtual ruler of England for much of the period from 1219 to 1232.) When Richard progressed into Connacht, the part of the province closest to his Munster base became the core of his new estate. Hence, southern Galway was heavily settled. His principal manor was at Loughrea, and he also built castles at Galway itself and at Meelick and Portumna. In classic fashion, other parts of the province were subinfeudated, handed out in smaller portions to friends, relatives and allies. From Leinster came the Geraldines, the de Berminghams, and the Stauntons. From Munster came more Geraldines, Cogans, Barrys, Prendergasts, and Barretts, the latter ending up in the far north-western corner of Mayo. And from Meath came the le Petits, the Cusacks, and the de Angelos (or Nangles), who in time became so hibernicized that their name changed to Mac Oisdealbaig ('son of Jocelin') and hence Costello.

However, just as the de Angelos became Costellos, many of these men gaining lands in Connacht in the mid-thirteenth century were born and reared in Ireland. They saw themselves as English, but for many of them their contacts with England were on the wane. Connacht did not become a little England beyond the Shannon. What it did become, if it had ever been otherwise, was a land of war. Warfare was not a tactic employed with any regularity by Feidlim Ua Conchobair, who spent most of his career trying to prove his good faith.[7] When asked by Henry III he even led a large Irish contingent to fight in the latter's campaign against the Welsh in 1245. He negotiated continually to have his rights of tenure recognized, and in 1240 actually went in person to petition the king on the subject, probably the first Irish king since Diarmait Mac Murchada to attend the court of the king of England. He was fully prepared to pay his rent for the fairly meagre holding he had been granted, yet in 1249 he was temporarily banished from his lands and when he returned it was to a diminished estate, because the king even began now to make grants to Englishmen in the barony of Roscommon.[8]

The lesson of the mistreatment of Feidlim was not lost on his son, Áed na nGall. When Feidlim died the annals called him 'a man full of honour and valour, of respect and importance, in Ireland and in England'.[9] When Áed died the annals described him as 'a king who inflicted great defeats on the foreigners, and pulled down their palaces and castles'.[10] Áed Ua Conchobair was one of the first of a new breed of kings and kings' sons who were aware that their fathers' policy of compromise was no longer an effective response, and who opted for the path of resistance. Needless to say, resistance was not something new to the mid-thirteenth century. As far back as 1195 the Munster chronicler had praised Cathal Crobderg Ua Conchobair for coming and demolishing the settlers' castles in Munster, and the annalist adds that 'everyone expected that he would destroy all the foreigners on that expedition, and he arranged to come back, but he did not come'.[11] It was said of Domnall Mac Carthaig, the king of Desmond who died in 1206, that 'during the twenty years in which he held the kingship he never submitted to a foreigner', while Áed Méith Ua Néill's obituarist says of him that 'he was the man among the Irish who most killed and pillaged the foreigners and destroyed their castles'.[12] Opposition to colonial aggrandizement is, therefore, something which we can see in action from the earliest stages of the conquest.

That is not to say that as the thirteenth century progressed it did not intensify. By the 1240s the situation had begun to worsen considerably. These revolts were led, not by kings, but by the sons of kings. Of 1247 an annalist says that 'the foreigners of Connacht had not experienced for many a long year the like of the war these sons of kings waged against them in this year, for they did not forbear to ravage a single tract or territory of the foreigners of Connacht'.[13] Troubles continued in Connacht in the following year, but by now the risings had spread further afield. The Munster chronicle reports for 1248 that 'many of the kings' sons of Ireland were treacherously and shamefully slain this year'.[14] This served only to foment further unrest. By the summer of 1249 the war had been brought into Desmond by Finín Mac Carthaig, while further east 'the justiciar of Ireland led a great host into Leinster to attack the kings' sons who were spoiling and ruining the foreigners, but the Leinster princes paid no heed to him on this occasion'.[15] When the settlers slew the Ossory prince Donnchad Ua Gilla Pátraic later that same year, an annalist reported that 'this was a benefit to the foreigners, for many a one of them had he killed and raided and burned before that day; for he was one of the three Irishmen who [most signally] rose against the foreigners since their taking of Ireland'.[16] Connacht too was in turmoil in this year with, for the first time, the lead being taken by King Feidlim's son, Áed. It was his leadership which made these uprisings a real cause of disquiet to the lordship's governors, especially when he made common cause with Brian Ua Néill of Tír Eógain.

In 1255, after several years of parallel but unaligned rebellion, a vital alliance was formed between the two when Áed undertook a mission to Tír Eógain 'and made peace between his own father and the north of Ireland'.[17] They cooperated for mutual benefit: Connacht's aim was to assert suzerainty over Bréifne, which they quickly achieved; as for Ua Néill, his aim was to annex the former kingdom of Ulaid which had now been subsumed into the earldom of Ulster, and he had the support of Áed Ua Conchobair in attempting to do so. Their alliance, and the general native recovery taking place at this time, was partly a response to a new wave of English expansion, licensed and promoted by Henry III, in which John fitz Geoffrey, justiciar from 1245 to 1256, played a key role.[18] In 1258 Áed and Brian met at Cáel Uisce on the Erne, where they were joined by the son of the king of Thomond, Tadc Ua Briain. There, Ua Conchobair and Ua Briain abandoned their own dynasties' ancestral claims and acknowledged Brian Ua Néill's right to 'the kingship of the Irish of Ireland', while even the Dublin government acknowledged that he (presumptuously, as they saw it) bore the title 'king of the kings of Ireland'. This was an extraordinary meeting which amounted to an attempt to revive the high-kingship after seventy-five years in abeyance, and it may well have been inspired by a similar, though more representative, gathering in Wales in that same year which led to the assumption of the title 'Prince of Wales' by Llywelyn ap Gruffudd of Gwynedd.[19]

In the following year Áed Ua Conchobair travelled to Derry and obtained as a bride the daughter of the Hebridean lord, Dubgall Mac Ruaidrí, bringing with her a dowry of 160 galloglasses: Ua Conchobair was strengthening his army in preparation for a major campaign. Later in 1259 he met again with Ua Néill at Devenish, an island on Lough Erne. We have no record of what they discussed but their plan appears to have had as a first move a strike at the capital of the earldom of Ulster, Downpatrick, and after the hoped-for successful accomplishment of this goal, with the destruction of colonial power in Ulster would come an assault on the Connacht colony, on Ua Conchobair's behalf. However, the plan backfired. Tadc Ua Briain died prematurely in 1259, causing an annalist to remark that this was 'good news for the foreigners'.[20] In the following year the attack on Downpatrick was a disaster, with Brian Ua Néill losing his life in the contest, and the fact that his head was sent off to Henry III in London is a measure of the significance that was attached to the victory. This, of course, spelled the end of the alliance, but it seems that it did not entirely dash Áed Ua Conchobair's hopes. In 1263 the king of Norway, Hákon IV, sailed south to defend his claim to

123

overlordship of the Western Isles in the face of opposition from the king of Scotland. Hákon was joined by Dubgall Mac Ruaidrí, whose son-in-law was, of course, Áed Ua Conchobair. According to King Hákon's saga, messengers came to him from Ireland to the effect that the Irish were willing to maintain the Norse king's army until Ireland was freed from the power of the English. Norse sources say that Hákon was dissuaded from taking up the offer, but when he died in 1264 the Irish annals, then being compiled in Connacht, report that he did so 'on his way to Ireland'.[21]

The events of these years show the lengths to which some Irish kings and kings' sons were prepared to go to in order to overcome the colonial domination to which they had been subjected. They were enabled to do so partly at least because of the misgovernment of the lordship at this time. In 1254 Henry III granted his eldest son, Edward, a vast estate that included Ireland, Gascony, the Channel Islands, the earldom of Chester, the city of Bristol, and various lands and castles in England and Wales. Henry retained for himself the title 'lord of Ireland', but Edward in effect held the land of Ireland as part of a condominium. Edward took over many of the rights of lordship in Ireland, but his father still retained, and occasionally continued to exercise, the powers that legally belonged to him as lord of Ireland. In a sense, Ireland had two lords. Sometimes Edward would appoint a chief governor, and sometimes Henry would. Sometimes decisions were made under Edward's seal, and sometimes they were made under the great seal of England. It was a messy affair, but it did set one crucial precedent. The charter by which Edward was granted Ireland stated that it was his, 'provided that the land of Ireland shall never be separated from the crown of England, and no one but Edward and his heirs, kings of England, shall ever claim or have any right in that land'.[22] This was important. Whereas Henry II had once contemplated, as earlier discussed, the transference of Ireland to a cadet branch of the English royal house, Henry III deliberately granted Ireland to his eldest son, who would succeed him as king of England, so that henceforth England and Ireland would remain tied in such a way that the king of one was *ipso facto* lord of the other.

This had advantages and disadvantages. The advantage was that the future constitutional position of Ireland was secure; there could be no doubt about royal policy towards it or about its place in the Plantagenet scheme of things. The disadvantage was that Ireland's lord would inevitably be an absentee. As king of England, Ireland was only a small part of his estate, and (depending on the particular king and on conditions in England) far from the top of his list of priorities. This was the case from the start of Edward's takeover of power. From what we can tell Edward showed little sustained interest in Ireland. In the period from 1254 until he became king in 1272, Ireland had eleven different chief governors. This compares with the period from 1232 (when his father came of age) to 1254 when Ireland had only two governors.[23] These changes of personnel brought instability, and Ireland was unstable enough without that.

It would be wrong, of course, to exaggerate the ill-effects of Edward's rule, and it should be said that the changes of governor and frailty of government in this period were partly the product of the protracted crisis in England from 1258 to 1267, usually known as the barons' war.[24] Nevertheless, undoubtedly the loosening of the reins of power under the lordship of Edward only served to heighten Irish restiveness. Furthermore, increasingly from this point onwards we find dangerous and destabilizing disputes starting among the Anglo-Irish, one faction of the baronage lining up against another. In 1264 something not far short of civil war broke out in Ireland, a civil war which split the lordship in two, led on one side by the de Burghs and on the other by the Geraldines. The native Irish were secondary to this, although both sides did have Irish allies. What was happening was that families like the de Burghs and the various branches of the Geraldines, who had by now been in Ireland for generations, were splitting along factional lines, each trying to gain political ascendancy over the other, each seeking to be the real power behind the administration, each quarrelling over land.

The most important baron in Ireland at this point was Walter de Burgh, who was already lord of Connacht when the Lord Edward made him earl of Ulster in 1263. Ulster enjoyed the distinction of being the only earldom in Ireland and had been vacant since the death of Hugh de Lacy in 1242, but now, in theory at least, de Burgh controlled all Connacht and Ulster. The problem was that various members of the Geraldine family had landed interests in both Connacht and Ulster; Maurice fitz Gerald, for example, was, as we have seen earlier, trying to expand into north Connacht and Donegal. In 1264, Walter de Burgh seized the Geraldine castles and manors in Connacht, while the Geraldines responded by seizing the justiciar and some other nobles who were assembled for a council at Castledermot, co. Kildare. This was unprecedented. Widespread disturbances broke out as a result and, according to the annals, 'a great part of Ireland was ruined' between both sides. When a new justiciar was appointed, he began to prepare Dublin to withstand a siege, but the crisis ended – at least this phase of it – when the various factions were persuaded to come to Dublin in April 1265 to discuss the affair. Eventually it was agreed that all those who had been dispossessed or expelled from their lands as a result of the disturbances should recover them without question; the leading barons on each side swore an oath to abide by the agreement, and peace was restored.

This had been a private war, a war fought in pursuit of the private interest of the individuals concerned, and each had a private army. Each had his own retainers and each kept his own band of hired mercenaries, and, of course, as these private armies proliferated, so the threat of war increased. Needless to say, the government frequently passed laws designed to control the spread of such armed retinues, or to prohibit them altogether, but the fact was that for war against the Irish and for faction fights with rival Anglo-Irish alliances, a powerful baron could not stay powerful for long without them. However, with private armies ready to serve their masters whether the enemy was Irish or English, the Geraldine–de Burgh feud was set to continue and, though silent for a generation after 1265, it subsequently re-emerged. Walter de Burgh died in 1271 and was succeeded by his young son Richard, the famous Red Earl. Richard de Burgh was a man of considerable stature in both Ireland and England. The only man who could possibly compete with him in Ireland was the leader of the Geraldine faction, John fitz Thomas, who eventually was made earl of Kildare, and who started the great Kildare rise to power. These two men were inveterate enemies and in 1294 fitz Thomas caused turmoil in Ireland by capturing the earl of Ulster and imprisoning him in his castle of Lea, co. Kildare. War broke out and the country fell into a state of lawlessness. With de Burgh out of the way, there was nobody to stand in fitz Thomas's path as he unleashed his followers on the rampage, destroying their enemies' property, and burning and looting as they went about their master's business. These events demonstrated just how ruthless John fitz Thomas was and that there were few lengths to which he would not go in order to increase his own power and influence. He was building up his own power-base by destroying that of his rivals, and in doing that he was prepared to encourage revolts by the Irish, provided, of course, that they agreed to leave his estates intact and only overran the lands of his enemies.

He retained the earl of Ulster in prison for three months. It took a special sitting of parliament in Kilkenny in March 1295 to secure de Burgh's release. Even then the disturbances continued. It was only when the king threatened to seize the lands of any Anglo-Irishman inflicting damage on another that a truce was declared and peace restored. In 1298 the problem was eventually solved. One of the sources of the de Burgh–fitz Gerald quarrel lay in Connacht. De Burgh was lord of Connacht but the Geraldines, as already noted, had extensive holdings there which led to tensions between them. Under an agreement that was worked out by the justiciar in 1298, John fitz Thomas undertook to stop his efforts at expansion into Connacht. He agreed to swap all the lands he claimed in Connacht for lands in Leinster and Munster which Richard de Burgh held, but which he too now agreed to give up. It was a very simple solution. Under it, the Geraldines would be supreme in Leinster and Munster and the de Burgh ascendancy in Connacht would be secure. To seal the matter John's son was married to the earl's daughter, and the great feud was at an end.

This long-running feud was allowed to destabilize the colony partly because Edward I showed no great interest in solving it and in improving the government of the lordship. It would be an exaggeration to say that the only real interest Edward had in Ireland was in exploiting Irish resources, but there is an element of truth in it.[25] When he ran up debts he used the revenues collected on his behalf in Ireland to pay them off. When he led an army on expedition in Wales or Scotland or Gascony or Flanders, he expected Ireland to supply food for his troops. He did this from the very moment that he had become lord of Ireland: within a year he was ordering his officials in Ireland to supply large quantities of wheat to Gascony; they were to postpone paying for them all as long as possible, and all available revenue was to be sent to him. He was, of course, well within his rights in doing this, since as lord of Ireland the revenues of Ireland were his to dispose of as he wished, and perhaps the government would not have sought to raise so much if it was intended to use them for Irish purposes alone. So it was that a vicious circle began to take shape: revenues raised in Ireland, which could usefully have been spent there, were leaving the country; as a result, there was less money left in Ireland for running the government. The evidence would appear to indicate that from this point onwards crime, disorder and warfare increased (though this is perhaps partly a reflection of the more detailed documentation that survives for this period), and this may have been exacerbated by the fact that the government had less money to spend. Because of increased warfare and lawlessness, the profitability of the colony shrank: contemporary reports frequently refer to the destruction of crops, the fact that the cultivators of the crops were either dead or had fled, that fields went untilled, and revenues uncollected. Ultimately, therefore, less money came into the exchequer, so that there were fewer resources available for Edward to siphon off.

The fall-off in government revenues is quite stark. In the period from 14 May 1250 to 29 September 1251, the treasurer of the Dublin administration recorded receipts of £5052. We have no record of treasurers' accounts until 1271 and 1272, when the receipts were £2085 for the first year and £2593 for the second. Therefore, in the period since 1254 when Edward took charge of Ireland, the Dublin government's revenues had been halved.[26] The sheriffs were meant to account annually for the receipts in each county but often their accounts were outstanding for years on end. They blamed it on the disturbed state of the country, saying that they could not claim rents from property where the crops had been destroyed or the tenants had run off, and this may frequently have been the case. But it was often the case too that the sheriffs and other agents of the government, all the way up to the justiciar himself, were corrupt. In the 1280s an official audit of the Irish exchequer's accounts found that no one could gain an appointment without the justiciar receiving a consideration. It was also reported that the then justiciar, Stephen de Fulbourne, was using government receipts to buy vast quantities of foodstuffs and provisions at very cheap prices, and shipping them to Wales where Edward was on campaign, and willing to pay an exorbitant price for them, but that de Fulbourne was keeping the profit for himself. One has to be careful not to adopt too simplistic a view of such 'corruption' because de Fulbourne, for example, was an efficient manager of the treasury, and he succeeded in restoring the solvency of the Dublin government by returning the lordship to a position where the annual receipts at the exchequer in Dublin amounted to somewhere between £5000 and £6000, minuscule by English standards, but enough to keep the administration functioning reasonably effectively.[27]

It would have done so, that is, if King Edward had not found himself in the late 1270s and early 1280s embarked on a conquest of Wales which demanded enormous financial resources, while virtually all of the last decade of his life was spent attempting to repeat the exercise in Scotland, again at enormous cost. During the first Welsh war of 1277, Ireland played a very limited role; it did not contribute much towards the cost of the war, and neither was there any considerable military participation by Anglo-Irish armies. But part of the reason for the failure of the Irish lordship to contribute is that while Edward was in Wales in 1277, conducting a blitzkrieg against the prince of Wales, Llywelyn ap Gruffudd, his justiciar in Ireland was engaged in a remarkably similar exercise only eighty miles or so away against the king of Leinster, Muirchertach Mac Murchada. We can see the cross-purposes at which the English king and his Irish justiciar were working from letters that each sent to the other at this point: King Edward wrote to his justiciar in Ireland seeking supplies for his use in Wales; but not only were there no supplies to spare in Ireland, but the justiciar asked Edward to send him 2000 Welshmen who could be settled in Ireland and used by the chief governor when he was campaigning against the Irish.[28]

When war broke out in Wales again five years later, there was greater Irish participation. If we tot up all the monies sent from Ireland to Wales in the twelve months from November 1282 to November 1283, it comes to nearly £9000; this, it must be remembered, at a time when the normal revenues raised annually in Ireland rarely exceeded £6000. What is more, when the war was over Edward began building the magnificent series of castles that dominate the landscape of North Wales to this day. It is estimated that they cost the extraordinary sum of £80 000, nearly £30 000 of which came from Ireland. This was, of course, spread over a number of years, but even so it represented a huge drain on the resources of the lordship.[29]

The irony was that while all this money was leaving Ireland, and while Anglo-Irish barons were going off to serve in Edward's wars, and therefore leaving the Dublin government without money or manpower, the very fact that Edward was fighting a war in Wales, and that the Welsh were enjoying some successes, caused an outbreak of what appear to have been copy-cat revolts in Ireland. During the course of the 1282–3 war in Wales, the head of the Munster Geraldines, Thomas fitz Maurice, wrote to Edward I's chancellor, saying 'because of the war in Wales the Irish are more exalted than usual; some of them have been moved to war, others are getting ready to make war'.[30] It would be hard to find a clearer statement of the effects on the Irish of the stirring news from Wales. At the very least it shows that something like a siege mentality existed among the Anglo-Irish settlers who believed, rightly or wrongly, that a rebellion among the Welsh was likely to lead to a rebellion among the Irish. Again, it is part of a vicious circle. Edward was fighting a war against the Welsh, and bringing revenue from Ireland to finance it, but the Welsh war was encouraging the Irish to rebel, and there were not resources enough in Ireland to quell their uprisings.

Having conquered the Welsh, Edward found himself in the mid-1290s drifting into a war in Scotland. When that war broke out Ireland ended up making a greater contribution to it than to any of Edward's other adventures. In the years that followed, a constant stream of requests for money, supplies and soldiers reached Ireland from the king. Only small contingents of men from Ireland had served in the Welsh wars, but that changed when the war started in Scotland. The first campaign was in 1296, and over 3000 men left Ireland to take part, mostly infantry, but including over 300 mounted men-at-arms, at a total cost of nearly £7500.[31] To convince the Anglo-Irish to go to Scotland was no easy task. Edward desperately needed them, so they could strike a hard bargain, or simply refuse to go if it did not suit them. In the 1296 campaign, for instance, the earl of Ulster got the highest rate of pay ever given to an earl in these wars and, because he was at this stage closely aligned with the Bruce family, he only fought in Scotland in 1296 because the Bruces were on the English side; when the campaigns were against Bruce he simply asked for a price that Edward I was unwilling or unable to pay, and thereby avoided going.

One of the reasons Ireland was forced to contribute so much to the Scottish wars was because of its proximity. Edward would set up the headquarters of his commissariat near Carlisle or in Galloway once he entered Scotland on the west. The ports of north-east Ireland from Drogheda to Carrickfergus were ideal for directing supplies of food and men to the front. Royal purveyors were employed, whose job was to find the provisions necessary to feed the vast armies that accompanied the king; if they could not buy food and provisions, they seized it, promising to pay for it at a later date, though frequently payment never arrived. In the spring and autumn of 1298 the treasurer of Ireland paid out over £4000 to the royal purveyors, along with vast quantities of grain, meat and wine which were shipped to Carlisle. But in that same year the total receipts of the Irish exchequer amounted only to £5671. This indicates the drain on the government's resources that these campaigns imposed. If one adds to that the numbers of soldiers from Ireland who fought in Scotland, and the cost of their wages, one can readily appreciate why the government ended up in very straitened financial circumstances.[32]

There were other unfortunate consequences. To encourage men to leave Ireland to serve in his wars, Edward began by paying their wages. Then these men started to drive a harder bargain, and Edward could find himself promising to pardon all the debts they owed at the Irish exchequer: in 1303, the earl of Ulster owed over £11 000 and Edward wiped the slate clean to ensure his participation in a military campaign.[33] This was a common phenomenon not confined to Ireland, since the crown liked to build up the indebtedness of nobles in order to use pardons of debt as a form of patronage. But Edward now began to go one step further by starting to pardon men's crimes. Even murderers could get a pardon if they agreed to serve. He even ended up giving some people a pardon in advance!

All of this was ultimately quite damaging for the Anglo-Irish lordship. If we are not being altogether misled by the survival of colourful and sometimes gory court records from this period and by what one suspects are often overly pessimistic contemporary accounts, Ireland at the end of the thirteenth century was a country where lawlessness and disorder were rife and where the government was sometimes unable to cope. Contemporary accounts speak of the localities not being properly defended, of castles not being maintained, of the king's highways being overgrown, of bridges collapsed, and so on. Most important of all, the parlous state of the government's finances and the diversion overseas of so much of its energy and resources meant that the revival in the power of the Irish kings proceeded apace and the domination over them which the colonists had earlier wielded began to be lost.

6

A COLONY IN RETREAT

By the early fourteenth century the English colony in Ireland was experiencing the effects of neglect, and its government was not far from bankrupt as a result of the never-ending demands upon it by the absentee lord of Ireland. These conditions provided an ideal breeding-ground for an Irish resurgence. One particular manifestation of this, itself a product of the Edwardian wars, was the Bruce invasion, which began in May 1315 when a fleet-load of Scottish soldiers, who were veterans of the recent great victory over the English at Bannockburn, put ashore on the coast of what is now co. Antrim. They were led by Edward, the only surviving brother of Robert the Bruce; Robert had been king of Scots since 1306, and Edward had recently been ratified as heir presumptive to the Scottish throne. It was a major expedition, planned well in advance, and, although Scotland was then in the middle of a life-and-death struggle with England, for the next three and a half years a very significant proportion of Scotland's hard-pressed resources was devoted to it. Edward Bruce adopted the title 'king of Ireland', and was supported by several of the more important Irish kings, principally Domnall Ua Néill, king of Tír Eógain. He set up his own administration in Ireland, which was intended to replace that of the English colony based at Dublin, though in practice the Bruce government was never really effective outside its northern power-base. And for that three and a half years, Edward Bruce stayed in Ireland and tried to make his new kingdom a reality and to bring the English lordship of Ireland to an end, until, quite unexpectedly, he was killed in battle at Fochart, just north of Dundalk, in October 1318.[1]

The great question which has consumed the attention of historians is whether Robert I really envisaged turning his brother's invasion into a permanent conquest, or simply sought to exploit Irish dissidence as one of a number of levers designed to push the then king of England, Edward II, into acknowledging Robert's claim to be king of Scotland. Several explanations have been given by commentators through the ages: to cut off Irish supplies to the English; to create a diversion for Edward II by stirring the Irish into widespread revolt, or even better perhaps, encouraging the Welsh to do likewise; to satisfy the ambition of Edward Bruce; or to answer a plea by the Irish to help them end English rule. None of these suggestions lacks supporting evidence to sustain it. What we can say for certain is that Robert Bruce, right from the moment when he seized the Scottish throne, showed an interest in enlisting Irish support. More than likely, he spent the winter of 1306–7 on Rathlin island off the Antrim coast, and it seems that it was from there that he sent a letter to 'all the kings of Ireland, to the prelates and clergy, and to the inhabitants of all Ireland, our friends'.[2] In this now famous letter he says that 'we and you, our people and your people, have been free since ancient times, stem from one seed of birth, and are urged to come together in love, more eagerly and joyfully, by a common language and by common custom'. He adds that he is sending over 'our beloved kinsmen' to negotiate with the Irish 'about permanently strengthening and maintaining inviolate the special friendship between us and you, so that with God's will our nation (*nostra natio*) may be able to recover her ancient liberty'. Here he speaks of the Scots and Irish as a single nation. We know that he did get backing in Ireland at this point because an Irish king lost his life in the invasion of Galloway launched by Robert's brothers in the early weeks of 1307. Furthermore, he continued to have Irish support: in 1310 Edward II alluded to 'those adhering to Robert Bruce' in Ireland.[3] But it was the Bruce brothers who cultivated this support. A well-informed English chronicler refers to Edward Bruce, prior to his invasion of Ireland, as 'sending ahead letters to the inhabitants of that island, firmly proposing that he would be king in that land in the near future'. What is more, Archdeacon John Barbour, in his metrical biography of Robert Bruce, composed in the late fourteenth century, says that Edward 'send and had treting/ With the Erishry of Irland/ That in thar lawte tuk on hand/ Of Irland for to mak hym king'.[4]

Therefore, what we witness in the events of 1315–18 is a Scottish attempt to win support for their struggle with England by exploiting similar sentiment elsewhere. That sentiment lay in Ireland, and also in Wales. The contemporary biography of Edward II, the *Vita Edwardi Secundi,* says this of the Bruce invasion:

> Robert Bruce sent his brother Edward to Ireland with a picked force of knights, to stir up that people against the king of England, and subject the country if he could to his authority. And there was a rumour that if he achieved his wish there, he would at once cross to Wales, and raise the Welsh likewise against our king. For these two races are easily roused to rebellion; they bear hardly the yoke of slavery, and curse the lordship of the English.[5]

We have a copy of a letter almost certainly sent by Edward Bruce to Wales at this time, addressed to 'all those desiring to raise themselves up and liberate themselves from anguish when the time is right', in which he says that it is the duty of Christians everywhere to aid their fellow man, especially when, as he puts it, 'they stem from the same root of origin as regards kinship or country'.[6] How close this is to Robert's Irish letter which speaks of the Scots and the Irish as stemming from 'one seed of birth'. What we have here is an attempt by the Bruces to form an alliance with the Irish and the Welsh, against the English, based on contemporary perceptions of their common ancestral origin.

We know that the English expected a Scottish invasion of Wales to follow quickly on the heels of their invasion of Ireland, and efforts were made to protect the Welsh coast from attack. But apart from the odd raid on Anglesey, there was no large-scale invasion.[7] The reason for this is that the attempted conquest of Ireland got bogged down. The Bruces did have Irish support, and their arrival in Ireland did cause uprisings to break out all over the country, but they found it impossible to make that final push which would have been necessary in order to overturn the English lordship of Ireland. For instance, they never took Dublin, the centre of English government in the colony. When Edward Bruce was joined in Ireland by his brother Robert in the winter of 1316–17, they came as close as Castleknock, but the citizens set fire to the suburbs and pulled down churches to use the stone to strengthen the walls, so that the Bruce brothers, rather than risk a lengthy siege, passed Dublin by and headed south. Although it was another eighteen months before Edward Bruce was killed, one could say that the attempted conquest of Ireland ended on that day in February 1317 when the Scots refused the challenge of seizing Dublin.

But of course there were other reasons for Edward Bruce's failure. His occupation of Ireland coincided with one of the worst famines to afflict Europe in the later Middle Ages. For many, no doubt, political considerations came second to survival. It is also true that the Scots did not get sufficient support. Some of the Anglo-Irish colonists swapped sides during the invasion and joined the Scots, but most stayed loyal. And what Bruce needed was not just to defeat them – which he did in several battles and skirmishes – but to get them to join him, and to renounce their fealty to the lord of Ireland, Edward II. Without that, with just the support of what the government called the Irish rebels, the long-term prospects were poor.

However, even among the native Irish, support for Edward Bruce was not universal. His main Irish ally was, as already noted, Domnall Ua Néill of Tír Eógain. In 1317 the latter made his justly famous appeal to the pope, usually known as the 'Remonstrance of the Irish Princes', though the title *Lamentacio Hibernicorum* given to it in one manuscript version captures better the tone of the document.[8] In it Ua Néill says of the English that

> ... in order to shake off the harsh and insupportable yoke of servitude to them and to recover our native freedom which for the time being we have lost through them, we are compelled to enter a deadly war against the aforementioned, preferring under the compulsion of necessity to face the dangers of war like men in defence of our right rather than to go on bearing their cruel outrages like women. And in order to achieve our aim more swiftly and more fitly in this matter, we call to our help and assistance the illustrious Edward de Bruce earl of Carrick, brother of the Lord Robert by the grace of God the most illustrious king of Scots, and sprung from our noblest ancestors. And as each person is free to give up his right and transfer it to another, all the right which is recognised to pertain to us in the said kingdom as its true heirs we have given to him by our letters patent ... We have unanimously established him as our king and lord, and set him over us in the aforesaid kingdom.[9]

Elsewhere in this document Ua Néill describes himself as 'by hereditary right the true heir to the whole of Ireland'. But, of course, there was more than one king in Ireland, and others had reason to think that they too were the 'true heir' to the whole of Ireland. There were, therefore, plenty of people to challenge Ua Néill's right to hand that kingship over to Edward Bruce. Effectively, Bruce's support in native Ireland was limited to those who acknowledged Domnall Ua Néill's right to bestow the kingship of Ireland on the Scottish prince, and that meant that in practice Ua Néill's allies were Bruce's allies and Ua Néill's enemies were Bruce's enemies.

And perhaps that is why it did not last, why the attempted Scottish conquest collapsed with Edward Bruce's death. The invasion did, however, have long-term consequences. It wreaked a great deal of havoc and destruction throughout Ireland. The amount of revenue available for collection by the government was drastically reduced because of the damage done. What revenues did come in had to be spent, not just on repairing the damage, but on rewarding those who had stayed loyal. This fall-off in revenue was a serious matter. There were parts of Ireland from which the government collected taxes and rents before the invasion but from which it never again drew revenue in the medieval period. As a direct result of the Bruce invasion, therefore, the area of Ireland under the effective control of the Dublin government contracted. Parts of Ireland which were formerly in what the government called the 'land of peace' were now in the 'land of war', or were march-lands between the two, between the area where the king's writ continued to run, and the land of war where the Irish or rebel English ruled and the king's writ did not run.

Therefore, the Bruce invasion and the events surrounding it brought about a visible reduction in the size of the Anglo-Irish colony. It profoundly shifted the balance of power in Ireland. Prior to the invasion the most powerful man in the country had been Richard de Burgh, earl of Ulster and lord of Connacht, father-in-law of Robert Bruce (though by now they had had a parting of the ways). But in the battle of Connor in September 1315, the first serious engagement between the Scots invaders and the Anglo-Irish colonists, Richard de Burgh was ignominiously defeated and put to flight. The result was that, as an Irish annalist put it, de Burgh 'was a wanderer up and down Ireland all this year, with no power or lordship'.[10] He did, however, recover his position to some extent. Apart from the battle of Fochart at which Edward Bruce himself was killed, the most important battle in Ireland during the course of the invasion did not involve the Scots at all. It was fought at Athenry, co. Galway, on 10 August 1316 and was possibly the bloodiest battle in Ireland since the English invasion. Chroniclers say that over 10 000 Irish under their king, Feidlim Ua Conchobair, were slain, and that 1500 of their heads were cut off. The Irish who followed Feidlim into that battle were not from Connacht alone but came from as far afield as Munster, Offaly, Meath and Airgialla (modern co. Monaghan). Indeed, one could argue that Feidlim Ua Conchobair secured more widespread support in Ireland than the Bruces ever did: Irish sources call him 'chief king of Ireland by rightful inheritance' and 'the makings of a king of Ireland without opposition' and 'the man from whom the Irish had expected more than from any other Irishman then living'.[11]

But Feidlim was defeated in the battle of Athenry by the Anglo-Irish tenants of Richard de Burgh, which did a lot to restore the latter's fortunes. The Red Earl lived for another ten years, and was succeeded by his young grandson, William, known as the Brown Earl, who was reared in England. When the latter came to Ireland in 1328, at only sixteen years of age, he found it very difficult, not so much to keep control of the Irish (since, after the battle of Athenry, the Ua Conchobair kings were a spent force) but over his own Anglo-Irish tenants. These included his own kinsmen, de Burghs who had lived in Connacht for many decades and who, in some respects, acted and behaved no differently from the Irish of Connacht, and resented this external authority. In 1333, William was murdered by some of his own Anglo-Irish tenants in Ulster, in what appears to have been something of a private vendetta,[12] but the event indicates the extent to which law and order and respect for authority had broken down among the Anglo-Irish. They were part of the localities in which, for generations now, they had been settled, and they were not prepared to bow to impositions of outside authority, even if that came from their own lord, of whom they held their lands.

This event also ended the de Burgh earldom of Ulster and lordship of Connacht. Connacht to this day has its fair share of Burkes, but these are descended from cadet branches of the lords of Connacht, younger brothers, cousins and nephews of the earls. The main line died with the Brown Earl in 1333 because he left only an infant daughter. When she eventually married, it was to a son of Edward III, Lionel of Antwerp, duke of Clarence. Although he did lead an expedition to Ireland, given his status he was hardly likely to spend much time there, so that a further effect of the extinction of the de Burgh earldom was the handing over of power to an absentee, which caused a breakdown in authority and the emergence of other forces. This did not happen in such an obvious fashion in Connacht because of the dissipation in the Uí Chonchobair hegemony. But in Ulster, without the presence on the ground of someone of the stature of Richard de Burgh, there was nobody capable of repressing the ever-increasing power of the dynasty which came to dominate native Ireland in the later Middle Ages, the Uí Néill (O'Neills) of Ulster. They had provided the main opposition to the earls, and, after their extinction, sought to take their place, in effect to become earls of Ulster themselves (though for the time being they were insistent on bearing the title 'king'). In hindsight, therefore, we can view the Bruce invasion and its troubled aftermath as landmarks in the emergence of the Uí Néill line as the dominant force in native Irish politics.

The Bruce invasion was merely the most violent outbreak in a war which contemporaries believed had been ongoing for generations. The alarm-bells had begun to sound very clearly in the 1290s, and the Irish parliament that was held in 1297 had made plain, in the opening sentence of its recorded proceedings, that it was called 'in order to establish peace more firmly'.[13] Those assembled at the parliament were there to identify what it was that was causing the breakdown in law and order, and to offer remedies and their analysis of the problem, and the solutions they offered were repeated in similar terms in parliament after parliament for decades to come. It was this parliament which identified the physical shrinkage that was taking place in the size of the colony, which was happening because 'some great persons and others who have lands in the marches near the Irish, and other lands in the land of peace, remain and dwell in their manors in the land of peace, their lands in the marches being left waste and uncultivated and without a guard, and Irish felons, by means of such waste lands in their marches, pass freely through to perpetrate robberies, homicide and other mischiefs upon the English'. Therefore, it ordered that anyone who held land in the frontier zone on the fringes of the colony should properly guard their lands there and so prevent the further shrinkage of the colony. Those present at the parliament complained about local communities not being properly armed to resist Irish raids, about absentees living in England but draining the profits of their Irish estates, without leaving sufficient for the bailiffs to defend the land from attack, and it complained about the problem of degeneracy.

Gens is the Latin for a people, a nation; to become 'degenerate' is to lose a sense of belonging to that nation. For the colonists in Ireland, their survival depended – so the government thought – on them retaining a sense of their separateness from the indigenous inhabitants of Ireland. They were 'the English of the land of Ireland'; they were not the Irish who, by this period, were most definitely the enemy. For the English of the land of Ireland to survive, to prevent themselves from being overwhelmed by the Irish, it was vital to preserve this sense of differentness, to preserve their Englishness. The enemy, to be opposed, had to be recognized. The Irish enemy spoke the Irish language, dressed in the Irish fashion, and wore their hair and grew their beards in a manner that was different from the English. Therefore, all those who lived in Ireland but were of the English nation would, if necessary, have to be compelled to preserve their distinctiveness by avoiding these obvious traits of Irishness. And so the 1297 parliament banned those of English extraction from wearing Irish-type clothing or from sporting the *cúlán*, the peculiar hairstyle which was regarded as archetypically Irish. The view was, presumably, that if the Anglo-Irish were conforming to this extent, then they were doubtless becoming indistinguishable from the Irish in many less obvious facets of their lives. And that spelled great danger for the long-term survival of the lordship.

The problem of absenteeism was a similar cause of concern. The transfer into the hands of absentees of what had been the great de Burgh earldom of Ulster and lordship of Connacht did not cause the English presence on the ground to evaporate, but it certainly weakened it greatly; lesser men stepped into the earls' shoes, but they were not as answerable to central authority. Members of the Anglo-Irish gentry rose to power in Connacht and Ulster to fill the vacuum, but these men were, for all intents and purposes, free from outside interference, and less and less amenable to the dictates of government. From 1333 onwards Connacht and Ulster started to go their own way. Government control became weaker and weaker. The settler communities receded into themselves, fell back on their own resources, and developed their own methods for ensuring their survival. They could hardly be blamed if those methods involved adapting to their surroundings and conforming in many respects to the conventions of the society by which they were surrounded.

This weakening of authority was not confined to Connacht and Ulster. The fortunes of the colony had experienced a severe jolt in the mid-thirteenth century when several of the most important territorial blocs had to be subdivided between heiresses because they died out in the direct male line. The result of these partitions was that power became fractured. There were fewer grandees in the colony, people who had a large stake in it, and many English families came to inherit a relatively small landholding in Ireland, which was frequently too small to retain their interest, and too insignificant to bother defending or investing in. However, this process of subdivision was taken a step further in the fourteenth century. For instance, when the Marshal lordship of Leinster was divided into five shares in the mid-thirteenth century, the great Marcher family of de Clare, who were earls of Gloucester, received as their fifth share of Leinster the lordship of Kilkenny; but the last de Clare earl of Gloucester was killed at Bannockburn in 1314, and as a result Kilkenny in turn was divided in three between his sisters. Another fifth of Leinster had gone to the de Valence family who were earls of Pembroke. They received Wexford, which, like Kilkenny, was a substantial holding, and they did their best to defend it and to exploit it to the full; but the last de Valence earl of Pembroke died in 1324, so that Wexford was also divided in three. Carlow was part of another fifth share of Leinster that had gone to the Bigod family, earls of Norfolk; and then, in 1312, to Edward II's half-brother, Thomas of Brotherton, but in 1338 the latter died without male heirs and Carlow was split between two heiresses. This same sort of thing happened elsewhere. Meath was a great lordship founded by Hugh de Lacy, and when the direct de Lacy line died out it was split in two, one half going to the de Verdon family who already held a large stake in County Louth. However, in 1316 the head of the de Verdon family also died, leaving no sons, only daughters, between the four of whom his estate was eventually divided. In 1276 the Uí Briain kingdom of Thomond had been given by royal grant to Thomas de Clare, a younger brother of the influential earl of Gloucester, but the de Clares' efforts to colonize the province were brought to an end at the battle of Dysart O'Dea in 1318 when Thomas's son Richard was killed. Three years later his young heir died without issue and the lordship of Thomond was also divided among heiresses, thereby paving the way for a restoration of Uí Briain power which lasted in Thomond into the Early Modern period.

One can imagine the effects of this splintering of the great estates. The days when prominent English aristocratic families had a vast estate in Ireland were becoming part of the past. These heiresses had husbands for whom the defence of a small parcel of land in Ireland was not a worthwhile proposition. One by one, these small estates became vulnerable to the attacks of the Irish. In some cases the original Irish occupiers of these lands were still there, lurking in the badlands, awaiting an opportunity to recover their inheritance. The Meic Murchada family had been kings of Leinster before the province passed to Strongbow, then to the Marshals, then to the heiresses of the Marshals and their husbands, and then to their heiresses in turn. It is no coincidence that in 1328, for the first time since the English invasion, we hear of the inauguration of a Mac Murchada as king of Leinster. According to an Anglo-Irish chronicler based in Dublin, the Irish of Leinster gathered together and elected Domnall, son of Art Mac Murchada, as their king. He then ordered that his banner should be placed within two miles of Dublin (over which, of course, his ancestors had been king) and he then wanted to lead a conquest of all Ireland.[14] It was an important development, which shows the resurgence that was taking place in native Ireland, but it was a resurgence that was made possible because Leinster was now weak, divided and vulnerable, much of it in the hands of absentees who showed scant attention to their Irish acquisitions.

Since the great English aristocratic families had to a large extent severed their links with Ireland, and since much of the colony was now carved up between various other non-resident owners, it followed that others would emerge from within the colony as its natural leaders. During this period the face of Ireland as it was to remain for the rest of the Middle Ages began to take shape. Power came into the hands of a small number of Anglo-Irish barons who generally had little or no land in England but whose families had been in Ireland since the early days of the conquest. John fitz Thomas, the baron of Offaly, was made earl of Kildare in 1316; James Butler was made earl of Ormond in 1328; and Maurice fitz Thomas, the head of the Munster Geraldines, was made earl of Desmond in 1329. The significant thing about the grant of these earldoms is that they were made in tail male, which meant that they could not be inherited by heiresses; if an earl died without sons his estate was not divided between female relatives, but would pass to his closest surviving male relative. This meant that the splintering of the great conglomerations of lordships which had taken place in Ireland throughout the previous century was brought to a halt, and the Geraldine earls of Kildare and Desmond, and the Butler earls of Ormond, were assured a continuous possession of their estates (provided they resisted the urge to commit treason), so that for the next two centuries the history of the Anglo-Irish lordship is essentially their history. They were the men who dominated the colony and, to a large extent, the country, and the origins of their tremendous power lie in these years.

These men grew in importance partly because the government depended on them to keep the peace and maintain order, in effect, to govern in their localities. The revenues available to central government were shrinking all the time, from £5000 or £6000 during the reign of Edward I to about £2000 during the reign of his grandson, Edward III. One must be careful not to draw too sharp a contrast between the 'centralized' government of the thirteenth century and the 'decentralized' structure that emerged thereafter, but it was inevitably the case that the decline in revenue led to less effective government and to a reduction in the range of activities and functions performed by the government. If it is government's basic function to provide for the citizen's welfare in life and limb, then government in the Anglo-Irish colony in the fourteenth century was failing. In theory, the government was an itinerant one; its parliaments, councils, and some of its courts (though not, as we have seen, the Dublin bench or, for that matter, the important office of the exchequer) were intended to circulate around the country, the justiciar at its head dispensing justice and maintaining order as he went. In practice, apart from the occasional assembly in Drogheda or Trim or Naas or Kilkenny, the location of government was becoming more and more restricted to Dublin, the effective area of operations of that government was becoming limited to parts of Leinster, Meath, and Louth (though throughout the reign of Edward III the government still exercised considerable control over Munster),[15] and real authority in the localities was being delegated to the resident magnates.

The government itself occasionally organized large-scale military expeditions, especially against the Irish of the Leinster mountains and those in the foothills of the Wicklow–Dublin mountains who presented the greatest threat to Dublin and to the heart of the colony. But elsewhere, peacekeeping tended to be left to the local magnates and gentry. Relying on the magnates had advantages for the government since they had their finger on the local pulse and knew what was necessary to restore peace and to maintain order. Also, more importantly, the local barons usually ended up paying for their peace-keeping operations, and for a cash-starved administration this was a crucial consideration. But there were drawbacks. If the local lords were to be relied on to police their own areas, necessarily they were being allowed more independence of action than the government might previously or in other circumstances have been prepared to tolerate. The government, in allowing a local lord to proceed in his own way to handle relations with rebels – whether Irish or degenerate English – in his own area, had, in a sense, to trust him, knowing full well that this would lead to certain abuses of power, to which they were forced to turn a blind eye.

One of the most notorious examples of that was the first earl of Desmond, Maurice fitz Thomas. This man, while allegedly acting as an instrument of royal authority in the extreme south-west, in reality maintained a vast private army which he encouraged to ravage the countryside in pursuit of food and drink, and which he billeted on the local inhabitants wherever they went, precisely the same sort of onerous exaction (what later became known as 'coyne and livery') practised by native Irish kings. His cause was joined by several important Anglo-Irish figures and by some of the chief men among the Meic Carthaig and Uí Briain families. He led his armies to war against Anglo-Irish enemies and, allegedly, got himself involved in a plot to have himself crowned king of Ireland, and to share the country out among his friends. After a long career of murder and robbery and alleged treason the rebellious first earl of Desmond ended his career in 1356 as chief governor of Ireland.[16] Even if we allow for the undoubted fact that some of the earl's actions came in response to the provocative activities of royal officials, and that others reflect local tensions over the ownership of certain estates in the south-west,[17] nothing illustrates better than his career what a risk was involved in delegating power to the local magnates, and, at the same time, how utterly dependent on them the government was.

At one stage in his career an opponent of the earl of Desmond described him as a 'rymoure', a poet, perhaps a poet in Gaelic verse since one of his own sons, Gerald, known in Irish sources as Gearóid Iarla ('Gerald the Earl'), was one of the best-known Irish poets of the fourteenth century.[18] If the accusation is true (and it should be said that the only verses by him which still survive are in French),[19] it is an indication of the extent to which even people at the highest levels of the colonial community were adapting themselves to Irish society. If those on the highest rung of the social ladder were adopting features of the behaviour, speech and appearance of the native Irish who surrounded them, one can well imagine how much more so this was the case in regard to those lower down the scale, at least in those areas which were not heavily colonized. In such places, intermarriage with the Irish must have been quite common, and must have produced children with a diluted sense of Englishness, for whom it would be harder to regard the Irish as the enemy. Therefore, in 1346, messengers were sent by the Irish government to Edward III, asking that marriages between the two nations be prohibited, and he then issued an order that 'no marriages shall take place between English and Irish without the special licence of the king or justiciar'.[20] This kind of legislation culminated in the famous Statutes of Kilkenny passed in 1366, but it was largely worthless. It was attempting to turn back the tide; it was attempting to take a man who had been raised in an Irish milieu, whose mother might be Irish, who was surrounded by Irish-speaking people, and who may have spoken Irish himself since he left the cradle, and to make him English. And that is something that legislation on its own cannot do.

Besides, although the Anglo-Irish in many parts of Ireland were being assimilated into Irish life, and adapting themselves to their surroundings, they still were not Irish and did not see themselves as such. When, as seems to have been the case, the first earl of Desmond was accused of being an Irish rhymer he was gravely insulted.[21] His sense of identity as being one of 'the English of the land of Ireland' was offended by the accusation that he was a Gaelic poet and hence a fully-fledged Irishman. It is a subtle distinction. The Anglo-Irish were clearly not English but neither were they Irish. Some of the Anglo-Irish, in certain parts of the country and at certain levels of society, were more Irish than some other Anglo-Irishmen were. What we are witnessing is not a process of hibernicization *per se*; it is more a process of forced adaptation to circumstances. That adaptation was necessary for survival, and it did involve hibernicization (just as a degree of anglicization of the Irish population took place in those parts of the country that were heavily settled), but not to such an extent that all of these people lost their sense of Englishness. Some did, but right the way through the Middle Ages and into the Early Modern period the Old English, as they came to be called, survived, very like the Irish in many ways, but still conscious of their distinctiveness, still proud of their English origins, and very much aware of the debt they owed to their English inheritance.

In the face of the many difficulties the colony was experiencing in the mid-fourteenth century attempts were made to effect a recovery. An important set of ordinances for Ireland was enacted by the English government in 1331, unusual since the latter did not normally legislate directly for Ireland. These are a good measure of the perilous state of the colony's affairs. Under these ordinances, the same legal system was to apply to both Irish and English, perhaps a belated recognition of the fact that if the Irish were to be made amenable to the law, they should be introduced to the benefits of the law. Magnates were henceforth not to be allowed to billet their private armies on the countryside, the justiciar was to make an annual enquiry into the officials of the Dublin administration, and any of them who were corrupt or incompetent were to be punished and removed, and anyone who held land in Ireland would have to provide for its defence.[22] As usual, however, these reforms proved ineffective. What they do tell us is that under Edward III the English government was likely to take a more interventionist role in Irish affairs than that taken by any lord of Ireland since the reign of King John. Potentially this had great benefits for the colony, if it meant that more attention would be paid to its problems, that the Irish exchequer would not continue to be drawn upon to finance royal warfare elsewhere, and that real reform of the inefficient Dublin administration would be introduced. The negative side of this, though, soon became plain. Ironically, while the Anglo-Irish colonists wanted English help, and wanted the king to provide a remedy, there was only so much interference in their affairs which they were prepared to tolerate. But Edward III came to the conclusion that one of the main causes of the problems facing the lordship was the corruption and incompetence of Irish government officials. So, starting in the 1330s and continuing to the 1350s, he appointed a series of Englishmen as justiciars. These, of course, came over to Ireland with little or no understanding of the situation and few contacts in the colony, bringing with them an entourage of followers who got whatever favours it was within the justiciar's power to give. This naturally produced resentment among the Anglo-Irish, though it is ironic that they should boast so loudly of their loyalty to the crown, yet complain equally loudly when the king sent Englishmen of his own choosing to Ireland to institute the very reforms for which they had called.

It is in the 1340s that there emerges a serious rift between the English born in Ireland and the English born in England. The people of England had little sympathy or understanding for the Anglo-Irish, and the Anglo-Irish resented the English, a resentment which came to the surface in 1341 when King Edward sent over a justiciar charged with revoking all grants of Irish lands made since 1307 (which he would then have regranted to those in the king's favour), and with enforcing a law that only those who held land in England would be appointed to office in Ireland (a mechanism which would give the king greater leverage over them).[23] This caused such a storm of protest that the Dublin chronicler says that 'a great dispute arose in the land, and the land of Ireland was on the point of separation from the land of England'. The chronicler adds that 'before that time there never was such a notable and manifest division between the English born in England and the English born in Ireland'.[24] A parliament was called, which met at Kilkenny, and a list of petitions was drawn up in which the Anglo-Irish complained to the king about 'those who are sent from England to govern them, who have little knowledge of the land of Ireland, and who come here with little or nothing by which they can live and maintain their position, and so they use their offices to support themselves by extortion, to the great destruction of your people'.[25] Edward, who was then at war with France, did not risk further disruption, and abandoned his scheme of reform.

Edward's great preoccupation was what is now known as the Hundred Years War, the dominant theme of his long reign as king of England. It was only when the Treaty of Brétigny in 1360 brought hostilities with France to a temporary halt, coinciding with a break in the Scottish war, that Edward was free to deal with other less pressing problems, including Ireland. Here, intervention was sorely needed. The early years of the century had witnessed one of the most severe famines in living memory, when it was reported that men resorted to cannibalism to survive. This was followed by a series of bad harvests and, to cap it all, the outbreak of the Black Death in 1348–9, with periodic recurrences of plague thereafter. The effect of these natural disasters was to produce a prolonged agricultural depression and a massive shrinkage in population levels. This, combined with the raids of Irish and rebel English, meant that lands which had formerly been put to use were now abandoned, manors, villages and many of the smaller, more rural boroughs were deserted, and, instead of the inward migration of colonists, the colony began to experience a gradual haemorrhage of manpower.

A great council was held at Kilkenny in July 1360 at which a message for the king was drawn up outlining the main problems faced by those in charge of the government of Ireland, and asking for Edward's help.[26] According to those who drafted this document a considerable part of the country was held by absentees, who took profit from it but did not defend their lands, the result being that not only their lands but those of their neighbours were being overrun by the Irish. The country, they say, is impoverished because of the constant warfare, and because of the oppressive behaviour of the king's ministers. Debts owed to the crown mount up because of the general poverty of the country, and, as a result, the treasury is empty, the justiciar being too busy attending to the war in the country to hold pleas, which formerly yielded large sums in fines. The threat from the Irish was such that, so they believed, 'the Irish of Leinster and elsewhere had agreed among themselves that each Irish captain would begin the war in his own marches at a certain time, so that in this way each of them would be able to conquer the lands of the lieges [the loyal men] in his own locality'. They believed, in other words, that there was a concerted plan on behalf of some of the Irish to take advantage of the weakness of the government. Not only that but the degenerate Anglo-Irish were now joining the Irish in their war, and offering them great assistance because they could guide them into the 'land of peace' and help in its destruction.

Because of all of these problems, and more besides, they appealed to Edward for help. They told him that they had done their utmost to defend his rights and his landed interests in Ireland, and now needed him to send them military aid. They expected, in view of the desperate state of their own finances, that such a military expedition would be paid for entirely by the English exchequer. Furthermore, for the first time, they asked for an English chief governor. The most important absentee lord was none other than Edward's son, Lionel, who, as already noted, had married the daughter of William de Burgh and thus became in her right lord of Connacht and Ulster. It was not long afterwards that Edward decided that Lionel would be sent to Ireland as his lieutenant with a substantial army recruited from England.

This was the first time that a member of the English royal family had led a military expedition to Ireland in over one hundred and fifty years, and was therefore an important development. Edward later explained his motivation by saying that Ireland was a land that had been profitable in the past, and it was his hope that it would be so again in the future.[27] In other words, now that there was a lull in the fighting with France, but aware that the war might erupt again, the king wanted to use the intervening period of peace to turn the Irish government and economy around, so that it could once more be a source of revenue. Therefore, when war with France broke out again, Ireland would be able to make a useful contribution. In King Edward's view, spending a lot of money on Ireland in the short term would not be a waste; it would be an investment for the long term.

Though technically earl of Ulster, Lionel had never been to Ireland and probably had little knowledge of the country. He was twenty-two years of age when he was appointed lieutenant

but had little previous experience, either militarily or adminis-
tratively. Yet, it fell to him to reform the administration of
Ireland in order to make it once more a source of profit to the
English crown, and it fell to him also to begin the process of
reconquest. He did not bring an especially large army with him
to Ireland, though it did cost a vast amount of money. Between
May 1361 and February 1367 the total amount paid on his
expedition was £52 000, of which £43 000 (or 83 per cent) came
from the English exchequer. This was a massive investment by
Edward in Ireland. In spite of it, Lionel's expedition achieved
little of lasting effect. He was successful in securing submissions
from a number of Irish lords, but they were short-lived. While
there was a large government army in their neighbourhood the
Irish were at peace – that went without saying – but take that
army away and the peace evaporated. Therefore, Lionel cannot
be said to have been a military success, because he failed to
provide a long-term solution to the government's problem, and,
in fact, after his departure conditions may well have been worse
than they were before. Bearing in mind that such documents
have a propaganda element and are not to be taken too literally,
it is worth noting that in 1368 the Irish council stated that 'the
Irish and others, our enemies, ride in hostile array through
every part of the land, committing robberies, homicide, and
arsons, pillaging, spoiling and destroying monasteries, churches, castles, towns and fortresses, without showing reverence or
respect to God or the Holy Church or to any person, to the
great shame and loss of the king and of his loyal subjects, so
that the land is at the point of being lost, if remedy and help are
not immediately supplied'.[28] This, one must remember, was
within two years of Lionel's departure, and it was as if he had
never been there. It seems, then, the English government
misread the nature and extent of the Irish problem if they
thought that it could be cured by such an expedition.
Something a good deal more radical was needed.

Lionel also attempted to reform the administration, his
most revolutionary move being to shift some of the organs of
government, including the exchequer, from Dublin to Carlow.
The theory of this was that Carlow was equidistant from the

two main cores of the effective lordship – the area around Dublin and the south Leinster–east Munster region. It was also on the Barrow, which was an important navigable artery of the colony. The move soon proved disastrous, however, and by the end of the century the exchequer was back in the safer confines of Dublin castle.

In fact, the only thing for which Lionel's campaign tends to be remembered today is the parliament over which he presided at Kilkenny in 1366, at which the famous Statutes of Kilkenny were passed.[29] Part of the legislation passed at Kilkenny was novel, but most was not and can be traced back to pronouncements made as early as 1297. But the Statutes are important because they represent an attempt to gather together and to make consistent a whole series of enactments designed to deal with the colony's problems, which had been passed at various stages throughout the preceding two-thirds of a century. They deal with economic matters, with the reform of the administration, with the relationship between church and state, with the preservation of public order, and, most notoriously, with the thorny question of the separate identity of the Anglo-Irish, and the method by which it might best be protected. Undoubtedly these amounted to a policy of racial exclusiveness on the part of the English in Ireland. For instance, they forbade Irishmen from being appointed to certain church offices or from being received as members of religious houses in the 'land of peace'. They forbade Englishmen from using the Irish language, from the Irish mode of riding without saddles, and from adopting an Irish style of dress, or from patronizing the Irish learned classes of poets and musicians. They forbade marriage, concubinage and fosterage between the Irish and the English, and other forms of contact. Clearly the intention was to maintain a sharp distinction between the two societies in Ireland, to ensure that the English were identifiable by their use of the English language and customs and that Irish enemies and intruders were recognizable as such. If the Irish are the enemy, then association with them is dangerous, and this is what the Statutes of Kilkenny sought to prevent.

But, as with Lionel's expedition in general, the Statutes of Kilkenny failed in their purpose. Lionel is of significance as marking a turning point in Anglo-Irish affairs with the commencement of a period of large-scale military intervention in Ireland, largely financed by the English exchequer, under William of Windsor from 1369 to 1372 and from 1374 to 1376, and under King Richard II in person in 1394–5 and 1399. It also marked the start of a systematic attempt to reform the financial administration of Ireland, to make Irish revenues more productive, and to provide a solution to the problem of absenteeism. However, Lionel's military successes were temporary and the financial recovery that took place while he was in Ireland did not endure. He failed because his efforts took place, as we have seen, against a background of economic and demographic decline which affected Ireland no less so than it did the rest of western Europe in the fourteenth century, and in circumstances in which even the English government could not afford to maintain a large enough army in Ireland for long enough to provide a lasting solution. From the colony's point of view that solution lay in a permanent large-scale military commitment, but that was a commitment that the late-medieval kings of England were neither prepared nor, perhaps, able to make.

7

EQUILIBRIUM

Attempts by Edward III to solve England's Irish problem were of little avail. A resurgence was taking place within native Ireland over which neither he nor his ministers had any control. This was a political resurgence, and it was also a cultural one. While Lionel of Clarence was in Ireland trying to stem the tide, a Gaelic poet, in an inauguration ode for Niall Mór Ua Néill, wrote that 'Ireland is a woman risen again from the horrors of reproach … she was owned for a while by foreigners, she belongs to Irishmen now.'[1] Yet, the poet was wrong. This Irish resurgence freed them in a sense from the shackles of English lordship, but this did not result in a universal recovery of land. In later medieval Ireland, with few exceptions, the most important men remained Anglo-Irish lords: the Geraldine earls of Kildare and Desmond, the Butler earls of Ormond, the various branches of the de Burghs in Connacht, the Tuits in Meath, the Savage family in Ulster, the le Poer family in Waterford, the Barrys and Roches in Cork, and others besides. Some of the fiercest fighting in this period was between Irish kings, whose enemies remained not Anglo-Irishmen but neighbouring Irish dynasties or their own collateral rivals. The cultural revival was in some ways more impressive, since it is here that the Irish really triumphed, the colonists conforming in large measure to the norms of Gaelic society, becoming patrons of the Gaelic learned classes, and in

time being accorded a place of honour in poets' and hereditary historians' scheme of things.[2]

It was into this situation that Lionel of Clarence intruded
himself in 1361 and after four years of ultimately fruitless campaigning his father was forced to concede, in February 1365,
that his lordship of Ireland was now 'sunk in the greatest
wretchedness'.[3] It was a familiar refrain, so familiar, in fact,
that one can but conclude that the contemporary belief that
the Irish colony was on the point of extinction was greatly
exaggerated. It struggled on. In the summer of 1369 Edward
again invested a considerable sum in Ireland in the form of an
army led by an experienced military commander, William of
Windsor.[4] Prior to Windsor's departure for Ireland the king
passed an ordinance to the effect that all those who held lands
in Ireland should reside there; and those who could not reside
there should, nevertheless, supply men-at-arms to protect their
Irish lands. The penalty for failing to do this by Easter 1369
was forfeiture of these estates. This ordinance, if anything,
served to worsen the situation, since those to whom it applied
simply disengaged from Ireland altogether by selling off their
estates there, or accepted their forfeiture, the long-term result
of which was that the lands were mismanaged by royal officials,
overrun by the Irish and rebel English, and unable, therefore,
to provide income for the crown. It is important to see the sale
of these absentee lands as, in part, a manifestation of prevail-
ing economic conditions. The several outbreaks of plague and
famine earlier in the century had reduced the population to
such an extent that labour in places became scarce. With this,
in England and, from what we can tell, in Ireland too, came a
movement away from demesne farming, whereby lords ceased
direct management of outlying estates, and instead leased
them out to others.[5] This was what the lordship's absentee
landowners were engaged in, and the effect of the 1369 ordinance was to accelerate the process.

After Windsor's arrival in Ireland, he led a campaign in
Leinster and it was probably this campaign which resulted in
the capture of its king, Diarmait Láimhderg Mac Murchada,
who was subsequently put to death. Thereafter, Windsor went

to deal with the Irish of Thomond who had broken out in revolt, burnt the town of Limerick, and imprisoned the earl of Desmond and other Anglo-Irish.[6] Here too Windsor seems to have been successful in bringing the Irish to submission. Anglo-Irish resentment at his high-handedness, however, forced William's withdrawal from Ireland, though in 1372 it was reported that

> almost all the Irish of Munster, Connacht and Leinster, and many English, rebels and enemies, had risen openly to war after the departure of William of Windsor, lieutenant of the king in Ireland, and had confederated to make a universal conquest of the whole of Ireland before the same lieutenant should come from England.[7]

When he did return, Windsor spent his time not at war with the enemy but trying to get the Anglo-Irish to bear responsibility for the cost of his campaigns by extracting subsidies from them (which they pointedly refused to pay), and defending himself from charges of extortion. His expeditions, no less so than that of the duke of Clarence, failed to turn the tide.

After the accession in 1377 of Edward III's ten-year-old grandson, Richard II, a range of devices was experimented with, each with the limited objective of turning Ireland into a source of profit for the English crown, each – far from proving successful – barely getting off the ground.[8] Then, in the summer of 1394, rather unexpectedly, Richard announced his decision to go to Ireland in person. The intention was by no means unique (more than one of his predecessors had expressed similar hopes, and on more than one occasion), but in putting it into effect Richard became the only king of England to visit Ireland between 1210 and 1689, and he did so twice. In announcing his imminent departure for Ireland, he also ordered all those who held lands or ecclesiastical offices there, as well as all craftsmen, artisans and labourers who were from Ireland but who were now resident in England, to return home. By then it had become normal practice to order absentees to provide for the defence of their lands, but this ordinance was, in effect, an attempt to halt the process of depopulation of the colony which recent migration to England had brought about. In this respect, of course, it failed, as did all of the many later attempts both to repatriate those from Ireland who now lived in England, and to curb emigration from Ireland. This first Irish expedition by Richard was the largest the country had ever seen, bringing perhaps as many as 6000 troops, which were augmented considerably by others raised in Ireland. Clearly, he had high hopes of bringing about a permanent settlement of affairs, and stated prior to his departure that the purpose of his Irish expedition was 'the punishment and correction of our rebels there and to establish good government and just rule over our faithful lieges'.[9]

Richard and his army landed at Waterford early in October 1394. His immediate aim was to secure by military superiority the submission of the king of Leinster, Art Mac Murchada Cáemánach, and his sub-kings, which he succeeded in obtaining by the end of the month, as a result of a violent though brief campaign in which Mac Murchada's men were slain, their settlements burned, and their cattle stolen (to a total, or so we are told, of 8000). Campaigning continued in the following months, with English forces seeing action in Kilkenny in December and in Kildare in April. In Munster a decisive victory was obtained over Mac Carthaig, while the Connacht lord, Ua Ceallaig of Uí Maine, and Mac Domnaill, the Hebridean captain of Ua Néill's galloglasses in Ulster, offered to serve Richard against his enemies.[10] The strength of the king's army contributed to this: the Irish annals, in commenting on the vastness of Richard's forces, say that 'such a fleet did not come to Ireland since the Norse fleets came'.[11] Froissart says that 'when the Irish saw such a large force entering the country, they found it advisable to acknowledge the king of England'.[12] In general, with or without his show of strength, the Irish were willing to cooperate with Richard, most seeing him as a possible protector against colonial aggression. For instance, Ua Catháin of Ciannachta (in co. Derry) told the archbishop of Armagh that he had previously only attacked the colonists in retaliation for their attacks on him. The south-midlands lord, Ua Conchobair Failge, explained his earlier rebellious activities by saying that 'I found none to do justice between the English and me', and stated that he would remain loyal in future and would 'do justice to the English who may complain of me, similarly having like justice from them'. From Ulster, Niall Mór Ua Néill wrote to Richard, saying:

> When I heard of your joyful coming to the land of Ireland I greatly rejoiced and now rejoice, hoping to obtain justice for many injuries done by the English marchers to me and mine, and if I have in anything offended against your Majesty's subjects, I have not done it to deny your lordship, which I have ever recognised and now continually recognise, and if I could have had justice from any minister of yours for the injuries done to me, I would never have made the reprisals which I have made.[13]

He asked Richard to act 'as shield and helmet of justice between my lord, the earl of Ulster, and me', while his powerful son, Niall Óg, also wrote to the king, listing the wrongs that he had suffered at the hands of the colonists, and noting Richard's promise to see justice done. Furthermore, some lesser Irish lords were happy to use Richard as a means of renouncing their submission to traditional superiors and establishing a direct personal link with the crown; Ua Cerbaill of Ely, for instance, wrote that 'I am your immediate servant and special subject, absolutely exempt from the lordship of other Irishmen',[14] while Feidlim Ua Tuathail of north Leinster, whose ancestors had always resented the overlordship of the Meic Murchada family of Uí Chennselaig, wrote to Richard claiming that he was his direct subject and complaining of the hostile actions of the men of Uí Chennselaig.[15]

These and other appeals to the king from Irish lords appear to have convinced him that the latter had genuine grievances and that the Irish problem could not be resolved without addressing those grievances and adopting a conciliatory approach. In an important letter which he wrote on 1 February 1395, Richard informed the English council of his new conviction that 'the said Irish rebels are rebels only because of grievances and wrongs done to them on one side and lack of remedy on the other; if they are not wisely trusted and put in good hope of grace they will probably join our enemies'.[16]

Art Mac Murchada Cáemánach represented the greatest threat to the security of the colony since he dominated Leinster, both Irish and Anglo-Irish, and, at a time when Carlow was the recognized capital of the lordship, he had the power to paralyse government if he so chose. Clearly, the English crown resented the revival of the kingship of Leinster that had taken place in recent generations. Art Mac Murchada's grandfather had been condemned in the 1350s for 'calling himself king or prince of Leinster', while in 1370 his uncle was described as an 'Irish enemy of the lord king ... called by the Irish "King of Leinster"'. In the period from 1354 to 1375, six of the leaders of the Meic Murchada family were killed directly or indirectly by the Dublin government, a measure of the fear which their resurgence generated.[17] When not executing or assassinating them, the government, as in the case of Art, regularly resorted to buying their silence, yet, though Art's seal is said to have borne the ambitious inscription 'By God's Grace King of Leinster', he was prepared to work within the system, and, in particular, was anxious to gain possession of the barony of Norragh, co. Kildare, to which his Anglo-Irish wife was heiress.[18] Her marriage to Art was technically illegal, since it was in breach of one of the Statutes of Kilkenny which outlawed marriages between the two nations, and she therefore forfeited her lands, said to have been worth £100 per annum, because 'she adheres to McMurrough, one of the principal enemies of the king in Ireland'.[19] As a consequence of his submission to the king, Art was confirmed in possession of Norragh, and was granted an annual stipend of 80 marks (an amount he had been receiving for many years, allegedly in return for securing the safety of the road between Carlow and Kilkenny, in fact a payment that was little short of a bribe). In return he and his subordinate sub-kings of Leinster agreed to relinquish those lands which they had illegally occupied and to join the king's army in a campaign to conquer other areas occupied by rebels. But it seems likely that Art was less than committed in his submission and the Four Masters confirm that after the king's departure he renounced his fealty. He had several grounds for complaint. Part of Richard's efforts at strengthening the colony involved securing the return of settlers who had migrated to England, and this renewed attempt at colonization, the restoration of old claims to land, and the grants of land in Leinster which Richard made to those who served him well – all, in time, would have helped undermine Mac Murchada's dominance. Furthermore, although Richard recognized Art's position of pre-eminence in Leinster, the personal and direct bonds which he made with the subordinate Irish rulers of Leinster, the likes of Ua Broin and Ua Tuathail of the Wicklow massif, again served to undermine Mac Murchada's role as the apex of the pyramid of power in his kingdom.

Mac Murchada's lukewarm attitude to the settlement being imposed by King Richard was clearly felt by others. One of the leading Irish lords of Connacht, Ua Conchobair Donn, stated that he was submitting to the king 'against the will of diverse Irish of my lordship'. Ua Néill of Ulster, in the letter which he sent to Richard, stated that 'I cannot trust my own people since they see me turning away from them to your Majesty'; he had gathered together the lesser Irish lords of Ulster to consult with them about his proposed submission, but claimed that there then arrived 'envoys from Ua Briain, Ua Conchobair, Mac Carthaig and many others of the southern Irish, urging us strongly not to go to the king'.[20] While we cannot say for certain that this embassy took place, Ua Néill is unlikely to have concocted the story, and his remarks can perhaps be used as evidence of less than unanimous support among the Irish for the royal intervention.

Because Richard II's reign over England was so unstable he could not commit more time to the Irish situation, and, with his departure, events were likely to resume their earlier course. If Richard was not personally in Ireland, he was not in a position to act as protector of the Irish lords in the manner which they had been led to expect, a situation which had immediate implications for Ulster. Since the death of the last de Burgh earl in 1333 the earldom had been in the hands of absentees and was now the possession of Roger Mortimer, the young earl of March. The Mortimers are in many respects an exception to the general rule of disinterested absentees in that they made consistent attempts to exploit their landed inheritance in Ireland. King Richard had to be careful to steer an even course between the conflicting aims of Mortimer and Ua Néill, who had secured his supremacy in the north of Ireland precisely because Mortimer's predecessors had been absentees, leaving a power vacuum into which the Uí Néill kings fitted themselves. The latter, in effect, had usurped the role of the earls, taking from the lesser Irish lords of Ulster the services they had formerly owed the earl. It was to this new supremacy that Mortimer now presented a challenge. In 1393 Mortimer accused Niall Óg Ua Néill of planning a general conquest of Ireland, and calling himself 'king of Ireland'.[21] When Richard arrived in Ireland Niall's father wrote to him seeking protection against Mortimer 'in case he be provoked by stern advice to exact more from me than by right he should', while, when news of the king's departure reached Ulster, Niall Óg wrote to Richard expressing fears that Mortimer might launch an assault on him, saying 'on the one hand, if I do not resist in obedience to your Majesty, he will make war on me … on the other hand, if I resist him, my rivals will say that I have become rebel and traitor to your Majesty'.[22] It was a difficult situation, and one which was made worse by the fact that when Richard did leave Ireland he appointed Roger Mortimer as his lieutenant. It was not long, therefore, until he and others antagonized the Irish, thereby causing an eruption of warfare in Ulster, Leinster, and elsewhere. The annals report for 1396 that Mortimer, in the company of the earls of Ormond and Kildare, launched an assault on Ulster and plundered and burned Armagh. There were attacks too on Annaly in co. Longford and on Bréifne, while the Four Masters report a treacherous but failed attempt to capture Mac Murchada (though Mortimer himself was killed in battle against the

Irish of Leinster in 1398). Clearly, King Richard's settlement was in tatters.

Richard returned to Ireland in 1399, this time with a smaller army, and his forces suffered a reverse in Leinster at the hands of Art Mac Murchada's men, his army almost starving on their march to Dublin. Some fruitless negotiations with Art took place, and King Richard was no further towards finding a settlement when news reached him of the invasion of England by Bolingbroke (soon to be Henry IV), and quickly returned home to face his deposition.[23] In the end, therefore, Richard II failed in Ireland as in England. To be fair to him, he showed some foresight in seeking to bring the Irish in from the cold, and in recognizing the legitimacy of some of their complaints. But, when their goals conflicted with the objectives of his English subjects in Ireland, he failed to find a means of squaring the circle. The Irish kings lost whatever faith they had had in Richard's settlement, a return to hostilities was inevitable, and the lordship reverted to its former state of endemic unrest. The oaths of fealty which the Irish lords had made were redundant, although they had undertaken to pay large sums to the papacy if they should ever go back on them. This was remembered as treachery by the colonists whose parliament, a generation later, urged the king to seek papal approval for a crusade against the Irish in punishment. Art Mac Murchada Cáemánach was among those Irishmen whose career had resumed its previous pattern after Richard's fall, and who no doubt felt that the Irish had no monopoly on broken promises. Thereafter, periodic bouts of hostility on Art's part were matched by long intervals of relative peace and public negotiation. He operated in two worlds, now far from distinct. To the Dublin government and the Anglo-Irish of Leinster he may have appeared a menace who had to be either fought off or bought off, but to his Irish obituarist he was 'Art son of Art son of Muirchertach son of Muiris, lord of Leinster, a man who had defended his own province against the English and the Irish from his sixteenth to his sixtieth year; a man full of hospitality, knowledge and chivalry; a man full of prosperity and royalty; the enricher of churches and monasteries by his alms and offerings.'[24]

A report sent to England in the autumn of 1399 illustrates how transient Richard's successes had been. It was compiled by Alexander Balscot, the justiciar, and he, with customary exaggeration, stated that the lordship of Ireland was 'in danger of final destruction if it be not quickly relieved and succoured'. The author claims that 'the Irish enemies are strong and arrogant and of great power, and there is neither rule nor power to resist them, for the English marchers are not able, nor are they willing, to ride against them without stronger paramount power'. Mac Murchada was 'at open war'. He had led his forces to Munster to support the earl of Desmond in his quarrel with the earl of Ormond, and was returning to Leinster with reinforcements to renew his war there. In Ulster, Niall Óg Ua Néill was threatening war unless his hostages, including his eldest son, were released from custody. Added to these Irish lords were men of English extraction, including Geraldines, Butlers, Poers, Barretts, Berminghams, Daltons and Dillons, who wished to be called gentlemen but who were, in fact, no more than 'sturdy robbers', and who were joining the Irish in their attacks so that 'the law cannot be executed and no man dares to attempt to execute it'. There was no money to pay for troops to defend the king's lieges and what money came into the exchequer was mismanaged by illiterate and incompetent officials.[25]

The tone of this report was matched by many others to emanate from colonial Ireland in this age, and yet the final destruction they prophesied failed to come to pass. In fact, if anything, the evidence points to something of an economic revival in this period. The fourteenth century, in Ireland and elsewhere in Europe, was a period of apparently unrelieved decline, of famine, plague and economic slump (or so the surviving evidence would suggest) but the fifteenth century saw an improvement in conditions.[26] To this period belongs the construction of many of the tower-houses which pepper the landscape of Ireland in both rural and urban environments to this day (not all of which were constructed in lands occupied by the colonial community), and which made the country by the Early-Modern period the most castellated part of the British Isles. These are substantial stone edifices which have strong defensive features, indicative of the disturbed conditions in which they were built, but their construction was an expensive business and suggests considerable economic resources on the part of their owners. Furthermore, in the fifteenth century more than forty religious houses were built, in particular, friaries for the Franciscan Observants, the great majority of which were founded by Irish rather than Anglo-Irish patrons. Patronage of the church depended on the wealth of the benefactor, and this argues for more prosperous and perhaps more settled conditions.[27]

That did not mean that the king's colony in Ireland was no longer under threat: far from it. Successive Lancastrian kings may not have regarded Ireland as of any great importance, but it became important when it became a security risk. Henry IV had considerable cause to worry about Ireland after his accession in 1399. On 16 September 1400 Owain Glyn Dŵr, a descendant of the princes of northern Powys, broke out in revolt and was proclaimed prince of Wales.[28] Shortly afterwards he wrote letters to some Irish kings, reminding them of their common kinship, and seeking their help against the oppression and tyranny of their common enemy, the Saxons. Owain admitted that he might be unknown to the Irish but, nevertheless, said he trusted them and that prophecy foretold that 'before we can have the upper hand on our behalf, you and yours, our well-beloved cousins in Ireland, must stretch forth a helping hand', adding that 'so long as we shall be able to wage manfully this war in our borders, as doubtless is clear to you, you and all the other chieftains in your parts of Ireland will in the meantime have welcome peace and calm repose'. Unfortunately for Owain, the messengers carrying the letters into Ireland (others were despatched to the Scots) were captured and executed, the letters ending up in the possession of Henry IV, who eventually put down Owain's revolt. But the incident, so similar to the intrigues that surrounded Edward Bruce's invasion of Ireland nearly a century earlier, proved the danger for the English kings inherent in an unstable and volatile Ireland.

If the interventions of Richard II and his immediate predecessors had shown anything it was that, even to maintain the English position in Ireland, let alone to improve it, demanded a huge injection of resources in money and manpower. The Irish government was incapable, because of incompetence, corruption and sheer shortage of funds (its annual income was now perhaps as little as £1000), of financing itself without subsidy.[29] But subsidies were something which, in the fifteenth century, under the cash-starved Lancastrian kings, were hard to come by. It has to be said that no concerted effort was made by them to remedy the Irish situation, largely because Ireland was regarded as unimportant by comparison with the government of England and Wales (in the face of a disloyal nobility and a series of conspiracies and rebellions) or the maintenance of the claim to the crown of France and the defence of English possessions there. Chief governors sent from England to Ireland found themselves having to finance their operations on credit. Even the new king's son, Thomas of Lancaster, who arrived in Ireland in 1401 as his father's lieutenant, was forced to pawn his jewels and plate in order to pay for his upkeep.[30] English chief governors ended up paying for their operations out of their own pocket, with little chance of having their debts repaid, while their retinues of soldiers had to be billeted on the inhabitants in lieu of pay, and those who supplied provisions or services to the king's army and officials in Ireland did so at their own risk.

In these circumstances, the government had to reconsider both the scale of its military commitments and the very nature of its operations. Efforts continued to try to get those who held lands in Ireland to return to protect them, but the very regularity of these orders is an indication of their ineffectiveness. If anything the drain was worsening, with parliament complaining to the king in 1421 that 'tenants, tradesmen, and labourers ... daily depart in great numbers from your said land [of Ireland] to the kingdom of England and remain there',[31] while the archbishop of Armagh stated some years later that 'there is more

167

gone out of the land of the king's liege people than be in'.[32] The major military offensives of previous years tended to be replaced by small-scale defensive measures, the aim of which was less that of reconquest and more to do with securing the colony's frontiers. In this new era of realism the boundaries of the area over which the government claimed effective control increasingly became confined to the coastal littoral from Dundalk to Dalkey, including portions of cos. Louth, Meath, Dublin and Kildare, an area which by the mid-fifteenth century was known as the English 'Pale', and which in part at least came by the late fifteenth century to be enclosed by an earthen bank and ditch. The emergence of the Pale, in some respects a frame of mind rather than a physical landmark, is of great significance, since effectively what the government was doing was recognizing that it could no longer continue to exercise its normal functions beyond this attenuated area. That did not mean that it was washing its hands of the rest of the country, merely that it was handing over the reins of authority in these areas to the great lords, and that included both Irish and English, who dominated the localities. This produced a new equilibrium in Ireland. The Dublin government did its best to maintain the rule of law within the Pale, and to keep the inhabitants of this cordoned enclave (and their stock) free from the raids and exactions of those beyond, but the rest of Ireland was largely given over to and dominated by a few men who exercised command over those under them by any means at their disposal and by a form of lordship that was sometimes little short of tyranny. Effectively, central government had defaulted on its commitment, and the rest of the colony beyond the Pale organized itself, for its own defence, into large individual semi-autonomous lordships, under the leadership of local magnates.

It was government policy, therefore, for most of the fifteenth century, to keep the frontiers of the Pale safe from external assault, and to force those lords on its borders (mostly Irish though not exclusively so) to submit by swearing fealty to the king, handing back captives or prey, and promising to desist from demanding 'black rent' (protection money) from its inhabitants. These methods allowed the activities of the Irish lords elsewhere to go largely unchecked. When Niall Óg Ua Néill died in 1403, the annals say that it had been expected that he 'would take the kingship of Ireland on account of the prowess of his hands and the nobility of his blood'. Thereafter, there was a succession dispute in Tír Eógain, which allowed the reigning king of Tír Conaill, Niall Garbh Ua Domnaill, to come to the fore in the north. He formed a great confederation of the Irish of Ulster and launched devastating raids on the lands of its absentee earl and, increasingly, on the Anglo-Irish of Louth and Meath (indeed, it was while on a raid in the Pale in 1434, in the company of Ua Néill in pursuit of prey and black rent, that Niall Garbh was eventually captured, only to end his days as a prisoner on the Isle of Man).[33] Niall Garbh is also notable for his marriage to a daughter of the Offaly lord, Calbach Ua Conchobair Failge, who ruled from 1421 to 1458, and who repeatedly harassed the colonists on the southern part of Meath; Calbach regularly obtained black rent from them, and resided in Rathangan castle which had been won back from the earls of Kildare. His marriage alliance with Ua Domnaill of Tír Conaill in the far north-west of Ireland is an indication of the inter-provincial associations, and ambitions, of these late medieval Irish lords. But all too often their gains were squandered by faction and (perfectly understandable) self-interest.

One of the biggest obstacles to their advancement undoubtedly stemmed from the fact that they occupied, by and large, the less fertile parts of the country and, even where this was not the case, operated methods of agriculture that were less intensive and less profitable than those which the great Anglo-Irish magnates were used to exploiting for their own benefit. This meant that most Irish lords were no match for the greatest of the Anglo-Irish grandees. It is in this period that the Irish began to drop the royal style from their titles, and increasingly we find them seeking alliance by marriage with the Anglo-Irish magnates. The White Earl of Ormond (d. 1452), for example, was related to both Mac Murchada of Leinster and Ua Néill of Ulster. By means of such alliances he could ensure peace for his lordship and build upon his position of power. As a result, the White Earl, who held the liberty of Tipperary, came to exert near total control over the so-called royal county of Kilkenny, and in a famous set of ordinances actually regulated the imposition of 'coyne and livery' and other such illegal exactions; these onerous demands are sometimes thought to be confined to the native Irish but in fact men like the White Earl depended on them to retain their supremacy.[34] In some respects it is hard to blame them for this, since they undertook much of the government's military commitments, with little or no chance of reimbursement, and compensated for the deficiency in central funding by allowing their armies to live off the countryside which they were otherwise protecting.

It is quite clear that in this period a change came in attitudes to the holding of high office among the Anglo-Irish magnates. Because of the repeated failure of government to reimburse those who held the chief governorship (or lieutenancy), it became hard to attract the right people to undertake the position. In the fourteenth century men like the earls of Ormond and Desmond had on occasion refused to take on the task, quite obviously, though they seldom admitted as much, because they would have to foot the bill themselves. But in the fifteenth century, the Lancastrian governments badly needed to recruit their governors from among those who were powerful landowners in Ireland, since they could not depend upon the availability of subventions from England, and would have had to utilize their own financial resources to support the administration. In order to coax the magnates into accepting the post, the degree of financial risk on the part of the incumbent was reduced, the obligation to account for revenue was removed, and lieutenants were given the prerogative of appointing and dismissing whom they pleased to some important offices of state. This had the effect of giving them control over the king's council in Ireland, and, through it, parliament. As a result, the chief governor was less and less answerable to outside control, and had wide-ranging rights of patronage at his disposal. As the dispenser of favours the chief governor had power, and although there might still be a financial outlay involved, it was this new stature that made the post of lieu-tenant attractive for the three great resident magnates, the earls of Ormond, Desmond and Kildare, and made the financial risk well worthwhile.

In the fifteenth century, therefore, the great magnates sought, by occupying the position of chief governor, to control the government and all the perquisites which went with high office. This had advantages since the participation of the great nobles in government meant strong and stable rule. The dis-advantage was that magnate government led to magnate domi-nation, and instead of government being impartial and open to all it became a cause of faction and power struggles. This was one of the root causes of the long-running feud between the White Earl of Ormond and John Talbot, later earl of Shrewsbury, since the appointment as lieutenant of the latter, an Englishman (albeit one with substantial Irish lands), meant a curtailment in Butler power after 1414. The White Earl made every effort to confound his opponent, allegedly packing the Irish parliament with his own followers, securing the appointment of his own lackeys as government officials, and inciting rebellion among both Irish and Anglo-Irish, all with the intention of securing his own reappointment as chief governor. The feud only ended (and even then not entirely) when a marriage alliance was agreed between both sides in 1444, but in the interval the conflict between them, each accusing the other of misrule, peculation, oppression, even treason, caused considerable harm.[35] Archbishop Swayne of Armagh said in 1427 that 'all this land is severed, and this debate between these two lords is cause of the great harms that be done in this country'.[36] What the archbishop was really witnessing was a shift in the balance of power. It was no longer the officials of the Dublin government who ruled the colony but rather it was the great lords who ruled the officials. To an outsider this might look like disorder, even chaos, but an impotent administration in Dublin did not mean an absence of power and, in its own way, order. An order of sorts existed in the country as the great magnates, Irish and Anglo-Irish, asserted ever-increasing control within their lordships, gained greater autonomy, and organized their communities to be as self-sufficient as possible in the absence of outside interference.

As the great lordships became more autonomous, and as communities fell back on their own resources and became more self-reliant, making a virtue of self-help, so what some historians would see as a separatist tendency began to emerge among the Anglo-Irish. This had been smouldering for generations, as resentment with interference from England and from English-born officials grew. In the mid-fourteenth century the animosity between the English by blood and the English by birth had been such that the Statutes of Kilkenny had sought to ban one from calling the other an 'English hobbe [fool]' or an 'Irish dog'. Before long this mutual misunderstanding had gained political expression. In 1375 Edward III had issued orders that each county in Ireland should elect two knights, each town two burgesses, and each diocese two representatives of the clergy, who were to come to the king in England to consult about the state of Ireland, and, of more immediate concern, to agree further taxation measures to help towards the defence of the lordship. However, although they made an exception in this case, most Irish communities disputed the right of the king to summon parliamentary representatives from Ireland to England, citing in their defence the 'liberties, privileges, rights, laws and customs of the church and land of Ireland'.[37] It was a defining moment. It highlighted the way in which the English of Ireland had not alone come to view themselves as a people distinct from the English of England but, rightly or wrongly, had come to view the lordship of Ireland as equally distinct from the kingdom of England.

This sentiment took an organized form in the mid-fifteenth century in the public assertion that Ireland was not bound by statutes out of England. At a parliament held in Drogheda in 1460, it was declared that

> the land of Ireland is, and at all times has been, corporate of itself by the ancient laws and customs used in the same, freed

from the burden of any special law of the realm of England save only such laws as by the lords spiritual and temporal and commons of the said land [of Ireland] had been in great council or parliament there held, admitted, accepted, affirmed, and proclaimed, according to sundry ancient statutes thereof made.[38]

It can be argued that what this statute amounted to was a statement of the legislative independence of Ireland.[39] It is true that there were exceptional circumstances surrounding its promulgation. Richard, duke of York, who had earlier enjoyed a relatively successful career as lieutenant in Ireland, had been attainted by the English parliament in 1459 for treason against the Lancastrian king, Henry VI, and was now a fugitive in Ireland, where Yorkist supporters dominated the government. His Irish supporters protected him, and reconfirmed him in the lieutenancy, and passed the famous 1460 statute partly to prevent English writs ordering York's arrest from having force in Ireland. But just as Richard used his following within the Irish parliament to shield himself from prosecution, so the Anglo-Irish, it would seem, used him, used his vulnerability, to make a declaration which was in accord with their own pre-conceived notions of autonomy – notions which had surfaced many times in the past and which were reflected in the fourteenth century in the petty jealousies that divided the 'English born in Ireland' from the 'English born in England'.

Since the establishment of the lordship of Ireland it had always been a land that was subject to the authority of the king of England, but had those assembled for the 1460 parliament succeeded in establishing the principle enunciated there, the lordship of Ireland would have emerged as a political entity separate from England, though still under the same crown. It is, however, important not to exaggerate the significance of the events of 1460. The precise constitutional position of Ireland was one over which there was much confusion (as is reflected in the different views which historians of the subject hold to this day). That confusion allowed stances to be adopted when circumstances suited, stances which were not necessarily part of an established policy but rather spasmodic reactions against perceived misrule. To view the 1460 declaration as part of a serious political movement reflecting 'nationalist' sentiment on the part of the Anglo-Irish would be to give it a status it does not deserve.

Richard of York did not long outlive the 1460 declaration, but after the Yorkist victory at Towton in March 1461, his son became the new Edward IV. This Yorkist success was disastrous for the Butlers of Ormond who had aligned themselves with the Lancastrian cause. The new king appointed the Geraldine earl of Desmond as chief governor of Ireland, though he was eventually charged with treason and was executed in 1468, at the bidding of the Englishman, John Tiptoft, whom King Edward appointed his deputy for Ireland in 1467. The execution of Desmond led to widespread unrest in Ireland. Quite the extent of his status in the eyes of both the Anglo-Irish and the Irish is revealed in the account of his death preserved by the Four Masters:

> Thomas, earl of Desmond, son of James son of Gerald, who had been justiciar of Ireland, the most illustrious of his people in Ireland in his time for his comeliness and stature, for his hospitality and chivalry, his charity and humanity to the poor and the indigent of the Lord, his bounteousness in bestowing jewels and riches on the laity, the clergy, and the poets, and his suppression of theft and immorality, went to Drogheda to meet the English justiciar and the foreigners of Meath. They acted treacherously by him and, without any crime [on his part], beheaded him. The greater number of the men of Ireland were grieved at the news of it.[40]

High praise indeed from a Gaelic annalist for an Anglo-Irish baron. With the Munster Geraldines in open revolt, and the Butlers temporarily forfeit, the only contender within Ireland for the office of king's deputy was the leading surviving Geraldine, Thomas fitz Maurice, seventh earl of Kildare, and from this point onwards, with few interruptions, an earl of Kildare was to govern Ireland until their power was smashed by Henry VIII in 1534.

The geographic location of Kildare's lordship was of significance in determining his appointment, since political influence in the colony was increasingly centred on the Pale, and the advancement of the interests of the Palesmen, and the winning of their sympathies, was crucial for the success of government. That is why when Edward IV recovered his throne in 1471, and sought effective but economically efficient government, he turned to the greatest nobleman in the Pale, the seventh earl of Kildare. Prior to this point Kildare had not been the most powerful of the Anglo-Irish lordships, though the earls of Kildare held a vast amount of land. Once they gained the deputyship the seventh, eighth and ninth earls in turn used their control of government to increase their lands further, by passing laws allowing them to occupy the lands of absentees, to use the rents and profits of absentee estates for their own ends, and to possess what lands they could recover from rebels. Kildare's enemies became the government's enemies, and government revenues were used to prosecute them. Kildare's friends too became the government's friends: when the seventh earl's sister married Conn Ua Néill an act of parliament was passed making Conn free under the law, their children to be treated as English. By a vast array of strategic marriage alliances, and by securing the right to billet their standing army on the countryside, and by gaining control of government revenues without an absolute duty to account for expenditure, the earls came to dominate Irish life, and did so within a very short space of time. One of the keys to their power lay in control of the council. In theory, the earls did not have the right to appoint and dismiss ministers of the council, but in practice they exercised just such a right.

We get an important insight into the state of Ireland shortly after the Geraldine ascendancy began, from an address sent to the king by the Irish parliament. The document begins with a gentle reminder to the king that he was honour-bound to defend his subjects in Ireland, and that England should make a contribution to its defence since Ireland was 'one of the members of his most noble crown, and eldest member thereof'. There follows a realistic assessment of the deterioration in the numbers of loyal subjects in the colony, who are described as 'but petty [in] number in comparison of the great multitude of their Irish enemies, English rebels, and Scots', the latter now settling in the north of the country in substantial numbers. Because of this, they say, it is necessary for the king or his lieutenant to lead an army of 1000 archers to the country, who would set the foundation for 'the whole conquest' of Ireland. The king should proclaim that 'all manner [of] persons of Ireland birth', except students in the English universities, should return 'to inhabit such countries as shall [be] conquered'. The supposed advantages for the king in this are then spelled out. Ireland had formerly yielded to the crown an annual revenue of 100 000 marks (a ludicrous exaggeration), which it could do again once fully conquered. The petitioners then hark back to the original English invasion of Ireland, saying that 'the first conquest thereof was obtained with a full small number of Englishmen', and, what is more, now 'all the cities, castles and walled towns are under the king's obeisance', although the Irish, English rebels, and Scots occupy the lands between. Even so, it argues, the latter are 'always divided within themself and not of one power'. If the king did proceed with such a reconquest of Ireland the profits would soon flow, which he could use in 'the subduing of his great enemies of France and Scotland and all their adherent friends'.[41] All in all, it is a relatively optimistic statement, and indicative of the recovery, however mixed, that the colony was making in the new equilibrium of the fifteenth century.

Attempts to remove or undermine the position of the eighth earl, known in Irish sources as Gearóid Mór, were made during the reign of Edward IV and the brief reign of his brother Richard III, as part of a policy aimed at reasserting royal control over the Irish administration, but in neither case was it carried out. It is, though, anachronistic to view this as a struggle by Kildare to achieve separatist or 'Home Rule' policies at the expense of the English crown. Under the earls of Kildare significant successes were obtained in pushing back the frontier with Gaelic Ireland; old castles were retaken from the Irish, new ones were erected to defend the territory gained, and the king's writ ran over a more extensive area.

This was, of course, Kildare expansion, but in doing so they were strengthening the English lordship of Ireland. That is why the earls of Kildare were retained as deputy: they provided a cost-effective method of safeguarding vital English interests in Ireland. A delicate balance existed between the aspirations of the earls and the interests of the king. The earls were not indispensable. As masters of the Pale the earls of Kildare helped to keep secure the administrative headquarters of the colony, but equally Kildare needed to occupy the position of deputy in order to enhance his own status within the colony. There were, therefore, mutual benefits for both king and earl in the Kildare supremacy.

After the battle of Bosworth in August 1485, and the accession of Henry Tudor as King Henry VII, the prospects of the Butler family in Ireland underwent a sea-change and it may have been this, or sincere Yorkist fervour, which encouraged the Great Earl to support the cause of the pretender Lambert Simnel and to secure his coronation in Christ Church cathedral in Dublin in May 1487.[42] Although the plot came to nothing in the end, it was a startling reminder of the dangers inherent in neglecting Ireland, and an illustration of the way in which Ireland had come to play a role that was critical to the conspiracies that dominated the age. Crucially too, instead of the customary title 'king of England and France, and lord of Ireland', Simnel was crowned 'king of England, France and Ireland', a measure of the extent to which the constitutional position of Ireland within the English realm was beginning to become an issue. Kildare had clearly acted treasonably, but again he survived, Henry Tudor being unwilling as yet to do without him. What forced Henry's hand was the appearance in Ireland in November 1491 of yet another Yorkist pretender, Perkin Warbeck, to whose cause Kildare was at best neutral.[43] The earl was dismissed from office almost immediately, and although he was eventually restored to the king's favour and to high office, in the interval Henry VII decided upon a major intervention in Ireland and a determined effort to strengthen royal control.

In August 1494 he nominated several new men to office in the lordship and on 12 September 1494 appointed Edward Poynings as his deputy. It was part of Poynings's mission to ensure that Perkin Warbeck did not receive sufficient support in Ireland by which to launch a Yorkist invasion of England. In this he succeeded, although Warbeck eluded capture for a few more years. Another of Poynings's tasks was to reform the financial administration of Ireland, so that the collection of revenue would become more productive and the auditing of accounts more efficient. In this, as might be expected, he and his officials were rather less than successful. But Poynings had one more task yet to fulfil. Henry Tudor had decided to reinstate Kildare, and intended both to clip his wings and to ensure that no governor of Ireland in the future could evade royal control in the manner in which the earls of Kildare had come to do. Therefore, Poynings was issued with explicit instructions as to legislation which Henry intended to have passed by the Irish parliament, comfortable in the knowledge that the new English officials dominating the Irish council would secure its passage.

The parliament met at Drogheda on 1 December 1494, and continued in session until the following March. The legislation passed confirmed the king's intention of asserting real control over the governance of his lordship. Ireland's chief ministers were henceforth to hold their offices at the king's pleasure, and not for life as Kildare had sought to secure for his cronies. Kildare had earlier also enacted that the Irish council could appoint a temporary justiciar in time of vacancy in the lieutenancy, but parliament now decreed that the treasurer should fill this role until a replacement was found. Furthermore, this parliament decreed that the government of Ireland was subordinate to that of England and that all royal commandments were to be duly obeyed. It annulled what it called the 'pretensed prescription' of the 1460 parliament, which had decreed that those resident in Ireland could not be summoned from the country by orders issuing from England, and that English seals were inoperative in Ireland; instead, the great seal of England, the privy seal, and signet, were henceforth to be obeyed in Ireland.

But it is for the ninth act, that has become known as Poynings's Law, that this parliament is best remembered, an act which thereafter changed the procedures for the passage of legislation by Irish parliaments. From now on, no parliament could be held in Ireland without the king's explicit licence, and no legislation could be enacted until the proposed legislation had been inspected and approved by the king and his council in England. The aim here was clearly to ensure that the Irish parliament never again (as had happened when Kildare secured the recognition of Lambert Simnel as king) passed measures which were contrary to the interests of the king of England. A constitutional check on the administration of the king's lordship of Ireland was thereby introduced. But inherent in the legislation was the assumption that the government of Ireland would again be entrusted to somebody of Kildare's ilk, since such stringent safeguards would have been unnecessary if government through loyal English officials such as Poynings was to become the norm. And therefore the Great Earl was soon reappointed but had to swear to abide by the provisions of Poynings's Law, so that if writs were issued out of England ordering the delivery to the king of those whom he considered rebels or traitors, those writs had to be obeyed.

Poynings's Law was passed to meet a certain set of circumstances (in particular, no doubt, to ensure that the supporters in Ireland of the pretender Perkin Warbeck did not use parliament, as had happened in the case of Simnel, to effect a *coup d'état*) and it is probably the case that its framers would have been surprised to know that it was still operative three centuries later. Nevertheless, Poynings's parliament was the most important to meet in Ireland from that which passed the Statutes of Kilkenny in 1366 to the Reformation Parliament of 1536. Although some of the enactments of the parliament were later repealed, and others were simply ignored, most did take effect, and as a result royal control in the lordship of Ireland was significantly increased. The legislation was not intended to be a direct challenge to Gearóid Mór or a deliberate assault on the powers of the chief governor. 'Direct rule' was not an option. The intention was simply to ensure that the king had knowledge of the decisions made in his name and the prime role in the decision-making process. That achieved, Kildare could be safely restored to office, as was to happen in August 1496. With proper safeguards built into the system, as Poynings had ensured, Kildare would be an asset to the king: a local magnate, able to provide strong and cost-effective government, yet constrained by law, and a water-tight promise of good behaviour, from overstepping the mark.

Before the king's council on 6 August 1496 the Great Earl swore certain articles: to defend the land of Ireland from the enemies, rebels and traitors of the king; to arrest any English rebels who had found refuge in Ireland, and to send them to England; to rule with impartiality; to observe Poynings's Law; and to put behind him old quarrels, especially that 'betwixt these two noble bloods of the land of Ireland called Butlers and Geraldines'.[44] In the new spirit of trust his terms of appointment were extremely generous. The earl was nominated as chief governor for a term of ten years, and thereafter at the king's pleasure. He was given the power to appoint whom he pleased to all offices save the chancellorship, and he was given a grant of all lands which he could recover from the Irish on behalf of the crown.

Gearóid Mór returned to Ireland in September 1496 and held a council at Drogheda a few days later. To this council messengers came from many Irish lords suing for peace, and several of them – one of the Uí Néill (O'Neills), Mac Mathgamna (Mac Mahon), Mág Aonghusa (Magennis), Ua hAnluain (O'Hanlon), and Ua Ragallaig (O'Reilly) – surrendered their eldest sons as pledges of their good behaviour and swore fealty to Henry VII. Later, though not entirely without military effort, similar pledges were obtained from the Irish of Leinster and the south midlands: Mac Murchada (MacMurrough), Ua Broin (O'Byrne), Ua Conchobair Failge (O'Conor Faly), Ua Mórda (O'More), and Ua Dímmussaig (O'Dempsey). The suspect Anglo-Irish earl of Desmond and the head of the Clanrickard branch of the Burkes of Connacht also made peace overtures, as did even Ua Domnaill (O'Donnell) in the far north-west. A contemporary observer was driven to comment of the earl that the king 'could have put no man in authority here that in so short space and with so little cost could have set this land in so good order as it is now'.[45] He was exaggerating but not excessively so. The earl remained true to his word in cooperating with Butler of Ormond, the king's interests in Ireland were protected, the ambit of central government was widened, and the inhabitants of the Pale were relatively free from war and deprivation.

It is perhaps not going too far to suggest that the colony by the year 1500 was more peaceful and more prosperous than it had been for two hundred years. But it was peace and prosperity of a sort. After nearly three and a half centuries Ireland remained unconquered, yet the English colony in Ireland had refused to die. Part of the explanation for its refusal to do so must lie in the continued belief which the English of Ireland had in the possibility of conquest. Despite periods of doubt and despair, the clamour for an all-out attempt at conquest remained. And so did optimism. In 1515 an Anglo-Irishman proudly boasted that 'the English have now a greater advantage than at the Conquest, for then there were not five piles or castles in all Ireland, where[as] at this day there are no less than 500'.[46] Though the writer failed to note that many of those five hundred castles were now in the hands of or had been built by Irishmen, his general point can be conceded: that a transformation had taken place in Ireland in the later Middle Ages and that transformation was brought about by the English presence.

NOTES AND REFERENCES

Abbreviations

AC   *Annála Connacht: the Annals of Connacht AD 1224–1544*, ed. A. M. Freeman (Dublin: Dublin Institute for Advanced Studies, 1944).

AFM   *Annala Rioghachta Eireann: Annals of the Kingdom of Ireland by the Four Masters, from the Earliest Period to the Year 1616*, ed. John O'Donovan, 7 vols (Dublin: Hodges, Smith & Co., 1851).

Ann. Inisf.   *The Annals of Inisfallen (MS Rawlinson B503)*, ed. Seán Mac Airt (Dublin: Dublin Institute for Advanced Studies, 1951).

ALCé   *The Annals of Loch Cé: a Chronicle of Irish Affairs, 1014–1590*, ed. W. M. Hennessy, 2 vols (London: Rolls Series, 1871).

ATig   'The annals of Tigernach', ed. Whitley Stokes, *Revue Celtique*, 16–18 (1895–7) (reprinted Lampeter: Llanerch Press, 1994).

AU   *Annála Uladh. Annals of Ulster; a Chronicle of Irish Affairs 431–1541*, ed. W. M. Hennessy and Bartholomew MacCarthy, 4 vols (London; Rolls Series, 1887–1901); *The Annals of Ulster (to AD 1131)*, ed. Seán Mac Airt and Gearóid Mac Niocaill (Dublin: Dublin Institute for Advanced Studies, 1983).

Brut   *Brut y Tywysogyon or the Chronicle of the Princes: Peniarth MS. 20 Version*, ed. Thomas Jones (Cardiff: Board of Celtic Studies, 1952).

INTRODUCTION

1. Sir John Davies, *A Discoverie of the True Causes why Ireland was never entirely Subdued, and Brought under the Obedience of the Crowne of England, untill the Beginning of his Majesties happie Raigne* (London: John Jaggard, 1612), pp. 116–18.

2. The classic discussion of the significance of the Viking incursions is D. A. Binchy, 'The passing of the old order', in Brian Ó Cuív (ed.), *The Impact of the Scandinavian Invasions on the Celtic-speaking Peoples c. 800–1100 AD*, Proceedings of the [First] International Congress of Celtic Studies (Dublin: Dublin Institute for Advanced Studies, 1975), 119–32.

3. For discussion, see Katharine Simms, *From Kings to Warlords. The Changing Political Structure of Gaelic Ireland in the Later Middle Ages* (Woodbridge: Boydell & Brewer, 1987), chap. 1.

4. Francis John Byrne, '*Senchas*: the nature of Gaelic historical tradition', *Historical Studies*, 9 (1974), 159.

5. See, for example, Eric St J. Brooks (ed.), *Knights' Fees in Counties Wexford, Carlow and Kilkenny* (Dublin: Irish Manuscripts Commission, 1950); H. G. Richardson and G. O. Sayles, *The Irish Parliament in the Middle Ages* (Philadelphia: University of Pennsylvania Press, 1952); G. J. Hand, *English Law in Ireland, 1290–1324* (Cambridge: Cambridge University Press, 1967).

6. Aubrey Gwynn, *The Medieval Province of Armagh, 1470–1545* (Dundalk: Dundalgan Press, 1946); some of Fr Gwynn's more important articles have been brought together in the collection *The Irish Church in the Eleventh and Twelfth Centuries* (Dublin: Four Courts Press, 1993). John A. Watt has produced two monographs devoted to ecclesiastical affairs, *The Church and the Two Nations in Medieval Ireland* (Cambridge: Cambridge University Press, 1970), and *The Church in Medieval Ireland* (Dublin: Gill & Macmillan, 1972).

7. See Art Cosgrove, *Late Medieval Ireland, 1370–1541* (Dublin: Helicon, 1981) and, for example, Steven G. Ellis, *Reform and Revival: English Government in Ireland, 1470–1534* (London: Boydell & Brewer, 1984); *idem, Tudor Ireland: Crown, Community and the Conflict of Cultures, 1470–1603* (London: Longman, 1985); *idem, Tudor Frontiers and Noble Power. The Making of the British State* (Oxford: Clarendon Press, 1995).

1 DWELLERS AT THE EARTH'S EDGE

1. The phrase is St Columbanus's, from his letter to Pope Boniface IV, written at Milan in AD 613: see G. S. M. Walker, *Sancti Columbani Opera* (Dublin: Dublin Institute for Advanced Studies, 1957), p. 38.

2. Giraldus Cambrensis, *The History and Topography of Ireland*, ed. J. J. O'Meara (Mountrath: Dolmen Press, 1982).

3. For Gerald, see especially Robert Bartlett, *Gerald of Wales, 1146–1223* (Oxford: Clarendon Press, 1982).

4. Bede, *A History of the English Church and People*, trans. Leo Sherley-Price (Harmondsworth: Penguin Books, revised edn., 1968), p. 136.

5. J. P. Mahaffy, 'Two early tours in Ireland', *Hermathena*, 40 (1914), 1–16.

6. G. G. Meersseman, 'Two unknown confraternity letters of St Bernard', *Cîteau in de Nederlanden, Achel et Westmalle*, 6 (1955), 173–8; Jean Leclercq, 'Deux épitres de St Bernard et de son sécretaire', in Jean Leclercq (ed.), *Recueil d'Études sur Saint Bernard et ses Écrits*, ii (Rome: Editiones Cistercienses, 1966), 313–18.

7. James F. Kenney, *The Sources for the Early History of Ireland: Ecclesiastical* (New York: Octagon Books, 1966 reprint), p. 582.

8. See D. A. Binchy, 'An archaic legal poem', *Celtica*, 9 (1971), 152–68.

9. Frank Mitchell, *The Shell Guide to Reading the Irish Landscape* (Dublin: Country House, 1986), pp. 117–21.

10. For this, see Charles Doherty, 'The monastic town in Ireland', in H. B. Clarke and Anngret Simms (eds.), *The Comparative History of Urban Origins in Non-Roman Europe* (Oxford: British Archaeological Reports, International Series, CCLV, 1985), pp. 55–63.

11. See Nancy Edwards, *The Archaeology of Early Medieval Ireland* (London: Batsford, 1990), chaps 1, 2.

12. See A. T. Lucas, *Cattle in Ancient Ireland* (Kilkenny: Boethius Press, 1989).

13. See Kathleen Ryan, 'Holes and flaws in medieval Irish manuscripts', *Peritia*, 7–8 (1987–8), 243–64.

14. See Michael V. Duignan, 'Irish agriculture in early historic times', *Journal of the Royal Society of Antiquaries of Ireland*, 74 (1944), 128–45; J. J. O'Loan, 'A history of early Irish farming', *Éire, Department of Agriculture Journal*, 60 (1963), 178–219; 61 (1964), 242–84; 62 (1965), 131–97.

15. A. T. Lucas, 'The horizontal mill in Ireland', *Journal of the Royal Society of Antiquaries of Ireland*, 83 (1953), 1–36.
16. See A. T. Lucas, 'Irish food before the potato', in *Gwerin*, 3 (1960), 8–43.
17. Kenneth Jackson, *The Oldest Irish Tradition: a Window on the Iron Age*, The Rede Lecture (Edinburgh: Edinburgh University Press, 1964).
18. See, for example, Liam Breatnach, 'Canon law and secular law in early Ireland: the significance of *Bretha Nemed*', *Peritia*, 3 (1984), 439–59; D. Ó Corráin, L. Breatnach, A. Breen, 'The laws of the Irish', ibid., 382–438; Donnchadh Ó Corráin, 'Irish vernacular law and the Old Testament', in P. Ní Chatháin and M. Richter (eds.), *Irland und die Christenheit/Ireland and Christendom* (Stuttgart: Klett-Cotta, 1987), pp. 284–307; Kim McCone, *Pagan Past and Christian Present in Early Irish Society* (Maynooth: An Sagart, 1990), pp. 84–106.
19. Fergus Kelly, *A Guide to Early Irish Law* (Dublin: Dublin Institute for Advanced Studies, 1988), pp. 19, 27.
20. See Donncha Ó Corráin, *Ireland before the Normans* (Dublin: Gill & Macmillan, 1972), pp. 28–32.
21. Kelly, *Guide to Early Irish Law*, p. 18, note 10; Liam Breatnach, 'Varia VI, no. 3: *Ardri* as an old compound', *Ériu*, 37 (1986), 192–3.
22. See Donnchadh Ó Corráin, 'Nationality and kingship in pre-Norman Ireland', in T. W. Moody (ed.), *Nationality and the Pursuit of National Independence*, Historical Studies 11 (Belfast; Appletree Press, 1978), pp. 9–10.
23. On the institution of kingship in early Irish society, see the text known as *Audacht Morainn*, ed. Fergus Kelly (Dublin: Dublin Institute for Advanced Studies, 1976).
24. Giraldus Cambrensis, *The History and Topography of Ireland*, p. 110.
25. Daniel Binchy (ed.), *Críth Gablach* (Dublin: Dublin Institute for Advanced Studies, 1941), para. 38.
26. See, for example, Máirín Ní Dhonnchadha, 'The guarantor list of *Cáin Adomnáin*, 697', *Peritia*, 1 (1982), 178–215.
27. ATig, AFM, s.a. 1166.
28. Ann. Inisf., s.a. 1040, 1050, 1068. See Ó Corráin, 'Nationality and kingship', pp. 22–3.
29. The fullest discussion is F. J. Byrne, *Irish Kings and High-kings* (London: Batsford, 1973).
30. G. H. Orpen, *Ireland under the Normans*, I (Oxford: Clarendon Press, 1911), p. 39.

31. Kelly, *Guide to Early Irish Law*, p. 27.
32. Kelly, *Guide to Early Irish Law*, p. 30.
33. Gearóid Mac Niocaill, 'The origins of the *betagh*', *The Irish Jurist*, 1 (1966), 292–8.
34. The definitive study of the subject is now Thomas Charles-Edwards, *Early Irish and Welsh Kinship* (Oxford: Clarendon Press, 1993).
35. See Donnchadh Ó Corráin, 'Marriage in early Ireland' in Art Cosgrove (ed.), *Marriage in Ireland* (Dublin: College Press, 1985), pp. 5–24.
36. For discussion of the subject, see Donnchadh Ó Corráin, 'Women in early Irish society', in Margaret Mac Curtain and Donnchadh Ó Corráin (eds.), *Women in Irish Society: the Historical Dimension* (Dublin: Women's Press, 1978), pp. 1–13; and now *idem*, 'Women and the law in early Ireland', in Mary O'Dowd and Sabine Wichert, *Chattel, Servant or Citizen. Women's Status in Church, State and Society*, Historical Studies XIX (Belfast: Institute of Irish Studies, 1995), 45–57.
37. Kuno Meyer (ed.), *The Triads of Ireland*, Todd Lecture Series XIII (Dublin: Royal Irish Academy, 1906).
38. Kelly, *Guide to Early Irish Law*, pp. 68–9.
39. D. A. Binchy, '*Bretha Crólige*', *Ériu*, 12 (1938), 44.
40. Helen Clover and Margaret Gibson (eds.), *The Letters of Lanfranc Archbishop of Canterbury* (Oxford: Oxford University Press, 1979), no. 10.
41. I have used the translation in John Watt, *The Church in Medieval Ireland* (Dublin: Gill and Macmillan, 1972), p. 7.
42. See Aubrey Gwynn, 'The first synod of Cashel', *Irish Ecclesiastical Record*, 5th ser., 66 (1945), 81–92; 67 (1946), 109–22.
43. H. J. Lawlor (ed.), *St Bernard of Clairvaux's Life of St Malachy of Armagh* (London: SCPK, 1920), p. 37.
44. Watt, *The Church in Medieval Ireland*, p. 37.
45. William Stubbs (ed.), *Gesta Henrici Secundi*, (London: Rolls Series), I, p. 28.
46. William Stubbs (ed.), *Opera Historica* (London: Rolls Series), II, pp. 350–1.
47. AC, s.a. 1233.
48. John of Fordun, *Chronica Gentis Scotorum*, ed. W. F. Skene (Edinburgh: Historians of Scotland, 1871–2), I, pp. 198–9; IV, p. 186.
49. Geoffrey Keating, *Trí Bior-ghaoithe an Bháis*, ed. Osborn Bergin (Dublin: Royal Irish Academy, 1931), p. 171.

2   A KINGDOM UNIQUE TO ITSELF?

1. Geoffrey Keating [Seathrún Céitinn], *Foras Feasa ar Éirinn,* 4 vols (London: Irish Texts Society, 1902–14).
2. Michael Richter, *Medieval Ireland: The Enduring Tradition* (Dublin: Gill & Macmillan, 1988).
3. D. A. Binchy, 'The passing of the old order', in Brian Ó Cuív (ed.), *The Impact of the Scandinavian Invasions on the Celtic-speaking Peoples c. 800–1100 AD* (Dublin: Dublin Institute for Advanced Studies, 1962), pp. 119–32.
4. The standard work on this is still A. T. Lucas, 'The plundering and burning of churches in Ireland, 7th to 16th century', in Etienne Rynne (ed.), *North Munster Studies* (Limerick: Thomond Archaeological Society, 1967), 172–229.
5. AU, s.a. 850.
6. See Seán Duffy, 'Irishmen and Islesmen in the kingdoms of Dublin and Man, 1052–1171', *Ériu,* 43 (1992), 101, 103, 114, 119, note 128.
7. See Donncha Ó Corráin, *Ireland before the Normans* (Dublin: Gill & Macmillan, 1972), pp. 1–9.
8. For the career of Brian, see John Ryan, 'Brian Bóruma, king of Ireland', in Rynne (ed.), *North Munster Studies,* 355–74.
9. See F. J. Byrne, *The Rise of the Uí Néill and the High-kingship of Ireland,* O'Donnell Lecture (Dublin: National University of Ireland, 1970).
10. See Ó Corráin, 'Nationality and kingship in Pre-Norman Ireland' in Moody, *Nationality and the Pursuit of National Independence.*
11. Aubrey Gwynn, 'Brian in Armagh (1005)', *Seanchas Ard Mhacha,* 9 (1978–9), 35–50.
12. See Donnchadh Ó Corráin, 'Dál Cais – church and dynasty', *Ériu,* 24 (1973), 52–63.
13. See John Ryan, 'The battle of Clontarf', *Journal of the Royal Society of Antiquaries of Ireland,* 68 (1938), 1–50.
14. See John Ryan, 'The O'Briens in Munster after Clontarf', *North Munster Antiquarian Journal,* 2 (1941), 141–52; 3 (1942–3), 1–52; 189–202.
15. See Donnchadh Ó Corráin, 'The career of Diarmait mac Máel na mBó, king of Leinster', *Journal of the Old Wexford Society,* 3 (1970–1), 27–35; 4 (1972–3), 17–24.
16. For this, see Duffy, 'Irishmen and Islesmen in the kingdoms of Dublin and Man'.

17. ATig, s.a. 1072.
18. *Brut*, s.a. 1072.
19. For what follows, see Seán Duffy, 'Ostmen, Irish and Welsh in the eleventh century', *Peritia*, 9 (1995), 378–96; and Marie Therese Flanagan, *Irish Society, Anglo-Norman Settlers, Angevin Kingship* (Oxford: Clarendon Press, 1989), pp. 61–9.
20. ATig, s.a. 1036.
21. Arthur Jones (ed.), *The History of Gruffydd ap Cynan* (Manchester: Manchester University Press, 1910); D. Simon Evans (ed.), *A Medieval Prince of Wales. The Life of Gruffudd ap Cynan* (Lampeter: Llanerch Press, 1990).
22. For this, see Ben Hudson, 'The family of Harold Godwinsson and the Irish Sea province', *Journal of the Royal Society of Antiquaries of Ireland*, 109 (1979), 92–100.
23. See Duffy, 'Irishmen and Islesmen in the kingdoms of Dublin and Man'.
24. See Benjamin Hudson, 'William the Conqueror and Ireland', *Irish Historical Studies*, 29 (1994), 145–58.
25. See Anthony Candon, 'Muirchertach Ua Briain, politics, and naval activity in the Irish Sea, 1075 to 1119', in Gearóid Mac Niocaill and P. F. Wallace (eds), *Keimelia: Studies in Medieval Archaeology and History in Memory of Tom Delaney* (Galway: Galway University Press, 1988), pp. 397–415.
26. See Donnchadh Ó Corráin, 'Irish regnal succession: a reappraisal', *Studia Hibernica*, 11 (1971), 7–39.
27. J. H. Todd (ed.), *Cogadh Gaedhel re Gallaibh* (London: Rolls Series, 1867).
28. George Broderick (ed.), *Cronica Regum Mannie & Insularum* (Douglas: Manx Museum, 1979), fol. 33v.
29. AFM, s.a. 1096.
30. See Rosemary Power, 'Magnus Barelegs' expeditions to the west', *Scottish Historical Review*, 65 (1986), 107–32.
31. Duffy, 'Irishmen and Islesmen in the kingdoms of Dublin and Man', 111.
32. Duffy, 'Irishmen and Islesmen in the kingdoms of Dublin and Man', 116.
33. *Brut*, s.a. 1127.
34. *Brut*, s.a. 1102.
35. William of Malmesbury, *Gesta Regum*, ed. William Stubbs (London: Rolls Series, 1889), II, pp. 484–5; Edmund Curtis, 'Murchertach O'Brien, high-king of Ireland, and his Norman son-in-law, Arnulf de Montgomery, *circa* 1100', *Journal of the Royal Society of Antiquaries of Ireland*, 51 (1921), 116–24.

36. James Ussher, *Veterum Epistolarum Hibernicarum Sylloge* (Dublin, 1632), no. XXXVII.
37. Orderic Vitalis, *Historica Ecclesiastica*, ed. Marjorie Chibnall, 6 vols (Oxford: Oxford University Press, 1969–80), VI, pp. 48–51.
38. AU, AFM, s.a. 1093.
39. J. E. Lloyd, 'Bishop Sulien and his family', *National Library of Wales Journal*, 2 (1941), 1–6; Bede, *History of the English Church and People*, p. 195.
40. Kenney, *Sources for the Early History of Ireland*, p. 551.
41. See, for example, Aubrey Gwynn, 'Ireland and the Continent in the eleventh century', in *idem*, *The Irish Church in the Eleventh and Twelfth Centuries* (Dublin: Four Courts Press, 1992), pp. 34–49.
42. For this, see Dennis Bethell, 'English monks and Irish reform in the eleventh and twelfth centuries', *Historical Studies*, 8 (1971), 111–35.
43. For the role of Canterbury in the Irish church and for the history of the Irish church in general during this period, see J. A. Watt, *The Church and the Two Nations in Medieval Ireland* (Cambridge: Cambridge University Press, 1970), chap. 1; Marie Therese Flanagan, *Irish Society, Anglo-Norman Settlers, Angevin Kingship* (Oxford: Clarendon Press, 1989), chap. 1; Aubrey Gwynn, *The Irish Church in the Eleventh and Twelfth Centuries* (Dublin: Four Courts Press, 1993).
44. James Ussher (ed.), *Veterum Epistolarum Hibernicarum Sylloge* (Dublin, 1632), no. XL.
45. See Duffy, 'Irishmen and Islesmen in the kingdoms of Dublin and Man'.
46. See John Ryan, *Toirdelbach O Conchobair (1088–1156), King of Connacht, King of Ireland 'co fresabra'*, O'Donnell Lecture (Dublin: National University of Ireland, 1966).
47. For his career, see Ó Corráin, *Ireland before the Normans*, pp. 159–66.
48. AFM, s.a. 1154.

3   ADVENTUS ANGLORUM

1. *Letters containing Information relative to the Antiquities of the County of Wicklow collected during the Progress of the Ordnance Survey* (National Library of Ireland transcript, 1927), p. 120 (370–1).
2. AFM, s.a. 1156.
3. AFM, s.a. 1166.

4. *The Book of Leinster*, I, ed. R. I. Best, Osborn Bergin, and M. A. O'Brien (Dublin: Dublin Institute for Advanced Studies, 1954), p. xvii.

5. J. J. O'Meara, 'Giraldus Cambrensis in Topographia Hiberniae. Text of the first recension', *Proceedings of the Royal Irish Academy*, 52, C (1948–50), 131; Giraldus Cambrensis, *History and Topography of Ireland*, ed. O'Meara, p. 52.

6. For discussion, see John Gillingham, 'The English invasion of Ireland', in B. Bradshaw, A. Hadfield, and W. Maley (eds.), *Representing Ireland: Literature and the Origins of Conflict, 1534–1660* (Cambridge: Cambridge University Press, 1993), pp. 24–42.

7. Goddard Henry Orpen (ed.), *The Song of Dermot and the Earl* (Oxford: Clarendon Press, 1892), pp. 23–5.

8. A. B. Scott and F. X. Martin (eds.), *Expugnatio Hibernica. The Conquest of Ireland by Giraldus Cambrensis* (Dublin: Royal Irish Academy, 1978), p. 27.

9. *Song of Dermot*, pp. 33–5.

10. AFM, s.a. 1167.

11. AFM, s.a. 1167.

12. AFM, s.a. 1167.

13. *Expugnatio Hibernica*, p. 25.

14. *Song of Dermot*, p. 11.

15. *Expugnatio Hibernica*, pp. 30–1.

16. *Expugnatio Hibernica*, p. 49.

17. *Song of Dermot*, p. 17.

18. For a full discussion, see Flanagan, *Irish Society, Anglo-Norman Settlers, Angevin Kingship*, pp. 95–111.

19. See Flanagan, *Irish Society, Anglo-Norman Settlers, Angevin Kingship*, p. 111.

20. ATig, s.a. 1169.

21. AFM, s.a. 1170.

22. *Song of Dermot*, p. 117.

23. *Expugnatio Hibernica*, p. 69.

24. *Song of Dermot*, pp. 137–9.

25. ATig, s.a. 1171.

26. *Expugnatio Hibernica*, p. 89.

27. *Expugnatio Hibernica*, p. 89.

28. See W. L. Warren, 'The interpretation of twelfth-century Irish history', in *Historical Studies VII*, ed. J. C. Beckett (London: Routledge & Kegan Paul, 1969), pp. 1–19 (at pp. 9–13).

29. Perhaps the best introduction to the world of Henry II and his dynasty is John Gillingham, *The Angevin Empire* (London: Edward Arnold, 1984); the phrase occurs on p. 29.

30. There has been a considerable amount of work on this subject, but perhaps the most comprehensive discussion is Flanagan, *Irish Society, Anglo-Norman Settlers, Angevin Kingship*, chap. 1.

31. Quoted in A. J. Otway-Ruthven, *A History of Medieval Ireland* (London: Ernest Benn, 1968), p. 47.

32. *Brut*, s.a. 1171.

33. Gervase of Canterbury, *Historical Works*, ed. William Stubbs (London: Rolls Series, 1879–80), I, p. 235.

34. Translated in Watt, *The Church in Medieval Ireland*, p. 36.

35. Watt, *The Church in Medieval Ireland*, pp. 37–9.

36. AFM, s.a. 1171.

37. *Book of Leinster*, I, ll. 5504, 3203–4.

38. *Expugnatio Hibernica*, p. 115.

39. *Expugnatio Hibernica*, p. 71.

40. *Expugnatio Hibernica*, p. 43.

41. *Expugnatio Hibernica*, pp. 41–3.

42. *Expugnatio Hibernica*, p. 231.

43. *Expugnatio Hibernica*, p. 69.

44. *Expugnatio Hibernica*, p. 149.

45. *Expugnatio Hibernica*, pp. 229–31.

46. *Expugnatio Hibernica*, pp. 63–5.

47. *Expugnatio Hibernica*, p. 135.

48. ATig, s.a. 1173.

49. J. E. Lloyd, *A History of Wales from Earliest Times to the Conquest*, 2 vols (London: Longman, Green and Co., 1911), II, pp. 545–6.

50. J. T. Gilbert (ed.), *Chartularies of St Mary's Abbey, Dublin*, 2 vols (London: Rolls Series, 1884–6), II, p. 305.

51. *Expugnatio Hibernica*, p. 233.

4   FROM KINGDOM TO LORDSHIP

1. A. J. Otway-Ruthven, 'Parochial development in the rural deanery of Skreen', *Journal of the Royal Society of Antiquaries of Ireland*, 94 (1964), 111–22.

2. See B. J. Graham, 'Anglo-Norman settlement in County Meath', *Proceedings of the Royal Irish Academy*, 75, C (1975), 223–48.

3. R. E. Glasscock, 'Mottes in Ireland', *Château-Gaillard*, 7 (1975), 95–110.

4. See D. C. Twohig, 'Norman ringwork castles', *Bulletin of the Group for the Study of Irish Historic Settlement*, 5 (1978), 7–9; T. B. Barry, 'Anglo-Norman ringwork castles: some evidence', in T. Reeves-Smith and F. Hamound (eds.), *Landscape Archaeology in Ireland* (Oxford: British Archaeological Reports, 116, 1983),

pp. 295–314. For an important study of the manifestations and implications of English settlement, see K. W. Nicholls, 'Anglo-French Ireland and after', *Peritia*, 1 (1982), 370–403.

5. See A. J. Otway-Ruthven, 'The character of Norman settlement in Ireland', *Historical Studies*, 5 (1965), 75–84; T. B. Barry, *The Archaeology of Medieval Ireland* (London: Methuen, 1987), chap. 4.

6. See Robert Bartlett, *The Making of Europe. Conquest, Colonization and Cultural Change 950–1350* (London; Allen Lane, Penguin Press, 1993); for the quotation, see p. 2.

7. *Brut*, s.a. 1172.

8. *Expugnatio Hibernica*, p. 141; *Song of Dermot*, pp. 235–43.

9. The text is printed from Roger of Howden's original in Flanagan, *Irish Society, Anglo-Norman Settlers, Angevin Kingship*, pp. 312–13; for a translation, see Edmund Curtis and R. B. McDowell, *Irish Historic Documents, 1172–1922* (London: Methuen, 1943)*, pp. 22–4.

10. Robin Frame, *Colonial Ireland, 1169–1369* (Dublin: Helicon, 1981), p. 17.

11. There is a valuable and detailed examination of these developments in Flanagan, *Irish Society, Anglo-Norman Settlers, Angevin Kingship*, pp. 254–60, though I have departed from her in some of my conclusions.

12. Orpen, *Ireland under the Normans*, II, pp. 33–4.

13. Conell Mageoghagan, *The Annals of Clonmacnoise*, ed. Denis Murphy (Dublin: University Press, 1896), p. 179.

14. J. F. O'Doherty, 'St Laurence O'Toole and the Anglo-Norman invasion', *Irish Ecclesiastical Record*, 50 (1937), 449–77, 600–25; 51 (1938), 131–46.

15. Flanagan, *Irish Society, Anglo-Norman Settlers, Angevin Kingship*, p. 260.

16. Ibid.

17. AFM, s.a. 1177.

18. Flanagan, *Irish Society, Anglo-Norman Settlers, Angevin Kingship*, p. 281.

19. William of Newburgh, *Historia Rerum Anglicarum*, ed. Richard Howlett, 2 vols (London: Rolls Series, 1884), I, pp. 239–40.

20. *Expugnatio Hibernica*, p. 191; see also Flanagan, *Irish Society, Anglo-Norman Settlers, Angevin Kingship*, pp. 263–4.

21. ALCé, s.a. 1185.

22. See W. L. Warren, 'John in Ireland, 1185', in J. Bossy and P. Jupp (eds.), *Essays presented to Michael Roberts* (Belfast: Blackstaff Press, 1976), pp. 11–23.

23. A. J. Otway-Ruthven, 'The chief governors of medieval Ireland', *Journal of the Royal Society of Antiquaries of Ireland*, 95 (1965), 227–36.

24. H. G. Richardson and G. O. Sayles, *The Irish Parliament in the Middle Ages* (Philadelphia: University of Pennsylvania Press, 1952).

25. J. F. Lydon, 'The Irish exchequer in the thirteenth century', *Bulletin of the Irish Committee of Historical Sciences*, new ser., 6 (1957–8), 1–2.

26. A. J. Otway-Ruthven, 'The medieval Irish chancery', *Album Helen Maud Cam*, 2 (1960), 119–38.

27. A. J. Otway-Ruthven, 'Anglo-Irish shire government in the thirteenth century', *Irish Historical Studies*, 5 (1946–7), 1–28.

28. Geoffrey Hand, *English Law in Ireland, 1290–1324* (Cambridge: Cambridge University Press, 1967); *idem*, 'English law in Ireland, 1172–1351', *Northern Ireland Legal Quarterly*, 13 (1972), 393–422; Paul Brand, 'Ireland and the literature of the early common law', *The Irish Jurist*, new ser., 16 (1981), 95–113.

29. The late W. L. Warren was convinced that they were; see 'King John and Ireland', in James Lydon (ed.), *England and Ireland in the Later Middle Ages* (Dublin: Irish Academic Press, 1981), pp. 28–39.

30. *Expugnatio Hibernica*, p. 241.

31. *Expugnatio Hibernica*, p. 81.

32. *Expugnatio Hibernica*, pp. 237–9.

33. Warren, 'John in Ireland, 1185' in Bossy and Jupp, *Essays presented to Michael Roberts*, p. 17.

34. See Seán Duffy, 'King John's expedition to Ireland, AD 1210: the evidence reconsidered', *Irish Historical Studies*, 31, no. 117 (May 1996). I have reached some conclusions which are at variance with those expressed by W. L. Warren in his important paper, 'King John and Ireland', in James Lydon (ed.), *England and Ireland in the Later Middle Ages* (Dublin: Irish Academic Press, 1981), pp. 26–42.

35. A. J. Otway-Ruthven, 'The medieval church lands of County Dublin', in J. A. Watt, J. B. Morrall, and F. X. Martin (eds), *Medieval Studies presented to Aubrey Gwynn S.J.* (Dublin: Cló Morainn, 1961), pp. 54–73.

36. G. H. Orpen, 'Castlekevin', *Journal of the Royal Society of Antiquaries of Ireland*, 38 (1908), 17–27.

37. Charles McNeill (ed.), *Calendar of Archbishop Alen's Register c. 1172–1534* (Dublin: Royal Society of Antiquaries of Ireland, 1950), p. 40.

38. Gwynn, *The Irish Church in the Eleventh and Twelfth Centuries*, p. 267.
39. Warren, 'King John and Ireland', in Lydon (ed.), *England and Ireland in the Later Middle Ages*, p. 38.
40. Watt, *The Church in Medieval Ireland*, p. 100.
41. Printed in translation in Watt, *The Church in Medieval Ireland*, p. 101.
42. Watt, *The Church in Medieval Ireland*, p. 105.

5 COLONIAL DOMINATION AND NATIVE SURVIVAL

1. See A. J. Otway-Ruthven, 'The organization of Anglo-Irish agriculture in the middle ages', *Journal of the Royal Society of Antiquaries of Ireland*, 81 (1951), 1–13.
2. See, for example, A. J. Otway-Ruthven, 'The character of Norman settlement in Ireland', in *Historical Studies*, 5 (1965), 75–84; and C. A. Empey, 'Conquest and settlement: patterns of Anglo-Norman settlement in north Munster and south Leinster', *Irish Economic and Social History*, 13 (1986), 5–31.
3. For de Courcy's career and background, see Seán Duffy, 'The first Ulster plantation: John de Courcy and the men of Cumbria', in T. B. Barry, Robin Frame and Katharine Simms (eds.), *Colony and Frontier in Medieval Ireland. Essays presented to J. F. Lydon* (London: Hambledon Press, 1995), pp. 1–27.
4. Ann. Inisf., s.a. 1210.
5. See Helen Perros, 'Crossing the Shannon frontier: Connacht and the Anglo-Normans, 1170–1224', in Barry, Frame, and Simms (eds.), *Colony and Frontier in Medieval Ireland*, pp. 117–38.
6. Otway-Ruthven, *History of Medieval Ireland*, p. 93.
7. See James Lydon, 'Lordship and crown: Llywelyn of Wales and O'Connor of Connacht', in R. R. Davies (ed.), *The British Isles 1100–1500. Comparisons, Contrasts, and Connections* (Edinburgh: John Donald, 1988), pp. 48–63.
8. See Robin Frame, 'King Henry III and Ireland: the shaping of a peripheral lordship', in *Thirteenth Century England IV. Proceedings of the Newcastle upon Tyne Conference 1991*, ed. P. R. Coss and S. D. Lloyd (Woodbridge: Boydell & Brewer, 1992), pp. 179–202.
9. AC, s.a. 1265.
10. AC, s.a. 1274.
11. Ann. Inisf., s.a. 1195.
12. Ann. Inisf., s.a. 1206; AU, s.a. 1230.
13. AC, s.a. 1247.
14. Ann. Inisf., s.a. 1248.

15. AC, s.a. 1249.
16. AC, s.a. 1249.
17. AC, s.a. 1255.
18. For an important study of this period, see Robin Frame, 'King Henry III and Ireland: the shaping of a peripheral lordship', in Coss and Lloyd, *Thirteenth Century England IV. Proceedings of the Newcastle upon Tyne Conference 1991*, pp. 179–202.
19. See Seán Duffy, 'The Bruce brothers and the Irish Sea world, 1306–29', *Cambridge Medieval Celtic Studies*, 21 (1991), 55–86.
20. Ann. Inisf., s.a. 1259.
21. Duffy, 'The Bruce brothers', 69–70.
22. For a discussion, see J. F. Lydon, *The Lordship of Ireland in the Middle Ages* (Dublin: Gill & Macmillan, 1972), p. 120.
23. See James Lydon, 'The years of crisis, 1254–1315', in Art Cosgrove (ed.), *A New History of Ireland. II. Medieval Ireland 1169–1534* (Oxford: Clarendon Press, 1993), p. 181.
24. For this, see Robin Frame, 'Ireland and the barons' war', in *Thirteenth Century England I. Proceedings of the Newcastle upon Tyne Conference 1985*, ed. P. R. Coss and S. D. Lloyd (Woodbridge: Boydell & Brewer, 1986), pp. 158–67.
25. See Lydon, *Lordship of Ireland*, chap. 6.
26. Lydon, 'The years of crisis' in Cosgrove, p. 189.
27. Lydon, 'The years of crisis' in Cosgrove, pp. 191–2; H. G. Richardson and G. O. Sayles, 'Irish revenue, 1278–1384', *Proceedings of the Royal Irish Academy*, 62, C (1962), 87–100.
28. G. O. Sayles (ed.), *Documents on the Affairs of Ireland before the King's Council* (Dublin: Irish Manuscripts Commission, 1979), no. 19.
29. Lydon, 'The years of crisis' in Cosgrove, p. 196.
30. Duffy, 'The Bruce brothers', p. 80.
31. James Lydon, 'An Irish army in Scotland, 1296', *The Irish Sword*, 5 (1961–2), 184–90.
32. James Lydon, 'Irish levies in the Scottish wars, 1296–1302', *The Irish Sword*, 5 (1961–2), 207–17.
33. James Lydon, 'Edward I, Ireland and the war in Scotland, 1303–1304', in *idem* (ed.), *England and Ireland in the Later Middle Ages*, pp. 43–61.

6 A COLONY IN RETREAT

1. For the Bruce invasion, see Olive Armstrong, *Edward Bruce's Invasion of Ireland* (London: John Murray, 1923); Orpen, *Ireland under the Normans*, IV, chap. XXXVII; James Lydon, 'The Bruce

invasion of Ireland', *Historical Studies*, 4 (1963), 111–25; Robin Frame, 'The Bruces in Ireland, 1315–18', *Irish Historical Studies*, 19 (1974–5), 3–37.

2. The letter is printed in Ranald Nicholson, 'A sequel to Edward Bruce's invasion of Ireland', *Scottish Historical Review*, 42 (1963), 30–40, and in A. A. M. Duncan (ed.), *Regesta Regum Scottorum, V, The Acts of Robert I* (Edinburgh: Edinburgh University Press, 1988), no. 564, and in translation in G. W. S . Barrow, *Robert Bruce and the Community of Realm of Scotland* (London: Eyre & Spottiswoode, 1965), p. 434.

3. Duffy, 'The Bruce brothers', 64–5.

4. See Seán Duffy, 'The "continuation" of the annals of Nicholas Trevet: a new source for the Bruce invasion', *Proceedings of the Royal Irish Academy*, 91, C (1991), 303–15.

5. N. Denholm-Young (ed.), *Vita Edwardi Secundi* (London: Nelson Medieval Texts, 1957), p. 61.

6. J. Beverley Smith, 'Gruffydd Llwyd and the Celtic alliance, 1315–18', *Bulletin of the Board of Celtic Studies*, 26 (1976), 463–78.

7. J. Beverley Smith, 'Edward II and the allegiance of Wales', *Welsh History Review*, 8 (1976), 139–71.

8. Trinity College Dublin MS 498 (formerly MS E.2.28), p. 384.

9. Walter Bower, *Scotochronicon*, general editor D. E. R. Watt, vol 6, N. F. Shead, W. B. Stevenson, and D. E. R. Watt (eds.) (Aberdeen: Aberdeen University Press, 1991), p. 401.

10. AC, s.a. 1315.

11. John O'Donovan (ed.), *The Tribes and Customs of Hy-Many* (Dublin: Irish Archaeological Society, 1843), p. 138; AC, s.a. 1316.

12. Robin Frame, *English Lordship in Ireland 1318–1361* (Oxford: Clarendon Press, 1982), pp. 144–6, 222–3.

13. Curtis & McDowell (eds.), *Irish Historic Documents*, pp. 32–8.

14. Gilbert (ed.), *Chartularies of St Mary's Abbey*, pp. 365–6.

15. There is an important discussion of the range and intensity of fourteenth-century government in Frame, *English Lordship in Ireland 1318–1361*, pp. 77–87.

16. See G. O. Sayles, 'The rebellious first earl of Desmond', in Watt, Morrall, and Martin (eds.), *Medieval Studies presented to Aubrey Gwynn*, pp. 203–29.

17. Robin Frame, 'The justiciarship of Ralph Ufford: warfare and politics in fourteenth-century Ireland', *Studia Hibernica*, 13 (1973), 7–47; *idem, English Lordship in Ireland 1318–1361*, pp. 267–74, 283–93.

18. See Gearóid Mac Niocaill, 'Duanaire Ghearóid Iarla', *Studia Hibernica*, 3 (1963), 7–59.
19. See Evelyn Mullally, 'Hiberno-Norman literature and its public', in Bradley (ed.), *Settlement and Society in Medieval Ireland*, pp. 332–3.
20. Frame, *Colonial Ireland, 1169–1369*, p. 132.
21. Evelyn Mullally has, however, suggested that what offended the earl was not so much being called a 'rymoure' in Irish but the social slur of being called a rhymer at all, in any language ('Hiberno-Norman literature and its public', in Bradley (ed.), *Settlement and Society in Medieval Ireland*, p. 333).
22. Otway-Ruthven, *Medieval Ireland*, p. 248.
23. See Robin Frame, 'English policies and Anglo-Irish attitudes in the crisis of 1341–1342', in Lydon (ed.), *England and Ireland in the Later Middle Ages*, pp. 86–103.
24. Gilbert (ed.), *Chartularies of St Mary's Abbey*, ii, pp. 383–4.
25. H. F. Berry (ed.), *Statutes and Ordinances and Acts of the Parliament of Ireland: King John to Henry V* (Dublin: Irish Record Office, 1907), pp. 344–5.
26. H. G. Richardson and G. O. Sayles (eds.), *Parliaments and Councils of Medieval Ireland* (Dublin: Irish Manuscripts Commission, 1947), pp. 19–22.
27. See Philomena Connolly, 'The financing of English expeditions to Ireland, 1361–1376', in Lydon (ed.), *England and Ireland in the Later Middle Ages*, pp. 104–21.
28. Berry (ed.), *Acts of the Parliament of Ireland: King John to Henry V*, p. 470.
29. Berry (ed.), *Acts of the Parliament of Ireland: King John to Henry V*, pp. 430–69.

7 EQUILIBRIUM

1. Cuthbert Mhág Craith (ed.), *Dán na mBráthar Mionúr. Cuid I: Téacs* (Dublin: Dublin Institute for Advanced Studies, 1967), pp. 1–2.
2. Katharine Simms, 'Bards and barons: the Anglo-Irish aristocracy and the native culture', in *Medieval Frontier Societies*, ed. Robert Bartlett and Angus Mackay (Oxford: Clarendon Press, 1989), pp. 177–97.
3. Quoted in James Lydon, *Ireland in the Later Middle Ages* (Dublin: Gill & Macmillan, 1972), p. 94.
4. See Maud Clarke, 'William of Windsor in Ireland, 1369–1376', *Proceedings of the Royal Irish Academy*, 41, C (1932–3), 55–130;

Sheelagh Harbison, 'William of Windsor, the court party, and the administration of Ireland', in Lydon (ed.), *England and Ireland in the Later Middle Ages*, pp. 153–74.

5. See, for example, J. L. Bolton, *The Medieval English Economy 1150–1500* (London: Everyman University Paperback, 1980), chap. 7.

6. Sheelagh Harbison, 'William of Windsor and the wars of Thomond', *Journal of the Royal Society of Antiquaries of Ireland*, 99 (1989), 98–112.

7. Lydon, *Ireland in the Later Middle Ages*, p. 99.

8. See Anthony Tuck, 'Anglo-Irish relations, 1382–93', *Proceedings of the Royal Irish Academy*, 69 (1970), C, 15–31.

9. For a narrative of the expedition, see J. F. Lydon, 'Richard II's expeditions to Ireland', *Journal of the Royal Society of Antiquaries of Ireland*, 93 (1963), 135–49.

10. Dorothy Johnston, 'Richard II and the submissions of Gaelic Ireland', *Irish Historical Studies*, 22 (1980), 1–20.

11. Séamus Ó hInnse, *Miscellaneous Irish Annals* (Dublin: Dublin Institute for Advanced Studies, 1947), p. 153.

12. John Joliffe (ed.), *Froissart's Chronicles* (London: Harvill Press, 1967), p. 369.

13. For these letters from the Irish, see Edmund Curtis, *Richard II in Ireland, 1394–5, and Submissions of the Irish Chiefs* (Oxford: Clarendon Press, 1927).

14. Johnston, 'Richard II and the submissions of Gaelic Ireland', 3, 10.

15. Curtis, *Richard II in Ireland*, p. 125.

16. N. Harris Nicolas, *Proceedings and Ordinances of the Privy Council of England, 1386–1410* (London: Record Commission, 1836), pp. 55–7.

17. Robin Frame, 'Two kings in Leinster: the crown and the MicMhurchadha in the fourteenth century', in Barry, Frame, and Simms (eds.), *Colony and Frontier in Medieval Ireland*, p. 156.

18. Edmund Curtis, 'The barons of Norragh, Co. Kildare, 1171–1660', *Journal of the Royal Society of Antiquaries of Ireland*, 75 (1935), 88–91.

19. *Calendar of Patent Rolls, 1392–3*, p. 362.

20. Curtis, *Richard II in Ireland*, pp. 113–14, 124–5, 133–4.

21. Johnston, 'Richard II and the submission of Gaelic Ireland', 17.

22. Curtis, *Richard II in Ireland*, pp. 131–2, 211–12; 134–6, 213–14.

23. Dorothy Johnston, 'Richard II's departure from Ireland, July 1399', *English Historical Review*, 98 (1983), 785–805.

24. AFM, s.a. 1417.
25. James Graves (ed.), *A Roll of the Proceedings of the King's Council in Ireland, 1392–93* (London: Rolls Series, 1877), pp. 261–9.
26. For a detailed study of this in an English context, see Christopher Dyer, *Standards of Living in the Later Middle Ages* (Cambridge: Cambridge University Press, 1989).
27. See T. B. Barry, *The Archaeology of Medieval Ireland* (London: Methuen, 1987), chap. 7.
28. See J. E. Lloyd, *Owen Glendower* (Oxford: Clarendon Press, 1931).
29. S. G. Ellis, 'Ioncaim na hÉireann, 1384–1534', *Studia Hibernica*, 22–3 (1982–3), 39–49.
30. F. C. Hingeston (ed.), *Royal and Historic Letters during the Reign of Henry IV* (London: Rolls Series, 1860), I, pp. 73–6.
31. Berry (ed.), *Acts of the Parliament of Ireland: King John to Henry V*, pp. 568–9.
32. D. A. Chart (ed.), *The Register of John Swayne* (Belfast: Public Records Office of Northern Ireland, 1935), p. 108.
33. Katharine Simms, 'Niall Garbh II O Donnell, king of Tír Conaill 1422–39', *Donegal Annual*, 12 (1977/9), 7–21.
34. C. A. Empey and K. Simms, 'The ordinances of the White Earl and the problem of coign in the later middle ages', *Proceedings of the Royal Irish Academy*, 75, C (1975), 161–87.
35. M.C. Griffith, 'The Talbot–Ormond struggle for control of the Anglo-Irish government, 1417–47', *Irish Historical Studies*, 2 (1940–1), 376–97.
36. *Register of Swayne*, p. 111.
37. Thomas Leland, *The History of Ireland* (Dublin, 1773), I, p. 368.
38. See Art Cosgrove, 'Parliament and the Anglo-Irish community: the declaration of 1460', *Historical Studies*, 14 (1983), 25–41.
39. A view propounded by Edmund Curtis who gave the title 'Aristocratic Home Rule' to the appropriate chapter of his *History of Mediaeval Ireland* (Dublin: Maunsel & Roberts, 1923), chap. XIII; see now, James Lydon, 'Ireland and the English crown, 1171–1541', *Irish Historical Studies*, 29 (1994–5), 281–94.
40. AFM, s.a. 1467.
41. Donough Bryan, *Gerald FitzGerald, the Great Earl of Kildare, 1456–1513* (Dublin: The Talbot Press, 1933), pp. 18–22.
42. See F. X. Martin, 'The crowning of a king at Dublin, 24 May 1487', *Hermathena*, 144 (1988), 7–34.
43. Agnes Conway, *Henry VII's Relations with Scotland and Ireland 1485–1498* (Cambridge: Cambridge University Press, 1932), pp. 42–62.
44. Conway, *Henry VII's Relations with Scotland and Ireland*, p. 226.

45. Quoted in Steven Ellis, *Tudor Ireland: Crown, Community, and the Conflict of Cultures, 1470–1603* (London: Longman, 1985), p. 85.
46. J. S. Brewer and W. Bullen (eds), *Calendar of the Carew Manuscripts, 1515–74* (London: Rolls Series, 1871), p. 5.

SELECT BIBLIOGRAPHY

This bibliography is not intended to be comprehensive; it comprises only a sample of the secondary literature on the subject in the form of some of the better-known books and essay collections. For guides to sources and further reading, see James F. Kenney, *The Sources for the Early History of Ireland: Ecclesiastical* (New York: Columbia University Press, 1929); Kathleen Hughes, *Early Christian Ireland: Introduction to the Sources* (London: The Sources of History Ltd, 1972); Donnchadh Ó Corráin, 'A handlist of publications on early Irish history', in *Historical Studies*, 10 (1976), pp. 172–203; P. W. A. Asplin, *Medieval Ireland c. 1170–1485. A Bibliography of Secondary Works* (Dublin: Royal Irish Academy, 1971); and *idem*, 'Bibliography', in *A New History of Ireland. II. Medieval Ireland 1169–1534*, ed. Art Cosgrove (Oxford: Clarendon Press, second impression, 1993), pp. 827–964.

Barry, T. B., *The Archaeology of Medieval Ireland* (London: Methuen, 1987).

Barry, T. B., Frame, Robin and Simms, Katharine (eds.), *Colony and Frontier in Medieval Ireland. Essays presented to J. F. Lydon* (London: Hambledon Press, 1995).

Bartlett, Robert, *The Making of Europe. Conquest, Colonization and Cultural Change 950–1350* (London: Allen Lane, Penguin Press, 1993).

Bartlett, Robert and Mackay, Angus (eds.), *Medieval Frontier Societies* (Oxford: Clarendon Press, 1989).

Bradley, John, (ed.), *Settlement and Society in Medieval Ireland. Studies presented to F. X. Martin O.S.A.* (Kilkenny: Boethius Press, 1988).

Bradshaw, Brendan, *The Dissolution of the Religious Houses in Ireland under Henry VIII* (Cambridge: Cambridge University Press, 1974).

——, *The Irish Constitutional Revolution of the Sixteenth Century* (Cambridge: Cambridge University Press, 1979).

Brady, Ciaran, (ed.), *Worsted in the Game. Losers in Irish History* (Dublin: Lilliput Press, 1989).

Bryan, Donough, *Gerald FitzGerald, the Great Earl of Kildare, 1456–1513* (Dublin: The Talbot Press, 1933).

Byrne, F. J., *Irish Kings and High-kings* (London: Batsford, 1973).

Carney, James, *The Irish Bardic Poet* (Dublin: Dolmen Press, 1967).

Charles-Edwards, Thomas, *Early Irish and Welsh Kinship* (Oxford: Clarendon Press, 1993).

Clarke, Howard (ed.), *Medieval Dublin*, 2 vols (Dublin: Irish Academic Press, 1990).

Clarke, H. B. and Simms, Anngret (eds.), *The Comparative History of Urban Origins in Non-Roman Europe* (Oxford: British Archaeological Reports, International Series, 1985).

Conway, Agnes, *Henry VII's Relations with Scotland and Ireland, 1485–1498* (Cambridge: Cambridge University Press, 1932).

Conway, Colmcille, *The Story of Mellifont* (Dublin: Gill, 1958).

Corish, P. J., *A History of Irish Catholicism*, 28 fascs in 16 (Dublin: Gill & Macmillan, 1967–72).

Cosgrove Art, *Late Medieval Ireland, 1370–1541* (Dublin: Helicon, 1981).

Cosgrove, Art (ed.), *Dublin through the Ages* (Dublin: Irish Academic Press, 1988).

——, (ed.), *A New History of Ireland. II. Medieval Ireland 1169–1534* (Oxford: Clarendon Press, second impression, 1993).

Curtis, Edmund, *A History of Medieval Ireland* (Dublin: Maunsel & Roberts, 1923).

de Paor, Máire and Liam, *Early Christian Ireland* (London: Thames & Hudson, 1958).

Davies, R. R. (ed.), *The British Isles, 1100–1500: Comparisons, Contrasts and Connections* (Edinburgh: John Donald, 1988).

——, *Domination and Conquest: the Experience of Ireland, Scotland and Wales, 1100–1300* (Cambridge: Cambridge University Press, 1990).

Dolley, Michael, *Viking Coins of the Danelaw and of Dublin* (London: British Museum, 1965).

——, *The Hiberno-Norse Coins in the British Museum* (London: Syllogue of Coins in the British Isles, Consecutive Series, 1966).

——, *Anglo-Norman Ireland, c. 1100–1318* (Dublin: Gill & Macmillan, 1972).

Edwards, Nancy, *The Archaeology of Early Medieval Ireland* (London: Batsford, 1990).

Ellis, Steven, *Reform and Revival: English Government in Ireland, 1470–1534* (London: Boydell & Brewer, 1984).

——, *Tudor Ireland: Crown, Community and the Conflict of Cultures, 1470–1603* (London: Longman, 1985).

——, *Tudor Frontiers and Noble Power. The Making of the British State* (Oxford: Clarendon Press, 1995).

Flanagan, Marie Therese, *Irish Society, Anglo-Norman Settlers, Angevin Kingship: Interactions in Ireland in the Late Twelfth Century* (Oxford: Clarendon Press, 1989).

Foster, R. F. (ed.), *The Oxford Illustrated History of Ireland* (Oxford: Clarendon Press, 1989).

Frame, Robin, *English Lordship in Ireland, 1318–1361* (Oxford: Clarendon Press, 1981).

——, *Colonial Ireland, 1169–1369* (Dublin: Helicon, 1981).

——, *The Political Development of the British Isles, 1100–1400* (Oxford: Opus, 1990).

Graham, B. J., *Anglo-Norman Settlement in Ireland* (Athlone: GSIHS, 1985).

Graham, B. J. and Proudfoot, L. J. (eds.), *An Historical Geography of Ireland* (London: Academic Press, 1993).

Green, Alice Stopford, *The Making of Ireland and its Undoing, 1200–1600* (London: Macmillan, 1908).

Gwynn, Aubrey, *The Medieval Province of Armagh, 1470–1545* (Dundalk: Dundalgan Press, 1946).

——, *The Irish Church in the Eleventh and Twelfth Centuries* (Dublin: Four Courts Press, 1993).

Hand, G. H. *English Law in Ireland, 1290–1324* (Cambridge: Cambridge University Press, 1967).

Hannigan, Ken and Nolan, William (eds.), *Wicklow: History and Society* (Dublin: Geography Publications, 1994).

Herbert, Máire, *Iona, Kells and Derry* (Oxford: Oxford University Press, 1988).

Hogan, Dáire and Osborough, W. N. (eds.), *Brehons, Serjeants and Attorneys: Studies in the History of the Irish Legal Profession* (Dublin: Irish Legal History Society, 1990).

Hughes, Kathleen, *The Church in Early Irish Society* (London: Thames & Hudson, 1966).

Kelly, Fergus, *A Guide to Early Irish Law* (Dublin: Dublin Institute for Advanced Studies, 1988).

Leask, H. G., *Irish Castles and Castellated Houses* (Dundalk: Dundalgan Press, 1941).

——, *Irish Churches and Monastic Buildings*, 3 vols (Dundalk: Dundalgan Press, 1955–60).

Lennon, Colm, *The Lords of Dublin in the Age of the Reformation* (Dublin: Irish Academic Press, 1989).

——, *Sixteenth-Century Ireland: the Incomplete Conquest* (Dublin: Gill & Macmillan, 1994).

Lydon, James, *The Lordship of Ireland in the Middle Ages* (Dublin: Gill & Macmillan, 1972).

——, *Ireland in the Later Middle Ages* (Dublin: Gill & Macmillan, 1972).

——, (ed.), *England and Ireland in the Later Middle Ages* (Dublin: Irish Academic Press, 1981).

——, (ed.), *The English in Medieval Ireland* (Dublin: Royal Irish Academy, 1984).

McCone, Kim, *Pagan Past and Christian Present in Early Irish Society* (Maynooth: An Sagart, 1990).

Mac Neill, Eoin, *Phases of Irish History* (Dublin, 1919; reprinted New York: Kennikat Press, 1970).

McNeill, T. E., *Anglo-Norman Ulster: The History and Archaeology of an Irish Barony, 1177–1400* (Edinburgh: John Donald, 1980).

Mac Niocaill, Gearóid, *Na Manaigh Liatha in Éirinn, 1142–c. 1600* (Dublin: Cló Morainn, 1959).

——, *Ireland before the Vikings* (Dublin: Gill & Macmillan, 1972).

Mac Niocaill, Gearóid and Wallace, P. F. (eds.), *Keimelia: Studies in Medieval Archaeology and History in Memory of Tom Delaney* (Galway: Galway University Press, 1988).

Mitchell, Frank, *The Shell Guide to Reading the Irish Landscape* (Dublin: Country House, 1986).

Nicholls, Kenneth, *Gaelic and Gaelicised Ireland in the Middle Ages* (Dublin: Gill & Macmillan, 1972).

Nolan, William and McGrath, T. G. (eds.), *Tipperary: History and Society* (Dublin: Geography Publications, 1985).

Nolan, William and Whelan, Kevin (eds.), *Kilkenny: History and Society* (Dublin: Geography Publications, 1990).

Nolan, William and Power, Thomas P., *Waterford: History and Society* (Dublin: Geography Publications, 1992).

Ó Corráin, Donncha, *Ireland before the Normans* (Dublin: Gill & Macmillan, 1972).

Ó Cróinín, Dáibhí, *Early Medieval Ireland 400–1200* (London: Longman, 1995).

Ó Cuív, Brian (ed.), *The Impact of the Scandinavian Invasions on the Celtic-speaking Peoples c. 800–1100 AD* (Dublin: Dublin Institute for Advanced Studies, 1975).

O'Flanagan, Patrick, and Buttimer, Cornelius G., *Cork: History and Society* (Dublin: Geography Publications, 1993).

O'Neill, Timothy, *Merchants and Mariners in Medieval Ireland* (Dublin: Irish Academic Press, 1987).

O'Rahilly, T. F., *Early Irish History and Mythology* (Dublin: Dublin Institute for Advanced Studies, 1947).

O'Sullivan, M. D., *Old Galway: The History of a Norman Colony in Ireland* (Cambridge: Cambridge University Press, 1942).

——, *Italian Merchant Bankers in Ireland in the Thirteenth Century* (Dublin: Allen Figgis, 1962).

Orpen, G. H., *Ireland under the Normans*, 4 vols (Oxford: Clarendon Press, 1911–1920).

Otway-Ruthven, A. J., *A History of Medieval Ireland* (London: Ernest Benn, 1968).

Richardson, H. G. and Sayles, G. O., *The Irish Parliament in the Middle Ages* (Philadelphia: University of Pennsylvania Press, 1952).

——, *The Administration of Ireland, 1172–1377* (Dublin: Irish Manuscripts Commission, 1963).

Richter, Michael, *Medieval Ireland: The Enduring Tradition* (Dublin: Gill & Macmillan, 1988).

Ryan, John (ed.), *Féilsgríbhinn Eoin Mhic Néill: Essays and Studies presented to Professor Eoin Mac Neill* (Dublin: Sign of the Three Candles, 1940).

Rynne, Etienne (ed.), *North Munster Studies* (Limerick: Thomond Archaeological Society, 1967).

Seymour, St J. D., *Anglo-Irish Literature, 1200–1582* (Cambridge: Cambridge University Press, 1929).

Simms, Katharine, *From Kings to Warlords: The Changing Political Structure of Gaelic Ireland in the Later Middle Ages* (Woodbridge: Boydell & Brewer, 1987).

Smyth, Alfred P., *Scandinavian Dublin and York*, 2 vols (Dublin: Temple Kieran Press, 1975–9).

——, *Celtic Leinster: Towards a Historical Geography of Early Irish Civilisation, AD 500–1600* (Dublin: Irish Academic Press, 1982).

Stalley, R. A., *The Cistercian Monasteries of Ireland* (London and New Haven: Yale University Press, 1987).

Walsh, Katherine, *A Fourteenth-Century Scholar and Primate: Richard FitzRalph in Oxford, Avignon, and Armagh* (Oxford: Clarendon Press, 1981).

Watt, John A., Morrall, J. B. and Martin, F. X. (eds.), *Medieval Studies presented to Aubrey Gwynn S. J.* (Dublin: Cló Morainn, 1961).

Watt, John A., *The Church and the Two Nations in Medieval Ireland* (Cambridge: Cambridge University Press, 1970).

——, *The Church in Medieval Ireland* (Dublin: Gill & Macmillan, 1972).

Whelan, Kevin (ed.), *Wexford: History and Society* (Dublin: Geography Publications, 1987).

INDEX

absentee landholders, 125, 140–5, 151, 152, 155–8, 167, 175
acculturation, 148–9
administrative records, 3, 8
Adrian IV, pope (1154–9), 25, 70, 92
Affreca, daughter of the king of Man, 114
agriculture, 10, 81, 111, 169
Aífe, daughter of Diarmait Mac Murchada, king of Leinster, 65
Ailill, king of Connacht, 23
Airgialla, 54, 55, 87, 139
Alexander III, pope (1159–81), 25–6, 72
All Hallows, Dublin, 105
Anastasius, papal librarian, 9
Angelo, de, family of, 120
Angevin 'empire', 93
Anglesey, 38, 137
Anglicization, 112, 148
Anglo-Irish separatism, 100–1, 150, 172, 176
Anglo-Saxon England, 49
Anjou, 60, 70
annals, 3–4, 14, 16, 18, 67, 85, 103, 159, 174
'Annals of Connacht', 26
'Annals of the Four Masters', 58, 68, 74, 162, 163
'Annals of Inisfallen', 85
'Annals of Loch Cé', 119
'Annals of Tigernach', 75, 76, 88
Annaly, co. Longford, 163
Anselm, archbishop of Canterbury (1093–1109), 25, 45, 50–1
anti-Irish bias, 107–9, 154
Antrim, co., 47, 113, 134
Aquitaine, 60, 70
arable-farming, 8, 12

archaeology, 3, 13
Ardee, battle of (1159), 55
Argyll, 117
Armagh, 34, 52, 54, 55, 76, 107, 109–10, 113, 163
Armagh, archbishops of, 50, 92–3, 159, 167 (*see also* Nicholas Mac Maíl Ísu, Tommaltach Ua Conchobair, John Swayne)
Armagh, co., 113
Athboy, co. Meath, 62
Athenry, battle of (1316), 139–40
Athlone, co. Westmeath, 99, 118, 119

Baginbun, co. Wexford, 67
Balscot, Alexander, justiciar of Ireland (1387–9, 1391–2), 165
Ballynagran, co. Wicklow, 57
Baltinglass, co. Wicklow, 9
Bannockburn, battle of (1314), 134, 143
Bannow Bay, co. Wexford, 63
Barbour, Archdeacon John, 136
barons' war (1258–67), 125
Barrett, family of, 120, 165
Barri, Gerald de (1146–1223), 7, 10, 17, 24, 59, 63, 67, 75, 80, 87, 94, 100, 104
Barri, Robert de, 63
Barry, family of, 63, 120, 156
Bavaria, 49
Bede (d. 735), 9, 48
Bermingham, family of, 120, 165
betagh, *see biatach*
biatach, 21
Bible, 15, 23
Bigod family, earls of Norfolk, lords of Carlow, 143
Black Death (1348–9), 151

'black-rent', 168
Book of Armagh, 34
Book of Leinster, 39, 58, 75
bóaire, 11, 21
Bolingbroke, Henry, afterwards
    Henry IV, king of England
    (1399–1413), 164
boroughs, 83, 151
Bosworth, battle of (1485), 177
Boyne, river, 109
Brega, 30
Brehon laws, *see* law
Bréifne, 27, 46, 53, 54, 55, 57, 62,
    86, 87, 122, 163
Bretha Crólige, 23
Brétigny, treaty of (1360), 151
Brian Bóruma (d. 1014), 17, 31–7,
    40
Briouze, Philip de, 91
Briouze family, 103
Bristol, 58, 124
Brotherton, Thomas of (d. 1338),
    earl of Norfolk, son of Edward
    I, 143
Bruce invasion (1315–18), 79,
    134–41, 166
Bruce, Edward (d. 1318), earl of
    Carrick, 'king of Ireland',
    134–8
Bruce, Robert (d. 1329), king of
    Scotland, 134–8
Bruce family, 131
burgesses, 83
Burgh, Hubert de (d. 1243), earl of
    Kent, 120
Burgh, Richard de (d. 1243),
    119–20
Burgh, Richard de (d. 1326), 'Red'
    earl of Ulster, 127–8, 131, 139
Burgh, Walter de (d. 1271), earl of
    Ulster, 126–7
Burgh, William de (d. 1205), 99
Burgh, William de (d. 1333),
    'Brown' earl of Ulster, 140
Burgh family, 125, 156
Burkes, 140; *see also* Burgh
Butler, James (d. 1338), 1st earl of
    Ormond, 145
Butler, James (d. 1452), 4th earl of
    Ormond ('White Earl'), 169,
    171

Butler, *see also* Ormond, earls of
Byrne, Francis John, 3

Cáel Uisce, near Beleek, co.
    Fermanagh, 116, 123
Cáin Lánamna, 22
Cambrensis, Giraldus, *see* Barri,
    Gerald de
cannibalism, 151
Canterbury, 49–51
Canterbury, archbishops of, 24, 45,
    50, 70; *see also* Anselm,
    Lanfranc, Theobald
Carlow, 97, 143, 153, 161
Carnfree, co. Roscommon, 19
Carolingian empire, 49
Carlisle, 131
Carrickfergus, co. Antrim, 103–4,
    112, 114, 131
Cashel, co. Tipperary, 52
Cashel, first synod of (1101), 25, 51
Cashel, second synod of (1171–2),
    26, 74, 104
Castledermot, co. Kildare, 126
Castlekevin, co. Wicklow, 106
Castleknock, co. Dublin, 68, 137
castles, 8, 83, 87, 165
cattle, 11, 13, 17, 21, 58, 88, 103,
    159
Cavan, co., 19
céilí (clients), 20–1
Cenél Conaill, 32, 35, 47, 54, 87
Cenél nEógain, 32, 35, 47, 54, 87,
    103
Cennétig mac Lorcáin (d. 951), 31
chancery, 96
Channel Islands, 124
Charlemagne, king of the Franks
    (768–814), Emperor (800–14),
    9
Charles the Bald, king of the Franks
    (843–77), Emperor (875–7), 9
charters, 8, 59, 118
Chepstow, Wales, 79
Chester, earldom of, 124
chief governorship, 94, 95, 105, 116,
    124–5, 129, 147, 149–50, 152,
    167, 170
Christ Church cathedral, Dublin,
    105, 117
Chronicle of the Kings of Man, 43

church, 14, 17, 20, 23, 29, 34, 48–52, 74, 76, 104–10, 154
church-reform, 13, 22, 24–5, 48–52, 72–4
Cináed mac Conaing, king of North Brega (d. 851), 30
Cistercians, 9, 55
Clan Donald (Clann Domnaill), of Scotland and Ulster, 117
Clann Cholmáin, Southern Uí Néill kings of Tara, 32
Clanrickard Burkes, 180
Clare, co., 33, 41, 112
Clare, Richard fitz Gilbert de, see Strongbow
Clare, Richard de (d. 1318), lord of Thomond, son of Thomas, 144
Clare, Thomas de (d. 1287), lord of Thomond, 144
Clare family, earls of Gloucester, lords of Kilkenny, 143
Clarence, duke of, son of Edward III, see Lionel of Antwerp
clientship, see céilí
Clondalkin, co. Dublin, 29, 67, 105
Clonfert, co. Galway, 33
Clontarf, co. Dublin, 68
Clontarf, battle of (1014), 35–6
Cogad Gaedel re Gallaib, 42
Cogan, Miles de (d. 1182), 68, 91
Cogan family, 120
coinage, 11, 103
colonization, 7, 84, 104, 111–13, 123, 162
Colmán Már (d. 558), son of Diarmait mac Cerrbeoil, Uí Néill high-king, 32
Cong, Augustinian abbey, co. Mayo, 93
Conn Cétchathach, ancestor of the Connachta, 31
Connacht, 19, 22, 31, 35, 46, 52, 54, 62, 75, 87, 88, 90, 92, 93, 97, 99, 103, 117–24, 126, 127, 139, 142, 152
Connor, battle of (1315), 139
Constance, 49
Cork, 29, 83, 90–1, 97, 112
corruption, 129, 149, 167
Cosgrove, Art, 6
Costello family, 120

council, 95, 146
Courcy, John de, lord of Ulster (1177–1204), 90, 113–15
'coyne and livery', 147, 170
crannóg, 11
crops, 12, 111
Cú Chulainn, 113
cúlán, distinctive Irish hairstyle, 142
Cumbria, 114
Cumin, John, archbishop of Dublin (1181–1212), 104
Curtis, Edmund, 5
Cusack family, 120
Cynan ab Iago, of Gwynedd, father of Gruffudd ap Cynan (d. 1137), 38–9

Dál Cais, 31, 33, 36
Dalkey, co. Dublin, 68, 168
Dalton family, 165
Davies, Sir John, 1–2
Declaration of Parliamentary Independence (1460), 172–3
degeneracy, 142
Deheubarth (South Wales), 41, 44, 62
demesne, 82, 157
derbfine, 22
Derbforgaill, wife of Tigernán Ua Ruairc (d. 1172), 57, 62
Derry, 123
Derry, co., 113
Desmond, 30, 53, 77, 90–1, 99, 122
Desmond, earls of, 145, 156, 158, 165, 180; see also Geraldines, Gerald fitz Maurice (d. 1398), Maurice fitz Thomas (d. 1356), Thomas fitz James (d. 1468)
De Statu Ecclesiae ('Concerning church order'), 50
Devenish, on Lough Erne, 123
Diarmait mac Maíl na mBó (d. 1072), king of Leinster, 36–40, 44
Dillon family, 165
divorce, 22
Donegal, co., 32, 116, 126
Donnchad mac Briain (d. 1065), king of Munster, 17, 36, 39, 91
Donngus, bishop of Dublin (1085–95), 50

Down, co., 47, 113, 123
Downpatrick, co. Down, 90, 113–14, 123
Drogheda, co. Louth, 131, 146, 172, 178, 180
Dublin, 3, 17, 29, 30, 34, 35–8, 40–3, 50, 53, 54, 58, 67–9, 75, 80, 82, 85, 87, 88, 89, 90, 93, 97, 103, 105, 126, 137, 144, 146, 153, 164
Dublin, archdiocese of, 104–6, 107; *see also* John Cumin, Donngus, Gilla Pátraic, Henry of London, Samuel, Lorcán Ua Tuathail
Duleek, co. Meath, 87
Dundalk, co. Louth, 135, 168
Dundrum, co. Down, 114
Dungarvan, co. Waterford, 89
Dysert O'Dea, battle of (1318), 144

ecclesia inter Anglicos, 110
ecclesia inter Hibernicos, 110
Echmarcach, king of Dublin (d. 1065), 37
economy, 10, 13, 81, 152, 155, 157, 165–6
Edward I, king of England (1272–1307), 124–5, 128, 145
Edward II, king of England (1307–27), 135–6, 143
Edward III, king of England (1327–77), 140, 145, 148–9, 152, 156, 172
Edward IV, king of England (1461–83), 174–6
Eichstadt, 49
Ellis, Steven, 6
Emain Macha (Navan fort), co. Armagh, 113
emigration, 151, 159, 162, 167
enech ('honour'), 62
England, 8, 28, 39, 41, 45, 49, 50, 74, 103, 112, 127, 136, 157, 179
English inhabitants of Ireland, 3, 148
English invasion of Ireland, 2, 13, 53, 56, 58–81, 84, 91, 139
Eóganacht, kings of Munster, 30–1, 34, 53
Erfurt, 49

Eriugena, Johannes Scotus, 9
Erne, river, 116
Europe, 9, 10, 11, 13, 15, 20, 22, 27, 37, 48–9, 51, 73, 84, 115
exchequer, 96, 107, 128, 132, 149, 153
Expugnatio Hibernica, 59, 62, 64, 75, *see also* Barri, Gerald de

factions, 115, 125–8, 171
famine, 13, 137, 151, 157, 165
Fermanagh, 116
Ferns, co. Wexford, 36, 58, 75, 107
feudalism, 20, 61, 73, 82, 119
feuds, 115, 125–8
Finglas, co. Dublin, 105
fitz Geoffrey, John, justiciar (1245–56), 123
fitz Godebert, Richard, 62
fitz Harding, Robert, reeve of Bristol, 58
fitz Stephen, Robert (d. *c.* 1182), 63, 75, 76–7, 91
flaith (lord), 20
Flanagan, Marie Therese, 6
Flanders, 62, 128
Flemings, 62, 63
Fochart, battle of (1318), 135, 139
Foras Feasa ar Éirinn, 28
forests, 10, 12, 67
fosterage, 23
Frame, Robin, 5
France, 59, 150, 152, 167
Francia, Frankish empire, 49
Franciscan Observants, 166
Froissart, Jean, 159
Fulda, 49
Fulbourne, Stephen de, chief governor of Ireland (1281–8), 129

Gaelicization, 148–9
galloglasses, 117, 123
Galloway, Scotland, 54, 131, 135
Galway, 120
Galway, co., 112, 116, 120
Gascony, 124, 128
Gerald of Wales, *see* Barri, Gerald de
Gerald of Windsor, steward of Pembroke, 44–5

Geraldines:
  Gerald fitz Maurice (d. 1398), 3rd
    earl of Desmond ('Gearóid
    Iarla'), 147
  Gerald fitz Maurice (d. 1513), 8th
    earl of Kildare ('Gearóid
    Mór'), 176–81
  John fitz Thomas (d. 1316), first
    earl of Kildare, 127–8, 145
  Maurice fitz Gerald (d. 1176),
    founder of the Irish
    Geraldines, 63, 101
  Maurice fitz Gerald (d. 1257),
    baron of Offaly, 116–17, 126
  Maurice fitz Thomas (d. 1356),
    first earl of Desmond, 145,
    147–8
  Thomas fitz James (d. 1468), 7th
    earl of Desmond, 174
  Thomas fitz Maurice (d. 1298),
    head of Munster Geraldines,
    130
  Thomas fitz Maurice (d. 1478),
    7th earl of Kildare, 174–5
Germany, 84
Ghent, Belgium, 49
Gilla Espaic, bishop of Limerick
    (c. 1107–40), 50
Gilla Pátraic, bishop of Dublin
    (1074–84), 50
Glamorgan, Wales, 79
Glasnevin, co. Dublin, 29
Glastonbury, Somerset, 49
Glendalough, co. Wicklow, 105–6
Gloucester, earldom of, 143–4
Godred Crovan (d. 1095), king of
    Dublin and Man, 42
Gofraid Méránach, see Godred
    Crovan
Golden Age, 48
government, central, 95–6, 103,
    128–9, 134, 137, 145–6, 153–4,
    167, 168, 179, 181
government, local, 96–7
Greenland, 9
Gregorian reform, 24, 48
Gregory VII, pope (1073–85), 40
Gruffudd ap Cynan (d. 1137),
    prince of Gwynedd, 38, 44
Gruffudd ap Rhys ap Tewdwr (d.
    1137), prince of Deheubarth, 44

Gwent, Wales, 79
Gwynedd (North Wales), 38–9, 41,
    44
Gwynn, Aubrey, 5

Hákon IV, king of Norway
    (1217–63), 123–4
Hand, G. J., 4
Harold Godwinesson (d. 1066), earl
    of Wessex, 39
Hebridean mercenaries, 35, 117,
    123
Henry I, king of England
    (1100–35), 44–5
Henry II, king of England
    (1154–89), 25, 58, 69–75, 78,
    85, 86–93, 106
Henry III, king of England
    (1216–72), 107, 111, 119, 123,
    124
Henry IV, king of England
    (1399–1413), 166
Henry VI, king of England
    (1422–61; 1470–71), 173
Henry VII (Henry Tudor), king of
    England (1485–1509), 177–8
Henry of London, archbishop of
    Dublin (1213–28), 105–9
Herefordshire, 82
Hiberno-Scandinavians, see Ostmen
high-kingship, 16, 17, 32–4, 36,
    39–40, 42, 51, 53, 54, 67, 90, 93,
    123
Honorius III, pope (1216–27), 109
honour-price (lóg n-enech), 15
horses, 12
hostages, 18, 40, 55, 67, 104, 165
Hughes, Kathleen, 5
Hundred Years War (1337–1453),
    150–1

Iceland, 9
inauguration, 17
incastellation, 83, 165–6
Inishowen, co. Donegal, 32, 54
Iorwerth ab Owain, lord of
    Caerleon, Wales, 79
Irish language, 4, 33, 142, 148, 154
Irish resurgence, 79, 121–4, 125,
    134, 156
Irish Sea, 37, 40, 86

Irish society, 3, 4, 8–27, 28

John, king of England (1199–1216), 91, 94–107, 114, 149
John of Fordun, 26
John of Salisbury, 70
John Paparo, Cardinal, 52
justiciarship, *see* chief governorship

Keating, Geoffrey, 27, 28
Kells, co. Meath, 97
Kells-Mellifont, synod of (1152), 52
Kerry, co., 97, 112
Kildare, co., 36, 97, 159, 168
Kildare, earls of, 127, 145, 156, 163, 169, 174; *see also* Geraldines, Gerald fitz Maurice (d. 1513), John fitz Thomas (d. 1316), Thomas fitz Maurice (d. 1478)
Kilkenny, 88, 97, 127, 143, 146, 150, 151, 154, 159, 170, 179
Kilkenny, Statutes of (1366), 154–5, 161, 172
Killaloe, diocese of, 108
Kilmainham, co. Dublin, 29, 68
kin-groups, 19, 21–2, 66
kingship, 15–20, 42, 47–8, 65–6
Kintyre, Scotland, 54

Lacy, Hugh I de (d. 1186), lord of Meath, 53, 78, 80, 82–3, 86, 93–4, 102, 114
Lacy, Hugh II de (d. 1242), earl of Ulster, 103, 114–16, 126
Lacy, Walter de, lord of Meath, 114
Lancastrian kings of England, 166, 167, 170
Lanfranc, archbishop of Canterbury (1070–89), 24, 40, 50
Lateran Council, Third (1179), 92
Lateran Council, Fourth (1215), 106
Laudabiliter, 70, 91
law, Brehon, 10, 12, 13, 17, 21–4, 33, 65
law, common, 1, 65, 97–8, 103, 118, 149
lawlessness, 127, 128, 132
Lea, co. Kildare, 127
legates, papal, 92, 93
legislation, 141, 178–9

Leinster, 35–6, 40, 45–6, 53–4, 57–8, 61, 65–7, 79, 86, 99, 107, 113, 122, 127, 130, 143, 157–65
Leitrim, co., 19
Leth Cuinn, northern half of Ireland, 31, 33, 52, 76, 87
Leth Moga, southern half of Ireland, 33, 52
liberties, 97
Liége, Belgium, 49
lieutenancy, 152, 163, 167, 171, 173; *see also* chief governorship
Liffey, river, 69
Limerick, 29, 31, 34, 40, 50, 54, 90–1, 97, 112, 120, 158
Limerick, co., 83
Lionel of Antwerp, earl of Clarence, 140, 152–7
Llywelyn ap Gruffudd (d. 1282), prince of Wales, 123, 130
local government, *see* government
Longford, co., 32, 82
Lough Corrib, 19
Loughrea, co. Galway, 120
Louis VII, king of France, 78
Louth, co., 97, 99, 109, 144, 146
Low Countries, 49, 59
Lusk, co. Dublin, 29, 105
Lydon, James, 5

Mac Carthaig, Diarmait (d. 1185), king of Desmond, 85, 102
Mac Carthaig, Domnall (d. 1206), king of Desmond, 121
Mac Carthaig, Finín (d. 1249/1250), 122
Mac Dermott's castle, co. Wicklow, 57
Mac Domnaill, galloglass captain, 159
Mac Duinn Sléibe, Eochaid (d. 1166), king of Ulaid, 55
Mac Lochlainn, Conchobar (d. 1136), 54
Mac Lochlainn, Domnall (d. 1121), king of Cenél nEógain, 47
Mac Lochlainn, Muirchertach (d. 1166), 54–6, 58
Mac Mathgamna (Mac Mahon), 180
Mac Murchada, Art (d. 1416), king of Leinster, 159–65

Mac Murchada, Diarmait (d. 1171), king of Leinster, 9, 27, 45, 53–68, 70, 74, 65, 77, 82, 86, 121

Mac Murchada, Diarmait Láimhderg (d. 1369), king of Leinster, 157

Mac Murchada, Domnall Cáemánach (d. 1175), king of Uí Chennselaig, 66

Mac Murchada, Domnall (d. 1340/1347), king of Leinster, son of Art, 144

Mac Murchada, Donnchad (d. 1115), king of Leinster, 58

Mac Murchada, Muirchertach (d. 1282), king of Leinster, 130

Mac Murchada, Murchad, brother of Diarmait, 68

Mac Murrough, *see* Mac Murchada, Meic Murchada

Mac Neill, Eoin, 5

Mac Ruaidrí, Dubgall, lord of Garmoran, 123–4

Mac Somurli [?Domnall], 117

Mac Turcaill, Ascall, king of Dublin (d. 1171), 68

Mág Aonghusa (Magennis), 180

Máel Ísu, bishop of Waterford (1096–1135), 150–1

Máel Sechnaill mac Domnaill (d. 1022), Uí Néill high-king, 31–3, 35, 36, 37

Máel Sechnaill mac Maíl Ruanaid (d. 862), Uí Néill high-king, 30

Magnus Barelegs, king of Norway (d. 1103), 43–6

Mainz, Germany, 49

Man, Isle of, 35, 37, 40, 42–3, 54, 103, 169

manors, 73, 83, 87, 96, 105, 106, 111, 151

manuscripts, 11, 13

Marianus Scotus, *see* Muiredach mac Robartaig

Marisco, Geoffrey de, 108

marriage, 22–7, 52, 65, 73, 104, 148, 175

Marshal, William (d. 1219), lord of Leinster, 107

Marshal lordship of Leinster, 143, 144

Mathgamain (d. 976), son of Cennétig mac Lorcáin, 31

Mayo, co., 116

Meath, 32, 46, 53–7, 77, 82–3, 86–7, 113, 139, 144, 168

Medb, queen of Connacht, 22

Meelick, co. Galway, 120

Meic Carthaig (Mac Carthys), kings of Desmond, 30, 53, 147, 159, 162

Meic Duinn Sléibe (Mac Dunleavys), kings of Ulaid, 68, 113

Meic Lochlainn (Mac Laughlins), kings of Cenél nEógain, 115, 117

Meic Murchada (Mac Murroughs), kings of Leinster, 37, 66–7, 144, 160–1, 180

Mellifont abbey, co. Louth, 55

Metz, France, 49

Mide, *see* Meath

military service, 21, 55, 64, 82

mills, 11, 12

Móin Mór, battle of (1151), 53

Monaghan, co., 139

monasteries, 29, 166

Montgomery, Arnulf de, 44–5

Montmorency, Hervey de, 67, 78

Mortimer Roger (d. 1398), earl of March, 163

motte-and-bailey castles, 83, 87

Muiredach mac Robartaig, 49

Murchad (d. 1070), son of Diarmait mac Maíl na mBó, 37

Munster, 17, 24, 30–1, 33, 42, 54, 88, 97, 99, 120, 127, 139, 146, 165

Naas, co. Kildare, 146

Nangle, family of, 120

Navigatio Sancti Brendani, 10

Newry abbey, co. Down, 55

Niall Noígiallach, ancestor of the Uí Néill, 15, 31

Nicholas Mac Maíl Ísu, archbishop of Armagh (1270–1303), 110

Nicholls, Kenneth, 5

Normandy, 78–9

Normans, 8, 38, 39, 44, 46, 49, 50
Norragh, co. Kildare, 161
North Channel, 114
Norway, 123
Nüremburg, Germany, 49

O'Brien, see Ua Briain
O'Connor, see Ua Conchobair
O'Connors, see Uí Chonchobair
ócaire, 21
O'Donovan, John, 57
óenach (assembly), 17
Offaly, 32, 82, 116, 139, 145
O'Melaghlin, see Ua Maíl Sechnaill
O'Neills, see Uí Néill
Orderic Vitalis, 45–6
Ormond, earls of, 145, 156, 163,
    165, 170, 171, 174, 181; see also
    James Butler (d. 1338), James
    Butler (d. 1452)
O'Rourke, see Ua Ruairc
Orpen, G. H., 4–5, 18, 59
Osraige (Ossory), 54, 88, 122
Ostmen, 17, 30, 34, 36–8, 41, 50–1,
    54, 58, 63–4, 68
O'Toole, St Laurence, see Ua
    Tuathail, Lorcán
Otway-Ruthven, A. J., 5
Owain Glyn Dŵr, 166
Oxford, Council of (1177), 91

Pale, 168, 175, 177, 181
papacy, 24, 91–2, 164; see also Adrian
    IV, Alexander III, Gregory VII
parishes, 73, 82, 104
parliament, 95, 127, 141, 146, 150,
    154, 164, 167, 170, 172, 175,
    178–9
pastoral farming, 12
Pembroke, Pembrokeshire, 44–5,
    62, 63
Pembroke, earldom of, 64, 143
Petit family, 120
peregrinatio, 49
pigs, 12
Pipard, Gilbert, 99
plague, 151, 157, 165; see also Black
    Death
Plantagenets, 91, 125
Poer family, 156, 165
poetry, 14, 15, 23, 156

polygamy, 23
population, 113, 151, 155, 157, 159
Portrane, co. Dublin, 105
Portumna, co. Galway, 120
Poynings, Edward, 177–8
Poynings's Law (1494), 178–80
Powys, Wales, 166
Prendergast, Maurice de, 63
Prendergast family, 120
Pseudo-Dionysius, 9
Pyrenees, 70

Ráith Bressail, synod of (1111), 52
Ralph of Diss, chronicler, 26
Rathangan castle, co. Kildare, 169
Rathcoole, co. Dublin, 105
Rathfarnham, co. Dublin, 68
Raymond le Gros, (d. *c.* 1188), 67
Reichenau, on Lake Constance, 49
'Remonstrance of the Irish Princes'
    (1317), 138
revenues, 128–33, 138–9, 145, 155,
    170, 175, 178
Rhys ap Gruffudd (d. 1197), prince
    of Deheubarth, 62
Rhys ap Tewdwr (d. 1093), prince of
    Deheubarth, 44
Richard II, king of England
    (1377–99), 155, 158–65, 167
Richard III, king of England
    (1483–5), 176
Richardson, H. G., 4
ring-forts, 10
ringwork castles, 83
roads, 10
Roche family, 62, 156
Roger of Howden, chronicler, 26
Rome, 39, 91, 108
Roscommon, co., 97, 112, 121

St Albans, Hertford shire, 50
St Bernard of Clairvaux (d. 1153), 9,
    24, 25
St Brendan the Navigator, 10
St Colum Cille (d. 597), 15, 75
St Davids, Wales, 48
St Gall, Switzerland, 49
St John Brooks, Eric, 4
St John the Baptist, hospital of,
    Dublin, 105
St Kevin, 106

St Laurence O'Toole, *see* Ua
    Tuathail, Lorcán
St Malachy (d. 1148), 25
St Mary's abbey, Dublin, 105
St Patrick, 74, 114
St Patrick's cathedral, Dublin, 105
St Patrick's Purgatory, Lough Derg,
    9
St Sepulchre, manor of, Dublin, 105
St Thomas's abbey, Dublin, 105
Salzburg, Austria, 49
Samuel, bishop of Dublin
    (1096–1121), 50
Saul, co. Down, 55
Savage family, 156
Saxons, 17
Sayles, G. O., 4
Scotland, 70, 84, 111, 128, 131–2,
    134, 151, 166
Scottish settlers in Ireland, 176
seafaring, 10
Senchas Már, 21
seneschals, 97
Shankill, co. Dublin, 29, 105
Shannon, river, 31, 99, 108, 118
sheep, 12
sheriffs, 96, 129
shires, 96–7
Sigurd, son of Magnus Barelegs,
    king of Norway, 43
Simms, Katharine, 5
Simnel, Lambert, 177, 179
Sitriuc Silkenbeard (d. 1042), king
    of Dublin, 38
Sligo, co., 112, 116–17
slógadh (hosting), 18
Song of Dermot and the Earl, 59, 61,
    62, 64, 67
Spain, 84
Staunton family, 120
Strigoil, Welsh March, 64
Strongbow (d. 1176), 45, 64–79, 82,
    86, 144
subinfeudation, 82
succession-disputes, 116–17, 120
Sulien, bishop of St Davids, 48
Swayne, John, archbishop of
    Armagh (1418–39), 171
Swords, co. Dublin, 29, 38, 105
synods, *see* Cashel, Kells-Mellifont,
    Ráith Bressail

Talbot, John, earl of Shrewsbury,
    171
Táin Bó Cúailnge, 22, 113
Tallaght, co. Dublin, 29, 105
Tara, co. Meath, 32–3, 54
taxation, 17, 74, 96, 139, 172
Termonfeckin, co. Louth, 110
Theobald, archbishop of
    Canterbury (1138–61), 70
Thomas of Lancaster, son of Henry
    IV, lieutenant of Ireland
    (1401–5), 167
Thomond, 31, 41, 53, 55, 68, 77, 88,
    90–1, 123, 144, 158
Thurles, co. Tipperary, 88
Tipperary, co., 97, 99, 120, 170
Tír Conaill, 32, 47, 49, 116, 117,
    169
Tír Eógain, 32, 46, 47, 54, 55, 58,
    103, 117, 122, 134, 169
tithes, 73
Topographia Hiberniae, 7, 17; *see also*
    Barri, Gerald de
tower-houses, 165
towns, 10
Towton, battle of (1461), 174
Travers, Robert, bishop of Killaloe
    (1217–26), 108
treasurer, 96, 129
Trim, co. Meath, 87, 97, 146
Tuam, archdiocese of, 52, 105–6; *see
    also* Felix Ua Ruadháin
tuarastal ('wages'), 54, 58
Tuit family, 156
túatha, 16, 18
Tyrone, 32, 109

Ua Briain, Amlaíb (Olaf) (d. 1096),
    son of Tadc, son of
    Tairdelbach, 43
Ua Briain, Diarmait (d. 1118), son
    of Tairdelbach, 41, 51
Ua Briain, Domnall (d. 1115), son
    of Tadc, son of Tairdelbach,
    43
Ua Briain, Domnall Mór (d. 1194),
    son of Tairdelbach, son of
    Diarmait, king of Thomond,
    68, 79, 85, 88–9, 102
Ua Briain, Muirchertach (d. 1119),
    son of Tairdelbach, king of

Munster, high-king of Ireland, 25, 40, 51–3

Ua Briain, Tadc (d. 1086), son of Tairdelbach, 41

Ua Briain, Tadc (d. 1259), 'of Cáel Uisce', son of Conchobar, 123

Ua Briain, Tairdelbach (d. 1086), king of Munster, high-king of Ireland, 17, 24–5, 36, 39–41, 51

Ua Briain, Tairdelbach (d. 1167), son of Diarmait, son of Tairdelbach, 53, 55

Ua Broin, of Uí Fáeláin, 162, 180

Ua Catháin, king of Ciannacht, 159

Ua Ceallaig, Máel Sechnaill (d. 1401), king of Uí Maine, 159

Ua Cerbaill, Donnchad (d. 1168), king of Airgialla, 55

Ua Cerbaill of Ely, 160

Ua Conchobair, Áed (d. 1228), son of Cathal Crobderg, king of Connacht, 118–19

Ua Conchobair, Áed na nGall (d. 1274), son of Feidlim, king of Connacht, 121–4

Ua Conchobair, Cathal Crobderg (d. 1224), king of Connacht, 103–4, 118–19, 121

Ua Conchobair, Conchobar (d. 1144), son of Tairdelbach, 53

Ua Conchobair, Feidlim (d. 1265), son of Cathal Crobderg, king of Connacht, 120–1

Ua Conchobair, Feidlim (d. 1316), son of Áed, king of Connacht, 139–40

Ua Conchobair, Ruaidrí (d. 1198), king of Connacht, high-king of Ireland, 17, 26–7, 54–5, 58, 62–71, 76, 77, 86–93, 101, 102, 103, 117

Ua Conchobair, Tairdelbach (d. 1156), son of Ruaidrí, king of Connacht, high-king of Ireland, 51, 53–5

Ua Conchobair, Tommaltach, archbishop of Armagh (1180–1201), 92

Ua Conchobair Failge, Calbach (d. 1458), 169

Ua Dímmusaig (O'Dempsey), 180

Ua Domnaill, Gofraid (d. 1258), king of Tír Conaill, 117

Ua Domnaill, Niall Garbh (d. 1439), king of Tír Conaill, 169

Ua Domnaill, Máel Sechnaill (d. 1247), king of Tír Conaill, 117

Ua Gilla Pátraic, Donnchad (d. 1249), of Osraige, 122

Ua hAnluain (O'Hanlon), 180

Ua Maíl Sechnaill, Magnus (d. 1175), king of Meath, 87

Ua Mórda (O'More), 180

Ua Néill, Áed Méith (d. 1230), king of Cenél nEógain, 103–4, 115–16, 121

Ua Néill, Brian (d. 1260), king of Cenél nEógain, 117

Ua Néill, Conn (d. 1493), king of Cenél nEógain, 175

Ua Néill, Domnall (d. 1325), king of Cenél nEógain, 134, 137–8

Ua Néill, Niall Mór (d. 1397), king of Cenél nEógain, 156, 160, 162, 163

Ua Néill, Niall Óg (d. 1403), king of Cenél nEógain, 163, 165, 169

Ua Ragallaig (O'Reilly), 180

Ua Ruadháin, Felix, archbishop of Tuam (1202–33), 106–7

Ua Ruairc, Tigernán (d. 1172), king of Bréifne, 27, 53, 55, 57, 62, 75–6, 86–7

Ua Tuathail, St Lorcán (d. 1180), 92, 104

Ua Tuathail, Feidlim, of Uí Muiredaig, 160, 162

Uí Briain (O'Briens), 40, 44, 53, 90, 144, 147, 162

Uí Briúin Aí, 19, 35

Uí Briúin Bréifne, 19, 35

Uí Briúin Seola, 19

Uí Chennselaig, 36–40, 58, 62–3, 160

Uí Chonchobair (O'Connors), 19, 35, 90, 117, 140

Uí Chonchobair Donn, 162

Uí Chonchobair Failge, 160, 180

Uí Fiachrach Aidni, 19

Uí Fiachrach Muaide, 19

Uí Flaithbertaig (O'Flahertys), 19

Uí Maíl Sechnaill, 32, 53, 55

Uí Néill, Northern, 15, 32, 35, 47
Uí Néill, Southern, 15, 31–3, 35
Uí Néill (O'Neills), 55, 115, 141, 169, 180
Uí Ruairc (O'Rourkes), 20, 35
Ulaid, 47, 54, 55, 87, 90, 113, 122
Ulster, earldom of, 114, 116–17, 122, 126, 139, 140, 142, 152, 160, 163
Uriel, *see* Louth

Valence family, 143
Verdon, Bertram de, 99
Verdon family, 144
Vienna, Austria, 49
Vikings, 2, 10, 13, 28–30, 35–6, 42, 43

Walafrid Strabo, 49
Wales, 7, 37–9, 41, 44–5, 48, 61, 62, 64, 69, 79, 84, 111, 112, 121, 123, 124, 128, 129–30, 135–7, 166, 167
Wales, Gerald of, *see* Barri, Gerald de
Wales, son of the king of, 62
Walter, Theobald, 99; *see also* Butlers, earls of Ormond
Warbeck, Perkin, 177–9

warfare, 18, 29, 30, 104, 121, 127, 128, 141, 151, 153, 156, 164
Waterford, 29, 34, 41, 50–1, 65, 67, 69, 77, 79, 83, 88, 89, 97, 99, 103, 159
Watt, John, 5
Welsh chronicles, 37–9, 71, 86
Wessex, 39
Western Isles, 35, 37, 42–3, 68, 123, 124
Westmeath, 32, 82
Westminster, 3
Wexford, 29, 37, 63–4, 67, 69, 89, 96, 143
Wicklow, co., 36, 37, 67, 105–6, 162
William the Conqueror, 41
William of Malmesbury, 45
Winchcombe, 49
Winchester, 49, 50
Windsor, Treaty of (1175), 88–93, 100, 117
Windsor, William of, 155, 157
women, 22, 24
Worcester, 49, 50
Würzburg, 49

York, Richard, duke of, 173
Yorkist support in Ireland, 173, 177–8

9670